THE ORIGINS OF
BRITISH SOCIOLOGY: 1834-1914

THE HERITAGE OF SOCIOLOGY

A Series Edited by Morris Janowitz

THE ORIGINS OF
BRITISH SOCIOLOGY:
1834-1914

by

PHILIP ABRAMS

An Essay with Selected Papers

THE UNIVERSITY OF CHICAGO PRESS

CHICAGO AND LONDON

Library of Congress Catalog Card Number: 68–54221

THE UNIVERSITY OF CHICAGO PRESS, CHICAGO 60637
The University of Chicago Press, Ltd., London W.C. 1

Acknowledgments

THIS BOOK was written during the spring of 1967 when I was holding a visiting appointment at the University of Chicago. I should like to take this opportunity to express my gratitude to the faculty and students in the Department of Sociology, and most of all to Professors Morris Janowitz and Edward Shils, for an experience of exceptional importance and value to me. In the context of this book I can hardly do better than borrow the words L. T. Hobhouse used to describe his own feelings on leaving another American university in 1911. As Hobhouse said: "The freshness, the vitality, the largeness of conception, the intellectual as well as social hospitality that characterize American academic life, have been to me stimulating and invigorating beyond all expectation."

Philip Abrams

Note

1834—THE YEAR of the *Report* of the Commission on the
Poor Law and the founding of the Statistical Society of London
—is about as rational a date for beginning a history of British
sociology as one could hope to find. 1914, however, is a quite
arbitrary stopping point. But origins must end somewhere and
from the 1920's onward the problems of developing social science
begin to take a rather different form—one best treated, as I hope
to do, in a separate study focused on the theme of professionaliza-
tion. On a few occasions, therefore, I have sketched lines of development beyond 1914, but for the most part I have accepted
the limits imposed by an unreal, even if conventional, historical
frontier.

Second, it must be noted that this book departs somewhat from
the general format of the series in which it appears. Being an
effort to present the development of a whole national school of
sociology rather than the work of a single thinker, it necessarily
took on a different form. The material to be presented was more
diverse, and a rather elaborate pattern of convergence and divergence between different strands of work had to be made clear. For
this reason the book consists of a rather long introduction, in
which historical analysis is combined with numerous short cita-
tions from representative works, followed by a relatively short
section of readings selected from those works which strike me as
having been historically decisive or intellectually distinctive in the
making of British sociology as a whole.

HERBERT SPENCER once said in the presence of Huxley and others: "You fellows would little think that I wrote a tragedy when I was young." Huxley said promptly: "I know what it was about." Spencer declared it was impossible as he had never shown or even spoken of it to any one before. Huxley persisted. Spencer put him to the test. Huxley replied: "It was the history of a beautiful induction killed by a nasty little fact."

Karl Pearson, *The Groundwork of Eugenics*, London, 1909

Contents

I. The Origins of British Sociology

Philip Abrams

1

INTRODUCTION

IN THE SUMMER of 1903 the energy and enthusiasm of a mixed bag of historians and philosophers, biologists, journalists, politicians and clergymen, town planners, geographers and businessmen, led to the founding of a Sociological Society in London. Thus Britain may claim to have had the first national sociological association in Europe. From 1905 to 1907 the Society published annually a volume of *Sociological Papers*. In these three volumes there are sixty-one definitions of the nature and aims of sociology. It is in this chaos that the origins of British sociology are to be found.

Insofar as there was a consensus among the pioneers it lay in the belief that sociology should be a science. As to how the science would be constituted there was less agreement. The great men to whom the young Society turned for advice on this matter were Durkheim, who produced a lecture on two types of sociological method, Toennies, who argued the importance of new techniques of statistical analysis, and Francis Galton, who hypnotized far too many of the members with his urgent advocacy of good breeding. While Durkheim and Toennies were talking about the nature of sociology, Galton, in his eighty-third year, was more concerned with what he wanted sociology to do. There was a deep-seated confusion about which type of question the Society should try to answer. And as there were among the members many different views of what sociology was, and very many different, vehemently held, and incompatible views about what sociology should do, the birth pains of the discipline were not surprisingly acute. Whether nature or nurture should he held responsible for certain sickly qualities of the infant that finally emerged is in large part the subject of this book.

I hope this essay contributes to historical sociology as well as to the history of ideas. It tries to do more than trace a sequence of intellectual development. My object has been rather to seize the social structure of a historical situation—to catch the interactions of social organization and social thought through time. The history of British sociology before 1914—indeed before 1945 —is in no sense a success story. What I have tried to make clear is that this failure was not at all an effect of inadequate intellectual resources. Many men of great capacity were deeply concerned with problems of social order and disorder at every level of generality. The critical difficulty was more immediately structural. It was a problem of institutionalization.

For sociology to emerge as a discrete and socially valued field of intellectual effort involving distinctive categories, procedures, and information, the organization of an existing thought world had to be reconstituted. But that thought world had an institutional as well as an ideological existence. And in a highly centralized society such as Britain, with an entrenched but adaptable ruling class, the institutional anchorage of presociological social thought was peculiarly firm. It was not so much the merits of old and new arguments that determined the fate of sociology in Britain as the difficulty of finding room for any large number of sociologists in an established, widely endorsed, and seemingly functional system of social roles. The society provided numerous outlets for social concern of a legitimate, satisfying, and, indeed, seductive nature; all these were disincentives to role-innovation. Above all it provided, for a large and apparently open class of "public persons," access to government. Use what indicators you will, it is clear that, whatever happened to the British economy, British government, both amateur and professional, grew continously and faster than any other throughout the nineteenth century. The political system was growing and malleable. Performing administrative and intelligence functions for government soaked up energies which might have gone toward sociology had such opportunities not been there.

But these opportunities carried their own cost. The problem of maintaining the credibility of intelligence in a context of political controversy is one which has still to be solved. The British intelligentsia, positively oriented to government and enmeshed in the country's social, ecclesiastical, and political elites, found a solution which directly discouraged the growth of sociology. They reduced the idea of intelligence to a matter of facts and figures, creating an empirical tradition of which the great monuments are government inquiries, massive but intellectually sterile levers of social reform. Statistician, administrator, reform politician—these were the roles the system encouraged. The ancient universities offered a fourth possibility, that of social philosopher. But formally and informally the universities were institutional adjuncts of the establishment—church and gentry. At Oxford and Cambridge social philosopher continued to mean moral philosopher working in an essentially classical tradition. Ever since 1660, in England at least, the thrust of intellectual innovation had been away from the universities and toward London, where the boundaries of intellectual activity were less rigidly set. The Royal Society provided a compelling paradigm. The form of organization recognized as establishing the propriety of intellectual change became that of the national society or institute based in London and enjoying royal or at least aristocratic patronage and a socially distinguished membership. The statisticians were greatly exercised by the need to establish themselves in this way. And the need or desire for this sort of recognition also had costs attached.

Meanwhile, sociologist remained a potential role. It could not emerge while the tasks a sociologist would perform were effectively dispersed among four other roles which were themselves well institutionalized and highly desired. Government and the universities were the only sources of patronage capable of sustaining a new profession. Since neither was available to sociology, the new activity, so far as it took institutional shape at all, tended to be institutionalized around a handful of highly charismatic individuals instead. And this in turn made it easy for sociology to dissolve into a cluster of schools, each stamped with the peculiar passions, biases, and eccentricities of its founder. The critical problem for sociology as it first developed in Britain was not in the first instance an intellectual one, a problem of theory or method. Rather, as J. A. Hobson saw in 1910, it was a problem of "the economy of our resources." And for reasons springing from the wider social and institutional setting of British sociology, its resources were both meagre and easily dissipated.

The plan of the essay, accordingly, is as follows: the primary focus is on the three organizations within which the most serious attempts to institutionalize social science were made during the eighty years before 1914—the Statistical Society of London, the National Association for the Promotion of Social Science, and the Sociological Society. In addition to examining the work and intellectual orientations of these agencies I deal extensively with their articulation with the wider social structure and especially with institutions of the political system. The secondary focus is on the work of seven individuals as it interacted with these institutions. These men, Comte, LePlay, Herbert Spencer, L. T. Hobhouse, Francis Galton, Charles Booth, and Patrick Geddes, seem to me to have had more direct influence, for good or ill, on the shaping of early British sociological practice than any others. I should have liked to lengthen the list by adding Edwin Chadwick, E. B. Tylor, Seebohm Rowntree, and the Webbs: but that would have meant writing a different sort of book. Important as they were, these individuals are treated mainly from the perspective of the social agencies in which they acted and by which their activities were contained.

The Problem of Positivism

Discussion of the growth of sociology in England has usually centered on the theme of the strength of positivism in nineteenth-century English thought.[1] This does not seem to me

[1]   N. G. Annan, *The Curious Strength of Positivism in English Political Thought;* Talcott Parsons, *The Structure of Social Action.*

a very helpful approach. To say that James Mill *and* John Stuart Mill, Spencer, Harrison *and* Hobhouse, the pioneers of the statistical societies, the ethnographers *and* the activists of the National Association for the Promotion of Social Science were all positivists is either trivial or wrong. It is true but trivial in the sense that there was a common determination to treat social questions in a manner assumed to be that of the natural scientist. With rather few exceptions the nineteenth-century English intellectual equated access to truth with a Baconian method of inquiry, a method rooted in the direct observation of facts. However, this equation could be modified in a great number of directions until positivism came to include a full spectrum of inductivist and deductivist positions. My own feeling is that there is nothing in positivism, in its minimal definition, that is intrinsically hostile to the development of sociology. What one must do is distinguish between varieties of positivism. It will then appear that some modes of positivism were actively conducive to the fruitful union of theoretical and applied sociology while others were not. The developmental positivism espoused by Hobhouse—and enjoying a return to favor today—clearly had creative possibilities. Some of the more naïve varieties of empirical positivism represented in the statistical movement did not.

What I have done in this essay is isolate three major dimensions of social thought. These provide the immediate intellectual structure within which the pattern of British sociology was formed. They are the dimensions of political economy, ameliorism, and social evolution. In each the broad positivist orientation is strong, while taking a distinctive color and direction. In each the history we discover is a history of controversy about the right method of work and about the meaning of available facts. Analytically separable, these themes were seldom intellectually separated. Each, however found its own distinctive institutional setting in the course of the eighty years before 1914: in the Statistical Society of London, the National Association for the Promotion of Social Science, and the Sociological Society. And that practical separation was consequential.

2

POLITICAL ECONOMY

THE RISE OF SOCIOLOGY in Britain must be treated first in terms of the vicissitudes of political economy. I use the expression to identify an implicit as well as an explicit ideology of mid-Victorian society. Its usual reference is narrower—to the formal programmatic accounts of the science of wealth developed by Malthus, Mill, Ricardo, Senior, Torrens and others devoted to filling out the master paradigm constructed by Adam Smith. But this work had its roots in a substructure of less plainly articulated axioms, assumptions, and principles, and these in turn provided the organizing basis for a wider-ranging public opinion and for the implicit perceptions of social order and purpose that guided public action. For the most part it is this broader reference that I shall use. Three central themes of political economy defined thus were critical in shaping the first efforts at a science of society in Britain, and we must start with them. They were: a deeply rationalist conception of social order; an atomism focused on the individual as the only significant unit of social analysis; and the idea of the Invisible Hand.

Information and Social Order

The elements of social knowledge, specified by Smith and accepted by his heirs, were the individual and the market—or more strictly, individual labor and the price mechanism. The Invisible Hand was the market reified, a force with the cogency of the laws of nature, generated by the activity of individuals and standing over against them as the source of social order, harmony, and integration. Society was represented by political economy as the unintended consequence of the free flow of individual self-interest, and whether the workings of the Invisible Hand were considered euphorically, as by Smith, or austerely, as by Malthus, it was agreed that the path to well-being lay in finding out those rational laws according to which it did its work—not in premature applications of human will through political action. Only when the natural laws of society were properly known would political legislation be appropriate. The first task was research.

The most general theory of society implicit in political economy was then, to borrow Dahrendorf's term, an integration theory. It postulated a fundamental consensus and community of interest among individuals and classes.[1] The central image of the Invisible Hand ruled out the need to recognize implacable conflicts of interest. Situations of overt conflict were problematic not because one had to take sides but because one had to determine how men had come to mistake their real interests. Conflict had to spring from ignorance or unreason, since it could not spring from real incompatibilities. In a curious mirror-image anticipation of Marx, the political economist saw conflict as a form of false consciousness. Malthus was very explicit about this: disagreements would turn out, when examined, to be a product of over-hasty generalization or of an inadequate study of facts and not, by contrast, of irreducible antitheses of value or interest. In the face of conflict, since the social order was axiomatically rational, the political economist resorted to information.

The great emphasis on laissez faire in the history of nineteenth-century thought has rather obscured this tendency of political economy. But the true political outcome of the ideology was two-

---

[1]   Thus Nassau Senior could conclude his case against trade unions by pointing out the malignancy of any agency that served to legitimate, institutionalize, or facilitate conflict, adding, "Our immediate object is to give freedom to the laborer: and we firmly believe that as soon as he is made master of his own conduct, he will use his liberty in the way most useful not only to himself, but to the rest of the community." Senior, *Historical and Philosophical Essays.*

fold: systematic intervention to enable or force men to square their lives with the natural laws of society where these were known but not working freely; and nonintervention where these laws, unencumbered by the remnants of an older, less enlightened society, were already working well. What was needed above all was not a laissez-faire government or an interventionist government, but an informed government, a government that had assimilated the principles of political economy and was fed constantly with the facts that would enable it to apply these principles wisely to cases. The readiness of political economists to turn statesman became notorious. But it is hard to find one of these men who *invariably* advocated laissez-faire. Laissez-faire was a partial application of the ideology. The role they appropriated was that of performing an unprecedented intelligence function for government. What they did invariably advocate was facts. And more facts. So Senior could be the active champion of poor-law amendment and the equally active opponent of factory laws; he could produce a classically pure statement of laissez-faire principle when asked what the government should do about trade unions; and he could advocate public medical services and government investment policies as a solution to the problems of Ireland. To discover the thread of consistency in the ideas of such a man we must see him in two further roles: as the member of the Poor Law Commission of 1832 who transformed a routine inquire-and-report enterprise into one of the most sweeping and meticulous official fact-finding investigations ever conducted in the area of social economics; and as an original member, along with Malthus, McCulloch, and Richard Jones, of the Statistical Society of London. Intelligence, not a particular mode of policy, was Senior's primary commitment.

Within the frame of reference of political economy the proper response to doubt and dissension was to mobilize empirical information. This was true politically. Henry Goulburn, Chancellor of the Exchequer from 1841 to 1846, told the Statistical Society that "during his political life he perpetually had occasion to prepare important documents for the public use," and that in doing so he had "felt in their full force the difficulties arising from a want of an authenticated collection of statistical knowledge." For him, the accumulation of such knowledge had become "an object of great national importance." And it was true academically. The broad consensual boundaries of political economy left room for disagreements on a wide range of particular issues: the whole problem of the basis of value; the concrete meaning of the all-important idea of enlightened self-interest; the proper role of the state; and above all, the meaning of the increasingly disturbing phenomenon of social disorganization known as "the condition of the people question." By 1830 a whole chain of controversies had become explicit inside the encompassing consensus. And as disagreements accumulated so did the appetite for facts, the belief that information would dispel the clouds of controversy. The alternative of course was to recognize the diminishing usefulness of Adam Smith's paradigm.

But what sort of facts? Here the atomistic conception of social order rooted in political economy was decisive. What facts could there be for the political economist but aggregated data about the circumstances and behavior of individuals? Political economy was to be perfected and disputes settled by the collection and classification of quantitative information about individuals. To further its growth and enable it to support practical conclusions the analytical science of economics needed an appropriate applied or descriptive science—the science of statistics. Malthus had urged the case for the systematic gathering of vital statistics as early as 1800. Jones renewed the appeal in 1833 in his inaugural lecture as professor of Political Economy at King's College, London. The British Association echoed him later in the same year. The following spring the felt need for statistics took organizational form. Sure that they were moving in a rationalized social universe, but aware of critical areas of ignorance and of the need to maintain a minimal unity of interpretation, political economists readily turned themselves into "facts-and-figures" men. Since the most significant objects in their universe were individual human beings, their conception of facts was determined by those objects.[2]

[2]   A general paradigm for this development is suggested by Harold Wilensky, *Organizational Intelligence*, 1967.

What made the need for statistics so much more pressing in 1834 was the continued growth of dissension among political economists. This in turn was directly related to their active involvement in problems of government. Political economy was from the first strongly policy-oriented, and it was the policy orientation more than anything else that inspired the development of specialized statistical work—but by reaction. It was precisely at the level of policy that the ambiguous nature of experience, the hazards of conflict, and therefore the need, as Malthus urged, for at least majority agreement among political economists, were most evident. By 1830 the divisive impact on political economy of a wide range of social issues—poor law, combinations, public health, child labor, emigration, factory conditions, education—had been recognized. Political economists were eager to make recommendations on these issues but found that they spoke with many voices. Conversely, the main assumptions of political economy had been largely assimilated by politicians. The problem was to keep political economy practical without plunging in into self-destructive scrutiny of its own fundamental positions. Consequently it was just those representatives of the school most involved in policy concerns who, whatever their own policy preferences, were most keenly aware of the need for social information in the form of statistics as the means of reconciling science and policy. Statistics was institutionalized under the direct patronage of the British political elite and with the active participation of its most distinguished officials.

3

STATISTICS

THE STATISTICAL MOVEMENT as represented by the Statistical Society of London thus rested on curious premises.[1] Its members were united in a common sense of the usefulness of quantitative social information. Many privately enjoyed a confidence, springing directly from the logic of political economy, that facts when discovered would speak with a single unequivocal voice to indicate practical conclusions. But meanwhile they played safe by formally excluding opinion from their proceedings. The implicit purposes of the Society were at once to bring political economy into politics, in the sense of generating relevant administrative intelligence, and to end politics, in the sense of obliterating conflicts of principle. Three things would be particularly

[1]   My general source for this section is the *Journal of the Statistical Society*, published from 1838, and in particular the *Jubilee Volume* of 1885; also *Annals of the Royal Statistical Society*, 1934. (Royal patronage was acquired in 1887.) It must be made clear that the Statistical Society of London was at best representative of a wider enterprise. The Manchester Society preceded it and in the early years, at least, did more impressive work. Then there was the Statistical Section of the British Association and a string of provincial statistical societies. There had also been a major development of statistical work within government before 1834, associated with the census, of course, but increasingly, too, with the Board of Trade. And one or two government officials played a decisive role in the broader promotion of statistics—the obvious example is G. R. Porter whose *Progress of the Nation* in edition after edition became the country's standard work of reference. The one thing the London Society had which other groups lacked was a capacity to bring together such officials with party politicians and a very distinguished group of private intellectuals.

important in its later intellectual history: its direct engagement with social policy, its orientation to the gathering and evaluation of facts as an alternative to the radical reconstruction of theory, and its close involvement with government.

The extent to which the founders of the statistical movement took it for granted that statistics meant social statistics is surprising. The new field of work was invariably defined substantively, not methodologically: it was seen as a form of applied economics, a realization of Malthus' intention "to prepare some of the most important rules of political economy for practical application by a frequent reference to experience." Although there were a few mathematicians among the original members, there were many more economists, politicians, peers, government officials, and doctors of medicine: their object was politically useful information about society, not, say, the development of mathematical method.[2] The great difference between statistics and political economy according to the manifesto printed in the first issue of the Society's *Journal* was that while both pursued the same end, a science of wealth, statistics:

neither discussed causes nor reasoned upon probable effects, but sought only to collect, arrange and compare the class of facts which can alone form the basis of correct conclusions with respect to social and political government.

a difference which, it was held, "absolutely excluded every kind of speculation." The same conception appears more bluntly in the original constitution of the Society:

The Statistical Society of London has been established for the purposes of procuring, arranging and publishing "Facts calculated to illus-

[2]   Compare the definition of statistics offered in the most recent of large dictionaries, *The Random House Dictionary*: "The science that deals with the collection, classification, analysis and interpretation of numerical facts or data and by the use of mathematical theories of probability imposes order and regularity on aggregates of more or less disparate elements." By contrast the conception of statistics found in the work of the London Statistical Society stands closer to the "social indicators" school of work represented today in the work of Russett, Deutsch, Bauer, Biderman, and others.

trate the Condition and Prospects of Society." The Statistical Society will consider it to be the first and most essential rule of its conduct to exclude carefully all Opinions from its transactions and publications—to confine its attention rigorously to facts—and, as far as it may be found possible, to facts which can be stated numerically and arranged in tables.

The close connection of the Society as a whole and of many of its most active members individually with government constantly reinforced this feeling for a pure empiricism. In its early years the Council of the Society often looked like a subcommittee of a Whig Cabinet. A significant element of its leading members, those who had most experience of intensive statistical research, was always made up of government officials. And serving, advising, and seeking to influence and ‘rationalize government all encouraged the style of work to which the Society was already predisposed—accumulations of facts systematically detached from fundamental speculations about the meaning of facts. There is a certain circularity here. Research presented as mere facts is more likely to be taken seriously by government than research that is speculatively engaged with the penumbra of meanings which the merest of facts must carry; it respects the division of labor between politician and adviser. Conversely, if the researcher's ambition is to perform an intelligence function for government he easily accepts current government definitions of the nature of intelligence. But in this case there is no need to try to break the circle. British statisticians and British statesmen were recruited from a common intellectual milieu; the frequency with which a single man filled both roles was high; most important, the diffusion of political economy was such that it was easy and instinctive for men in both roles to see eye to eye. For the early Victorians, from Professor Whewell, loftily admitting statisticians to the British Association on the understanding that they would eschew the "foul demon of discord" and confine themselves to "facts . . . mere abstractions . . . numerical results," to Mr. Gradgrind, murdering the innocents with the same medicine, "In this life we want nothing but Facts, Sir; nothing but Facts!," the peculiar salience of abstracted quantitative data was self-evident. "Nor need we doubt," as the Statistical

Society of Ulster was assured by one of its earliest speakers, "that the study of Statistics will, ere long, rescue Political Economy from all the uncertainty in which it is now enveloped."

These three elements, the abstracted conception of facts, the orientation to social issues, and the involvement with government, built into the first organization of the Statistical Society, worked on each other in decisive ways to shape its future development.

The Statistical Society

The intention of the original members had been to organize the work of the Society under four heads: economic statistics, political statistics, medical statistics, and moral and intellectual statistics. In the light of this comprehensive intention the pattern of work that actually emerged is revealing. It reflects the priorities of the active membership very plainly.

Of the 511 themes treated in papers read to the Society in its first fifty years only 11 are concerned with statistical method. Economic statistics are the largest single group (127 items). However these contributions cover the whole range of finance and taxation (53), production (49), and trade (25). The political category contains only 8 strictly political items, the other 72 being administrative and institutional. Ninety-five items fall into the category of medical statistics, or vital statistics as we should now say; 98 items can be placed in the last category, moral and intellectual statistics, but it is important to note that the great preponderance of these (90 contributions) are statistics of the "condition of the people"—poverty, crime, illiteracy, and so forth among the lower classes. Moreover, there was a significant division of labor between those members contributing to the economic category and those whose work fell into the moral and intellectual, or as it was soon renamed, social category.

In the field of social statistics, then, two types of work prevail: vital statistics and statistics of the condition of the poor. And in the first ten years this is an absolute predominance over all other types of work—the situation changed later largely because with the development of the Registrar General's Department vital statistics were absorbed by government with the Statistical Society confining itself to an advisory role. It is, in short, in the 1830's and not in the 1880's or 1930's that we find the peculiar pattern of British empirical sociology first set. It is there that we find the origins of the two branches of sociology which are still the most highly developed in Britain, demography and the sociology of poverty. And much of the early work, as we shall see, was already sociological in more than a descriptive sense.

The interest in vital statistics was largely oriented to departmental or other administrative needs. But in the 1830's we find the first of a series of efforts to standardize and generalize statistical materials, efforts by officials themselves for the most part, Porter's great reforms at the Board of Trade for example, or the work of Giffen a generation later. There was a new feeling for clean data, a new understanding of the need for large-scale comparative analysis. More important, there was a new sense of the relevance of vital statistics as a tool of social evaluation. Here the ideological bearing of political economy was again critical; it focused analysis on the issue of social progress, "the progress of the nation," and it suggested the appropriateness of measuring progress in terms of the differential experience of the classes of the nation (if only to show, as was Giffen's object in the paper of 1883 reprinted below, that contrary to appearances all classes, even the lowest, were in fact sharing in the national advance). It was political economy too, that suggested the need to use time-series tabulations linking economic and social indicators (market variables and life-chance variables) as one's primary measures of national progress. Thus we find some active members of the Statistical Society, mostly with medical backgrounds—Chadwick, Farr, Guy, and others—mobilizing vital statistics not just to map distributions of life expectancies or marriage rates among the different classes but to calculate relationships for different classes between, say, price fluctuations or entrepreneurial expansion on the one hand and sanitary conditions or occupational mobility, income or education on the other. The tendency of this work was, of course, to illumine with ever-growing clarity the ways in which life chances were mediated by socially structured experiences.

This is very clear in the long series of papers (1845–59) contributed by Guy on the duration of life in different occupational groups or in the controversy between Chadwick and Neilsen in 1844–45 over the influence of trade, locality and other factors on health and mortality "amongst different classes in different districts and countries." But for years the wider theoretical implications of the new mode of vital statistics were either not seen or ignored. Rather, emphasis settled on the business of producing more exact indicators, better methods of classification and data collection, improved life tables, higher levels of comparability between discrete bodies of data and the like. The ad hoc administrative orientation remained strong. The commitment was to statistics, not sociology.

Field Studies of "The Condition of the People"

A similar pattern appears more starkly when we look at the work done under the head of social statistics, the bulk of which was work on the condition of the poor. The Statistical Society began its study of society ambitiously. A program of "interrogatories" was designed by the Society in its first year with the intention that the Society should itself take on the collection of standardized data in all those areas of social life where ignorance of facts currently prevented the resolution of controversies. The most enthusiastic members were put to work preparing sets of questions in the areas of their special knowledge; Porter on savings banks and crime, Jones on rent, Senior on the laboring classes generally. And in July, 1836, the resulting questionnaires were approved and printed. They were distributed, however, not to a general sample of the population but to relevant authorities; the police, hospital, and poor-law administrators, school boards, factory commissioners, insurance societies, landlords, newspaper editors, magistrates and prison governors, and the Fellows of the Statistical Society in their various localities. The scale of the project is a good indication of the depth of men's sense of social ignorance in the 1830's as well as of the ambitions of the statisticians.

But it called for too much work from too few people and came to nothing: a handful of returns on different topics survive along with some of the interrogatories themselves. The one dealing with strikes was printed in the Society's *Journal* in 1838. Its open-ended empiricism is a model of serious intention and of survey design in the tradition of investigation from above that was to be the distinctive mode of social inquiry in Britain until the 1930's. The purpose was

to collect a statistical account of the various strikes and combinations which have existed in different parts of the United Kingdom for the purpose of altering the rate of wages, and of introducing new regulations between masters and men . . . to exhibit the condition of the workmen at the time of the commencement of the strike or combination, and the terms and conditions on which they resumed work; showing also, as far as the same can be statistically stated, the permanent effects of the several disputes upon the character and condition of the workmen.

Faced with such a task and with the presumed need to eschew explicit hypothesis, a natural history approach was adopted: "the members . . . after due deliberation, and with an anxious desire to avoid even the appearance of party bias, have prepared . . . a numerous list of queries, designed to elicit the complete and impartial history of strikes"—which was then transmitted to many "intelligent individuals." A perfectly coherent theory of strikes is of course *implicit* in the questionnaire—for example, in the assumption, at odds with a good deal of more recent industrial sociology, that whatever the ostensible causes of strikes, the real causes are to be found in the economic self-interest of the workmen.

Quite early on the difficulties of generating sufficient information by the method of interrogatories suggested another mode of inquiry to the statisticians. Again in the first instance the work was taken on directly by the Society, using paid agents. This was the field survey of particular local communities—a strategy primarily adopted for the study of poverty and the social concomitants of poverty. Following the reports of such studies through the early volumes of the Society's *Journal* is to see, step by step, the creation of a new method of research and with it the discovery of quite unanticipated and problematic new knowledge.

The decision to seek comprehensive data on particular communities as an alternative to partial data on the nation as a whole was important because it brought the statisticians one step closer to the professed object of their greatest concern, the condition of the people. Surprisingly, however, for three generations the first steps toward the direct study of the poor taken in the 1830's were not followed up, even though it became clear that there was much about the causes, meaning, and consequences of poverty that could *only* be learned by field survey methods. On the whole the Victorian statisticians did not see any great need to learn those things. They were looking for aggregate data on conditions or behavior not for experiential data, and accordingly their studies relied almost entirely on materials gathered from institutional administrators; their findings were inferences from the correlation of institutional statistics. The exceptional investigator might talk to school children as well as to school masters—E. W. Edgell, whose interest in moral statistics led him to seek direct measures of religiosity, was one who did— but both sides in the great debates of the midcentury, the debates about the relationship of crime to income for example, drew their evidence from information supplied by employers and policemen. The social survey in the form used by Booth was pioneered in the 1830's—in 1837 Porter found field investigations of the conditions of the working classes under way in Marylebone, Soho, Westminster, several rural parishes in Essex and Herefordshire, and the city of York.[3] But the administrative and rationalistic bias of the statisticians delayed its real development for sixty years.

The Ambiguity of Facts

Nevertheless the work on poverty and on the institutional contexts of poverty, schools, churches, workhouses, alehouses, and prisons, did create a cumulative tradition, largely because it was controversial. The statisticians were continually surprised by their own findings, and new insights, new studies, and new interpreta-

[3]   *Journal of the Statistical Society*, 1839.

tions sprang from their surprise. As early as 1840 it had been demonstrated that, at least at the lowest educational levels, crime and literacy varied together, not inversely. And such findings could not but challenge critical assumptions of political economy. Further fact-finding to resolve the difficulty was plainly called for.

The problem that emerged was to integrate the statistics of poverty with the analysis of economic system variables. The response can be traced through the London studies financed by the historian Hallam in the 1830's, Dansen's work on "Changes in the Condition of the People . . . and their Connection with Changes in the Prices of Food" of 1848, Seyd on "Currency Laws and their Effects on Pauperism" in 1871, Brabrook's set of papers on Friendly Societies and then Giffen's provocative "Progress of the Working Classes" in 1883. The work of Booth and Rowntree stands at the end of this tradition as well as at the beginning of something new. The concern at the center of these studies was to find an explanation for the incidence and distribution of poverty that squared with a self-regulating and optimistic conception of society. It was in this connection that Giffen's exercise in social accounting gave "comfort" to Gladstone—it disposed of the criticisms of men like Henry George (nobody yet noticed Marx) who insisted on finding structurally rooted conflicts of interest in capitalist economies.

But in the long run the poverty studies aggravated the problem they were meant to solve. The first thing to go was the effort to separate fact and opinion. The collection and presentation of even the simplest numerical distributions was so plainly shaped at every level by unspoken opinions, and the interpretation of facts was so inseparable from the evaluation of those opinions, that the statisticians quickly admitted the impossibility of reaching the level of pure empiricism aimed at in the 1830's.

The difficulty was revealed very nicely in the first paper to appear in the Society's *Journal*, "On the Establishment of Pauper Schools" by James Phillips Kay, Assistant Poor-Law Commissioner. The statistical facts presented by Kay concern the number of pauper children in workhouses, their level of education, and the costs, actual and estimated, of different methods of teaching them, with comparative figures from Belgium and Holland. The argument spun from this data is that pauper children should be removed from the workhouses (and their parents) and educated in special Schools of Industry, each school serving some ten workhouses. But the argument does not of course rest exclusively on the data. It rests also on some assumptions: that the future social and economic dependence of pauper children could be prevented only if they were fitted to "discharge their social duties" by training in "correct moral habits" as well as in useful skills: that the problem was one to be dealt with by central administrative action and at public cost: that the costs involved should be minimal: that "the outlay attending the maintenance of the pauperised classes," was a proper measure of "the extent and quantity of the moral evils incident upon the existence of pauperism"; and of course that "the great object to be kept in view of regulating any school for the instruction of the children of the labouring class, is the rearing of hardy and intelligent working men, whose character and habits shall afford the largest amount of security to the property and order of the community."

The exclusion of opinion was found to be doubly irksome. It encouraged the worst kind of gradgrindism. And it discouraged politically engaged persons from spending time on statistical research. What men in the grip of political economy most wanted to do was to mold policy; to make positive contributions in the sense of *informed* opinion to the policy process. The closer one was to political and official life the stronger this motive was likely to be. The members felt to be most valuable to the new Society and its new science were just those most involved in the public issues from which an explicit interplay of fact and opinion could not be excluded. The whole point of statistics for such men was to provide a basis for definitive opinions in the face of opposition. The idea embodied in the original motto of the Society ("Aliis exterendum")—that others should thresh out the harvest which the statisticians had gathered—implied a division of labor which for men like Chadwick, Porter, Purdy, of the Local Government Board, Farr, who became Superintendent of Statistics in the Registrar General's Office, Caird, Giffen, Craigie, R. W. Rawson, to say nothing of Dilke, Joseph Chamberlain, Lord Roseberry, and the host of other statisticians in "the front rank of public servants," as Booth was to put it, was not so much anomalous as simply unworkable.

But if the administrative and public service inclinations of the most distinguished statisticians quickly forced a recognition of the usefulness of at least ad hoc hypotheses, the issue was not quickly settled. It was debated solemnly in the 1840's and again in the late 1850's. By that time the tendency for new statistical data to generate new conflicts of opinion had become very clear. The storm caused by John Clay's demonstration in 1854 of a positive relation between rising prosperity and rising crime rates is the most famous example. In 1858 the Society dropped its early motto. But in 1865 the whole issue of the relationship of theory to information was being vehemently discussed once more. In that year and again in 1873 Guy, urging his colleagues to consider the "proper functions of a Statistical Society," still found it necessary to make a strong case for the explicit integration of fact and opinion. 1873 was also the year R. Biddulph-Martin presented a paper setting out a statistical case for the state ownership of railways, provoking "the longest discussion that has yet taken place within these walls," and causing several members to "doubt the expediency" of investigating such topics at all. The great debates on the meaning of the statistics of poverty and economic progress of the 1880's and 1890's were still to come, and beyond them lay the Majority and Minority Reports of the Poor Law Commission in 1909. But even such extreme evidence of the ambiguity of facts would not shake the distaste of a critical group of British social investigators for controversies of principle, or their faith that facts properly gathered would eventually speak for themselves. The strength of the tradition was such that even twenty years later the Webbs made it the basis of the true method of social science.

Pure Statistics

The achievement of Booth and Rowntree was to produce figures which revealed the structural connections of poverty as well as its extent. In tying poverty to unemployment, wage rates, and housing conditions and in suggesting that these and not personal viciousness or intemperance were the consequential links they forcefully introduced questions of principle on the basis of impeccable statistics. Like Edgell, Clay, and Biddulph-Martin, but more centrally and dramatically, they challenged the root beliefs of political economy. Even those who had advocated a marriage of fact and opinion in the past had not seen where they would finally be led. The questions that Guy had seen springing from the statistics of poverty in the 1870's are as interesting for what he left out as for what he included:

> What man possessed of sense, curiosity or fancy, could gaze unmoved on this mixed mass of poverty, destitution, and crime which makes up the lower stratum of our artificial society? How resist the question, what part of all this misery is the result of personal defects and vices—of sloth, unthrift, intemperance, incapacity; how much of slovenly habits, of dole-giving in the rich and less poor, how much of what may be called inaptitude in the State! How is it possible to resist the inquiry whether when more than three centuries ago, our ancestors established a poor law, they ought not rather to have given us a good police force.[4]

Booth and Rowntree drastically expanded the range of relevant questions. In the 1890's Booth was the ornament of the Statistical Society and the symbol of its tradition. He worked from the Society's offices, became its president and won its most distinguished award. But his great methodological innovation was not in numerical analysis (indeed not more than a third of *Life and Labour* has strictly quantitative value), but in renewing the tradition of house-to-house inquiry and case studies which the statisticians had pioneered and then allowed to languish. And more than anyone else he made explicit the crisis which had always lurked beneath the surface of the effort to combine uncritical empiricism with policy-oriented research under the aegis of the Invisible Hand.

The poverty debates had a powerful effect on the development

4   *Journal of the Statistical Society*, 1873.

of British sociology. But this effect was not entirely to the good. A new and damaging division of labor was opened up, producing an intellectual fission, implicit in the history of the Statistical Society from the start, between those who clung to figures and those who felt that the weight of the evidence already available called for an altogether new conception of society, and who turned increasingly to problems of sociological theory. The strictly statistical reaction, more and more specific after 1885, was to reassert the old faith, suspend judgment on the issues of contemporary debate, shy away from adventurous research enterprises and concentrate on the refinement of method. The path had already been indicated by Guy in the stormy atmosphere of 1873:

Assuming that we are justified in speaking of ourselves as a scientific body, with social man as our subject, and the most exact and precise knowledge attainable as our aim: what, it may be asked, can we do to perfect this scientific work? The time is deemed favourable to the reconsideration of the scientific work of the Society. What do these words mean? I take them to point to a larger introduction of the scientific element into all the work we do. . . . Now the scientific element of which I am speaking, is nothing else than the principles of the numerical method, of the logic of large numbers, seeking their application, as tests and correctives of all the numerical statements (tabulated or untabulated) which are brought before us. This division, or section, of universal logic has not yet, I venture to think, received the attention it deserves. . . . We should thus become more and more the scientific centre towards which would gravitate all who are prepared to make the sacrifice of time and thought required of those who prefer laborious truth to easy speculation. Outside of this narrow circle there would still be room enough for all honest workers anxious to promote social reforms on the basis of obvious wrong-doing, without waiting to ascertain in how many instances the wrong in question is being committed.[5]

In the middle decades of the century Guy was the leading exponent of a purer mathematical emphasis, but his own work on statistical methods hardly went beyond questions of the estimation of averages and the relationship between series. It is only in 1885 that a true collective commitment to the improvement of method appears. Edgeworth's rediscovery of probability curves and his refinement of the means of calculating error mark the beginning of the new age. Curiously, the *Jubilee Volume* of the Statistical Society reflects what was to come much better than it reflects what had gone before. Surveying the history of the Society, F. J. Mouat found the practical achievement of statistics much easier to record than the scientific; statistical work, he concluded, had established a new concept of social information and had disseminated it to all spheres of public life; "order, method and precision" had been injected into "all branches of legislation on social subjects"; above all, "statistics have become parliamentary . . . and administrative." But what we find in the *Jubilee Volume* is not a series of applied studies bringing together quantitative data on major social problems, nor the pattern of the past, but rather exercises in advanced statistical method by Edgeworth, Jeans, Levasseur, and Marshall—the distinctive emphasis of the future.

It would not be true to say that the statisticians now withdrew from their first concern with the condition of society. In the next thirty years vital statistics and social statistics still provide the largest element (37 per cent) of the work of the Society. There are five contributions by Booth and a set of further studies of the context of pauperism (wages, unemployment and consumption, cooperation, schooling, insurance, and pensions), which taken together provide as definitive a sociographic profile of a class as has ever been drawn. But what is true is that, at a time when the manifest evidence of social conditions might well have led to a crisis of ideology and to a major reconstruction of social theory, the statisticians found a way of preserving their own social assumptions uncriticized. As the interpretation of society, and therefore the determination of right courses of action became ever more problematic, the statisticians concluded that the search for reliable facts had also to become more complicated and exacting. And a corollary of this plunge into more sophisticated mathematics ("The History of Pauperism treated by Frequency Curves"), was an ability to perpetuate their antipathy to theory, to cling to the atomistic, optimistic perspectives of political economy as the organizing frame of reference for their research while still professing hostility to all "systems of opinion or doctrine"—including the rudiments of modern sociological theory already being constructed around them by men with less confidence in figures.

Investigation of social conditions did not of itself produce a new understanding of society—only a greater concern and a greater sense of the urgency of administrative and legislative action to bring society into line with what was essentially still Adam Smith's blueprint. Focusing persistently on the distribution of individual circumstances, the statisticians found it hard to break through to a perception of poverty as a product of social structure. They did not get near to conceptualizing it as Disraeli and Engels had done in the 1840's, as Dickens did in the 1850's or as the authors of the *Radical Programme* did in 1885. They did not and probably could not achieve the concept of structural victimization which has been so fruitful in the sociology of poverty developed in the United States since 1960.

Mouat was right to hold that by the 1880's the quantitative approach to social policy had taken hold of government. And those who espoused a quantitative approach saw administrative intelligence and action as the pivot of effective policy. This was true across the whole range of policy options from Lord Milner to the Webbs. The Webbs, indeed, are a critical case; government-sponsored empirical investigation to measure the problem and government machinery to deal with it became their prescription for all ills. Beatrice at least was to find the rubric for a democratic society not in the constitution of the Labour Party written by her husband but in the *Report* of Lord Haldane's Committee on the Machinery of Government. But as statistics became official those who had broken free of political economy tended to become anti-statistical. Many of those who called themselves sociologists in 1910 were in conscious revolt against the statistical science which ideally should have been among their distinctive tools. In the next half-century Bowley, Hogben, Glass and others would have to devote great efforts to closing a gap between sociology and statistics which, had the history of ideas been different, or the access of nineteenth-century statisticians to government less intimate, might never have opened. But in 1885 we find Giffen still using income tax returns as an adequate indicator of social structure.

Statistics and Social Policy

The central position of the statisticians was quickly made clear; they refused to be excluded from active involvement in the making of social policy; and they refused to admit the need for a more radically theoretical approach to social analysis. But the orthodox statisticians no longer monopolized the arena of discourse. Suddenly in the 1880's classical German writings on the nature and uses of statistics began to be translated; and there were native contributions by Hooper, Guy, Mouat, Rawson, Sidgwick and many more. The tendency of the discussion was divisive. For some, statistics was a helpful method of analysis but one which, given the general ambiguity and diversity of available data, could only specify problems, not interpret or resolve them; it was to be an adjunct of a more intellectually critical activity which was increasingly called Sociology. For others, and it was this group that continued to dominate the Statistical Society and, more importantly, the activities of government, including both research and patronage, the cogency of pure statistical work as a means of defining both problems and policies remained unquestionable; present doubts would be swiftly dispelled by a stricter attention to statistical method. This position is very plain in Rawson's attempt to use the Jubilee meeting as an "occasion for settling, if possible, the vexed question of the legitimate claim of Statistics to be acknowledged as a science." His own view was straightforward: "I am not prepared to make statistics the handmaid of social science, to degrade the parent into the position of a hewer of wood and a drawer of water in the service of its own offspring": specifically, "in claiming for Statistics a superiority of method over social science or sociology, I would point out that the latter may be studied by less precise methods than the former"—and for just that reason, of course, it was less scientific, less appropriate as a basis for "statecraft." Certainly, Rawson admitted, the meaning of the statistics so far gathered was often cloudy, but "mathematical principles of investigation are available, and, the more closely these are applied, the nearer will be the approach to mathematical precision in the results."

To yet others, R. H. I. Palgrave for example, speaking as President of the Section of Economic Science and Statistics of the British Association in 1883, another path suggested itself. Surveying the state of political economy he decided that the time had come for a renewal of theory: "endeavour to avoid the conclusion as we may, we are driven to admit that our science must be founded on theory, call it by what name you will: abstraction which lies at the root of the deductive, or hypothesis which forms the basis of the inductive method." Beyond such measured judgments lay a drastic bifurcation of intellectual activity. Booth and Rowntree straddled the gulf but fewer and fewer others did so—and Booth and Rowntree were special cases.

We should note before going on just what the new principles being mooted in the 1880's and found so threatening by the political economists were. They spoke of socialism—it was not only Liberal politicians but his statistical colleagues who hailed Giffen's work as "an easy method with the Socialists." But it was T. H. Green and Joseph Chamberlain they had in mind as much as Karl Marx. Palgrave found his main example of English socialism in the opinions of Canon Barnett:

His recommendations include a wiser administration of the poor law, so as to enable a distinction to be drawn between the man who had kept clear of parish relief up to a reasonable age and the man who had not. This, and a wider application of the principle of the Artisans' Dwelling Act and the Libraries Act are amongst the principal of his recommendations. They come to this, that the old age of the honest working man should be made secure against distressing want or degrading relief, and that the power of obtaining rational pleasures should be provided for him within reasonable bounds. *Some will think this will be going too far.* The question for the economist to consider is, How far can it be granted without impairing the great principle of self-help?[6]

6   British Association, *Transactions*, 1883.

The rejection of political economy implicit in the moralizing ac-
tivism of men like Barnett bothered the statisticians as much as
any direct confrontation of theories. The debates were still cen-
tred on facts and the meaning of facts. That was why Giffen's paper
was so important. The vote of thanks moved in reply to it went
straight to the point: his work, he was told, "rested on such solid
statistical facts that it had been listened to with much gratification
by the large audience that night who would sleep all the sounder
with the reflections afforded by [his] really comforting conclusions." The shift of emphasis toward purer and more sophisticated
mathematics followed easily.

Meanwhile the ameliorists and socialists refused to be either
comforted or put off. Barnett had worked in the slums. Chamberlain knew Birmingham. Facts speak for themselves at many levels
and with many voices. And reformers could more and more easily
find immediate opportunities, both in and out of the party system,
to change society; why wait for, let alone spend time on, more
perfect investigations of it. The grip of political economy on the
reform impulse had never been complete; but in the 1890's it was
almost lost. It was not so much the statisticians who changed in
this period as the political culture in which they existed. New
demands were articulated, new responses to social experience appeared, and in the face of this extended discussion the enterprise
of statistics was seen by many as only one strand—more or less
the official one, the mechanism of government action—in an increasingly diverse reaction to the problem of tying social knowledge to social change. It was not so much that the Statistical
Society narrowed its terms of reference as that other approaches
to social science developed outside it because they were not welcome within it. Methodology apart, the statisticians stood still
while the universe of social inquiry grew around them. Unfortunately the rooted intellectual inclinations and governmental
involvements of the statistical tradition made for a sharp, and
often hostile, separation of the statisticians, both in and out of
office, from the newcomers in what they still regarded as their
peculiar domain.

4

AMELIORISM

IF VICTORIAN ENGLAND produced Mr. Gradgrind and the Commissioners of Fact it also produced Charles Dickens. If it produced many men like Sir Robert Giffen it also produced some like Seebohm Rowntree. This is not a question of sharp antitheses. Again and again we find the concern for facts and for rationalization mixed up with a counteracting moral sensibility. The same minds display both tendencies. Lord Shaftesbury, champion of the "climbing boys" and "ragged schools," became president of the Statistical Society. Nevertheless, it is not a mere device of analysis to detach the moralizing orientation to society from the statistical. For many Victorians the moral perspective carried imperatives of its own at least as powerful as those of empirical science. Shaftesbury's understanding of society, the peculiar ways in which he linked knowledge and policy, owed more to Adam than to Adam Smith.

In the 1830's the scientific enthusiasm of the statisticians and a social concern of a more directly moral nature were very closely tied. The ambivalence is clear in the reports that have survived of some of the provincial statistical societies. The Royal Polytechnic Society of Cornwall gave the following elaborate reason for promoting an essay prize in statistics:

If "the proper study of mankind be man" the value of statistical information can no longer be doubted. It stimulates the benevolence and gives aim and effect to the energies of the philanthropist; it furnishes the legislator with materials on which to found remedial measures for social derangement, and plans for increasing the mass of social happiness. . . . From information thus furnished, it cannot be questioned that the public attention has been fastened, with an intensity never before given to the subject, upon the physical and moral degradation of the poorer classes . . . The appeal thus made has been nobly responded to; the dry facts have been interpreted; and means have been adopted for carrying the blessings of education, order, and virtue into these dark recesses where ignorance, vice, and misrule appeared to have fortified themselves in impenetrable obscurity.[1]

In such statements the value of statistics was great but secondary. It lay in pointing out "the fulcrum on which to rest the lever in our endeavours to remove the mass of sin and misery" that conscientious men sensed around them. Conversely the bait used to lure men to statistical work had two flavors: statistics, "enable us to associate more immediately scientific and intellectual pursuits with works of benevolence and the rich luxury of doing good." Impossible to resist the pull of those last six words!

On the other hand it is probably true that statistical societies flourished to the extent that statisticians managed to keep their moral impulses under control. Most of these societies perished quickly, depending as they did on the energies of quite small numbers of local businessmen and gentry. What moved the majority of such men to take an interest in social investigation was a traditional sense of their responsibility to do good, coupled with uncertainty about what doing good was in a society that had suddenly become extraordinarily large and complicated. Their concern had an important utilitarian dimension. They wanted to be sure that the proportion of their income devoted to philanthropy was used as rationally as the proportion that went to accumulation. Many of the people initially drawn to statistics came to view it, on this basis, as a poor investment. The costs of social science were high and they had to be privately borne. If one's moral understanding, constantly reinforced from the pulpit, already gave one a strong and coherent view of what ought to be done, elaborate social investigation could easily be seen as a waste of time, and still more as a waste of money that would be better used in direct philanthropy.

[1]   *Journal of the Statistical Society,* 1840.

The Cost of Social Knowledge

One had to be rich as well as committed to be both a sociologist and a philanthropist in Victorian England. One had to sense the need for information as a basis for policy and as a means of controverting rival policy positions; and one had to be able to fund large scale inquiries virtually without public subsidy. Henry Hallam privately financed the house-to-house surveys done in the name of the Statistical Society of London in the 1830's when the Society itself could not afford to. The Manchester Statistical Society was founded in 1833 by thirteen "gentlemen who felt a strong desire to assist in promoting the progress of social improvement." In addition to the desire, they had the means. The Society almost immediately undertook two massive inquiries, a survey of schools in the whole northern area and, using paid agents, a house-to-house poverty study of "the whole of the working population in six manufacturing towns . . . containing more than 300,000 inhabitants." In a famous remark Booth observed that intensity of feeling had to be added to statistics and statistics to intensity of feeling if a sociology capable of moving the world aright was to be created. But conscience and statistics would not have produced *The Life and Labour of the People in London,* if Booth had not also been rich. He was able to provide himself with the staff, "like an executive department of state," which the scale of the enterprise required. If Rowntree's research was felt to be definitive for policy in a way no one else's had been, it was not just because he was more meticulous or compassionate than others; he also had an income which allowed him when doing his Belgian study to employ 101 assistants for upward of 19 months.[2] Even now not much British social research has the kind of funding that the handful of great Victorian studies enjoyed.

The combination of solid wealth, intensity of feeling about social problems, and belief in the relevance of statistical investigation as a preliminary to action was a rare one. It was easy enough to find men and women with two of the necessary qualities. Few had

[2]   B. S. Rowntree, *Land and Labour: a Study of Belgium.*

all three. Perhaps because it was too easy for the rich to do good. We are dealing with a class that had long absorbed the role of public person. Its primary orientation was to measures not information. In the Statistical Society of London a commitment to information as such became institutionalized. Government departments took on a similar commitment if only because information-seeking, research, was one of the few legitimate ways of postponing action. But the immediate interest of most of the conscientious rich was to know what sort of measures would effectively deal with this or that well-known and pressing social problem. Only in exceptional circumstances was the nature of the social question itself so unclear that research obviously had to precede legislation. This was the case in the 1830's when men first realized that they were living in an industrial society. And it was so again in the 1880's when the victims of industrialism had become so articulate and so visible that something had to be wrong with the bland figures of national progress produced by the statisticians.

Yet even in such circumstances the development of an autonomous social science was unlikely. The society was too centralized. The political system was too well integrated with the upper echelons of the class system. When social analysis was needed it might briefly take the form of independent research, but this was quickly superseded by Royal Commissions, Advisory Committees, the engrossing of research by government departments. The potential sociologists invariably ended up as civil servants or chairmen of committees. Rowntree did not stop doing research after his first invitation to breakfast with Lloyd George in 1912. But he was given an official committee and for years his work was buried in volumes of state papers. He himself was happy to think that he had moved from the mere presentation of facts to an active engagement in policy.

Research in the Service of Policy

The image of the social scientist as a formulator of measures flourished, not surprisingly, in just that period when the sense of a need for basic information was least pressing. The initial ambivalence of the early statistical societies gives way in the 1850's to a new role model of the social scientist as a technician of policy. This is given institutional form in the National Association for the Promotion of Social Science. And the Association in turn dissolves amid the vehement policy debates of the 1880's.

We can briefly follow this development in the experience of the short-lived Statistical Society of Bristol. At the outset it provides a nice example of the early conjunction of motives. "The original design of the Society," says a report of 1839, "was twofold." First a strictly fact-gathering exercise concerned with the statistics of trade in the Bristol area. The report makes it clear that although this work was seen to be important it was not really of much interest. However, such data-gathering "would require no expenditure on the part of the Society," and hopefully, "however dry and forbidding statistical researches generally are, there will, nevertheless, spring up, every now and then, zealots, as it were, in the pursuit." Not in Bristol, however. After only two years of operation the fifty-five notables who made up the Society repudiated responsibility for statistical work proper as, "the leisure and taste for such tedious employment might not readily be met with." The second object that united these gentlemen was, however, "of much greater importance." It was the intensive study of the condition of the poor—a study directly oriented to reform.

The work was urgent because the felt complexity of society made it impossible to produce quick answers to pressing questions of moral and social conduct. Like the great continental sociologists, the Bristol statisticians saw an old order collapsing around them. As the structure of the emerging order was obscure, so was the meaning of social action. But whereas Toennies, Durkheim, LePlay and others tried to characterize the social revolution conceptually, these men had simpler purposes: they wanted to forestall violence and they wanted to rediscover the nature of effective charity. As Justices of the Peace, administrators of charitable institutions, and the like they had both the duty and the means to do these things. All they needed was the information that would allow them to make sound policy judgments. The method they turned to, therefore, was not abstraction but the social survey—in this case a survey of 4,700 families in the poorest Bristol parishes, "to ascertain what the actual exigencies are, and by an accurate exhibition of them, to rouse the community, and eventually the legislature, to take adequate measures to meet them."

Fifty years later Booth was to admit that one of the exigencies that made it necessary to understand and deal with poverty was that out of helplessness poverty bred socialism. So, in the 1830's the fear that poverty was the father of *sansculottism* was a powerful motive to social research. Quite explicitly the gentlemen of Bristol wanted to know, "what are the influences that increase or diminish the sanguinary character of this occult power?" and whether remedies might not "be applied which shall go far to extinguish its existence." The statistical societies would provide the means of formulating such remedies. But a more cogent motive was moral perplexity. Here the sense of contrast between an agrarian past and an industrial present was plainly important: "in a simple state of society, a man may know tolerably well what his duties to the poor are . . . but what shall be said of that artificial and complicated state of things when a nation manufactures for half the world—and when the consequence unavoidably is the enormous distance between the labourer and his virtual and subdivided employer?" Such statements remind us forcefully that the British elite was to the end of the nineteenth century a provincial elite which did not see the world quite in the manner of the intellectuals of the London Statistical Society. What was immediately salient for that elite was the problem of transposing its own role from a society in which:

the wealthier individual resides in the midst of his dependents, and the requisites of civilised life are produced and fabricated within a comparatively limited distance, say a patriarchal household, (so that) the ordinary visitations of Providence are easily known, and as easily mitigated. The orphan, the widow, and the unfortunate obtain a ready relief at the hands of a benevolent master or richer neighbour.

to one in which:

a person at the antipodes may feel his garment pleasant at his back, while yet the man to whom some portions of his gratitude is due may be pining with sickness at the distance of 12,000 miles ... (and where) the lowest orders of society are crowded together in the same locality and are removed from the benefits which a more immediate intercourse with their superiors would ensure.[3]

In a society of the new sort, clearly, "the principle of charity to the poor must undergo considerable modification, must indeed assume a new complexion and shape itself to more comprehensive objects." But how exactly? Research was worthwhile because it offered, as nothing else did, to point the way. It was, as one statistical doctor of medicine put it, "one of the most useful precursors to benevolent exertion." It was a central and well-publicized precept of political economy that indiscriminate benevolence did more harm than good. There was a real need therefore to know just what concrete actions would constitute doing good in an extended and differentiated world. This was not an academic issue. There was real anxiety in the debates that sprang up around the statistical demonstrations of Clay and others that giving money to the poor was merely giving them the means of drinking which led to crime which led to prison which led to deeper pauperism, with charity compounding misery all the while. It was essential to act. While research was appropriate as long as there was doubt about how to act, benevolent exertion was the real object.

Moral Principles—Social Measures

But the very power of this moral imperative tended also to short-circuit the process of social research. The belief system that generated the duty of benevolence went a long way toward defining the nature of benevolence. The social problem was easily translated into a moral problem. Just as it was necessary for the wealthy to be shown how to be moral, so it was above all necessary for the poor. In this perspective it was not poverty as such that was outrageous but rather poverty as a context for drunkenness, prostitution, depravity, and dependence—poverty as an obstacle to the moral development of the individual. What was needed was not

3 *Journal of the Statistical Society*, 1839.

the reorganization of society but the improvement of individuals. The problem was to design reforms that would so ameliorate social conditions that individuals would be enabled, or forced, to improve themselves.

The moral philosophy of utilitarian Christianity thus provided an alternative means of social understanding and action to empirical inquiry. As the costs and controversial nature of good empirical work began to be seen it was comforting to find that one had had other strong and clear guides to action available all the time. The Bristol Statistical Society exhausted its funds before it was able to write up the results of its modest survey. But the various and numerous philanthropic societies of the city continued to flourish and to disburse large sums. Indeed, as one disgruntled statistician pointed out, two thousand pounds were collected for benevolent purposes in the very week the Statistical Society proclaimed its bankruptcy—"and he greatly feared that if it were distributed without a proper precursor—enquiry—injury would be thereby done to society."

As the moralizing perspective took hold, we find a clearer focus on individuals instead of social organization as the relevant unit of analysis for all social problems. We find a shift of emphasis from research to legislation, from promoting the measuring of society to promoting social measures. We find a distinctive interest within social research on the collection of what are called "moral statistics"—essentially the mapping of depravity. We find social policy debates clustering around the issues of crime and criminal law, prison reform and prison administration, temperance, sexual conduct, schools and public health—all those issues that were seen as directly relevant to the central problem of setting the individual free or equipping him to be thrifty, self-reliant, orderly, clean, and, in a word, moral. We find a quite striking enthusiasm for the state —a spreading agreement that laws and administrative structures are the right and proper tools of improvement, even the improvement of individuals. We find an extraordinary growth of voluntary bodies concerned with the policies of moral improvement. These organizations engage themselves in the business of legislation. They collaborate with one another, pool their energies and slowly articulate a new conception of social science. Social science was effective philanthropy. Its strategies were the strategies of ameliorism. Finally, this conception is embodied in a great umbrella organization, the National Association for the Promotion of Social Science.

One of the early products of this movement was the journal *Meliora: a Quarterly Review of Social Science*, which achieved a circulation of 7,000 copies quarterly in its first year. It presents very clearly both the extent and the depth of the new view of social science as applied Christianity. The ambivalence about statistics is plain: on the one hand, "statistics, ... are the bones and sinews, the nerves and muscles of legislation; reforms are impossible without their aid"; statisticians on the other hand are imagined as "men with yellow wizened bodies, lean and withered souls . . . whose whole existence was spent in endless practice of the four rules of arithmetic." The moral imperative to social action and the morally based understanding of society are still plainer: "In every view of the subject it concerns the statesman, the patriot, and the Christian, to promote healthier and purer morals among the people, and medically to deal with the diseases which endanger our social welfare." The diseases in question were a short list endlessly insisted upon: ignorance, spiritual destitution, impurity, bad sanitation, pauperism, crime, and intemperance—above all intemperance. The singling out of drink as the critical social problem, often as the cause of all the others, was very representative of the new social science. England, the most prosperous nation in the world, "is confessedly the most drunken." Drink is presented as "the chief cause" of crime, pauperism, disease, and insanity.

Social Action Without Social Theory

The ameliorist was no more likely than the statistician to achieve an analytical sociology—but for a different reason. The statistician avoided the issue of social causes by limiting himself to a descriptive sociography and trusting to the long-run dynamics of the economy, helped by administrative common sense, to dispose of the social problems his research revealed. "It is for us," as Lord John Russell put it, "to investigate the great problems of political economy, which may often admit of exceptions but never of refutations." The ameliorist, by contrast, developed an applied sociology which had settled the issue of causes too quickly, too uncritically, and too atomistically. Social problems were rooted in individual moral weakness and in the conjunction of personal weakness and temptations offered to weakness by certain kinds of social situation. A two-pronged policy-science was called for: to show how individual character could be fortified against temptation; and to show how to eliminate vicious situations. It was, as it deployed itself in the 1860's and 1870's, an evaluative and experimental social science concentrated on policies of education and public health. Its typical works are comparative surveys of schools and teaching methods such as William Fraser's *The State of our Educational Enterprises,* and the dozens of model housing developments which sprang up as demonstration projects in and around each great city. But it never acquired a sociological theory of society.

It was not that the ameliorists lacked a sense of social structure. There are plenty of examples of good, piecemeal sociological reasoning—in the first issue of *Meliora* there is a cogent attempt to account for the growth of prostitution in terms of status-competition in the middle classes. But their moral perceptions were so strong and so clear that they seldom felt any need to examine at length, or to generalize, the structural links of which they were aware. Again and again we are launched into a promising analysis of the structural interconnectedness of social problems only to have the author suddenly shift his ground. The shift is not always in the same direction. But almost invariably the writer or speaker cuts his way out of the Gordian knot of social process by seizing on a solution or a main cause which is drawn, not from his analysis of society, but from his ulterior moral and political principles.

Very typical of this approach was the way *Meliora* solved the problem raised by Clay's demonstration of the relationship between high wages and high crime rates. Since the main cause of the relationship lay "in the ignorance and weakness of moral principle to be found among the working classes," the answer was to pay them their wages at a time when it would be difficult if not impossible for them to spend the money on drink—not, therefore, on Saturday as was the custom but before a working day.[4] Very typical too, was the distinction that quickly developed as a cardinal analytical principle of this mode of social science, between the steady, industrious, self-reliant, rational, and therefore deserving poor on the one hand, and the feckless, weak, drunken, loafing, and therefore actually or potentially criminal and undeserving poor on the other. This insight, which turns up again and again in the literature of ameliorism as a means of reducing perceived social problems to possible programs of reform was to become a pivot of policy, and of policy dispute, in the whole field of social welfare administration in the twentieth century. It is still more active than it should be. The idea that self-reliance was at all at odds with a socialization which, if the ameliorists had their way, would teach the poor nothing so well as to "know their place," is one of the few ramifications of the theme which did not get widely discussed.

When the logic of ameliorism was made explicit it often became clear that it was just the problem of character that made a science of philanthropy imperative. Sir Benjamin Brodie put the case very well in 1857.[5] There was, he observed, ample benevolence and probably ample means available to cope with outstanding social problems. The immediate need was to gain sufficient understanding of the articulation of these problems one with another for benevolence to be "judiciously directed." The essential thing to preserve was personal self-reliance. From this point of view "the immediate effect of an indiscriminate and careless charity must be to defeat its own object, and be injurious instead of beneficial." We then have some horror stories:

It was but a few days ago that a master tailor in London assured me that many of his journeymen who earn thirty-six shillings and sometimes forty shillings in a week, pass one and even two days in the week in the public house, expending a great part of their earnings in beer

4   *Meliora*, 1860.
5   NAPSS, *Transactions*, 1857.

and spirits, having the consciousness that their wives and children can never starve, as, whatever happens, the parish must maintain them.

Another account is of the "idle and lazy" moving in large numbers into a parish with numerous almshouses. In calling on his contemporaries to join him in a search for the "true principles of social economy," Brodie was asking for both research and action. He was calling for research which would effectively disentangle poverty, ignorance, disease, drunkenness, and crime and so open the way to action which would reduce each ill without aggravating others. He saw that mere police action in any one area would be no better than indiscriminate charity. For example, since prostitution was a product of more fundamental social disorder to attempt "to lessen this evil by merely carrying off and providing for its victims" would be futile; prostitutes would appear again "as fast as they were cut off." He had a clear understanding that "the questions which relate to the well-being of society hang one upon the other; so that to direct our attention exclusively to any one of them would not only answer no good purpose, but would actually mislead us." But he also had a means, short of evolving a full-blown sociology, of finding his way through the maze. The principle to be referred to at all times was that of personal independence and industry. To what extent did different groups and classes display these qualities? In what ways would different measures encourage or inhibit them?

The Appeal of Single Causes

The reasoning was not always as sophisticated as this. But always the ameliorist tended to shy away from the knowledge that social problems presented themselves as a structured set and seek instead a simplifying interpretation that would open the way to concrete problem-solving legislation. The commonest version of the leap from empirical analysis to principles, from the range of perceived problems to a single-cause remedy, was that which invoked the demon drink as the great subverter of characters. And this particular jump was made very easily indeed. What is more it was made by a great number of public men only *after* they had spent long and effective careers struggling with other aspects of the social problem. Lord Shaftesbury, in the last ten years of his life, provides almost as many instances of the habit of discovering drink as the master key to all social ills as do the publications of the United Kingdom Alliance. Having surveyed at length all the problems of public health, having made those problems seem gargantuan in their scope and intractability, he comes in a typical passage to this "great undeniable truth":

> If you go into these frightful places you will see there the causes of moral mischief, and I do verily believe that seven-tenths of it are attributable to that which is the greatest curse of the country—that which destroys their physical and moral existence, cuts through their domestic ties, and reduces them to pauperism, with all its various degradation—habits of drinking and systems of intoxication.[6]

The editors of *Meliora* found this a "guarded utterance"; their own estimate of the amount of social evil caused by alcohol was nine-tenths. Lord Brougham, originally very skeptical about temperance, came at the close of a long career of legal reform to the same view—explicitly as an alternative to accepting the idea of the fatuity of social action. Confronted with an increasingly complex and appalling tangle of problems the instinct of the ameliorist was to seize on some one feature about which something concrete could be done and then to formulate the measure. This was not a state of mind conducive to sociology—and it is doubtful to what extent it was conducive to reform. But it was hard to resist. To the upper-class visitor or spectator drink *was* the most visible thing wrong with the poor. Rowland Hill, a reformer whose wide interests involved colonial development and the post office, put the matter succinctly: "Into what path soever I strike, in whatever direction I go, the Demon Drink starts up before my face and stops the way."[7]

Even those who were not mesmerized by the problem of drink shared the same style of thought. G. W. Hastings, who was to be the moving force of the social science movement in the 1860's,

6   *Meliora*, 1859.
7   *Meliora*, 1860.

after tracing in graphic detail the "close connexion" between all
social problems, and deploring the tendency to attribute these
"terrible evils" to any one cause, nevertheless discovered a single
measure capable of working a radical improvement in social conditions—a reduction in the legal costs of transferring real estate.[8]
His thinking, within its frame of reference, was perfectly sound.
The measure would both permit and encourage the truly industrious and thrifty working man to escape from the environment
of degradation by giving him a realistic chance of buying a home
in the suburbs. Only research on the scale undertaken by Booth and
Rowntree, by demonstrating the unreality of the deserving-un-
deserving distinction in the face of the structured vicissitudes of
the social system, would have any serious effect on this mode of
social analysis.

The National Association

The summation of the ameliorist movement was the National Association for the Promotion of Social Science. It is important to pay some attention to this unduly ignored organization
because its influence was critical in frustrating the growth of
sociology in the mid-nineteenth century. NAPSS was a peak association almost unique in British political history. It was a union
of reform groups. And the belief that held it together was that
for every social problem there was an optimal ameliorating measure which could be scientifically arrived at by investigation and
by patient discussion between all interested parties. Once the
measure had been identified it was the purpose of the Association
to air it before the public and, more important, to reduce it to the
form of a draft Bill or Order in Council. In this form it would then
be presented, by way of friendly Members of Parliament, to the
legislature or executive as the proposal having the widest possible
informed consensus behind it. It was in fact a conspicuous example of what political scientists now call the aggregation of interests. It was an institutional filter for social concern. The orienta-

8   NAPSS, *Transactions*, 1857.

tion to measures was explicit and all-pervading. From 1857 to 1884 NAPSS organized annual congresses at which the great reform politicians appeared as chairmen of the various sections and urged audiences of thousands to get on with the work of preparing legislation. Between congresses the officials of the Association continuously fed the proposals generated by the movement to appropriate branches of government. Each year the president's report would move from a record of measures NAPSS had placed on the Statute Book in the past twelve months to a survey of measures still needed.

Within the class of public persons NAPSS was both brilliant and representative. In 1880, when it was already in difficulties, its Council included thirty-one Peers of the Realm, forty-eight MP's, nineteen Doctors of Law or QC's, fourteen Fellows of the Royal Society and numerous Baronets, Knights, Ministers of the Church of England, Professors, and Fellows of the Statistical Society. Clergymen and doctors of medicine were the most numerous occupational categories in its general membership. Thirty-eight corporate bodies belonged including several chambers of commerce, cooperative societies, temperance organizations and educational bodies, the Charity Organisation Society and the Vigilance Association for the Defence of Personal Rights. It had close and good relations with the Statistical Society, the two holding joint annual dinners at one time, and most of the key working statisticians, Guy, Farr, Newmarch, Heywood, were also active in the Association. So were third generation political economists such as Stanley Jevons. But the Association also mobilized people who were not touched by the statistical movement and often had grave doubts about it—the Christian Socialists, for example, Charles Kingsley and F. D. Maurice, and John Stuart Mill and John Ruskin. And it included, usually as more than symbolic members, the great politicians and functionaries of social reform: Brougham, Gladstone, Shaftesbury, Russell, Trevelyan, Chadwick, Kay Shuttleworth, Simon and Southwood Smith. Most of the distinguished foreigners who became its corresponding members were public men of the same type. But one at least combined active social reform with the cultivation of analytical sociology, and he, as I shall show later, was to have a critical influence in England—Frederic LePlay.

The Association was put together by a quite small group in the winter of 1856. Having persuaded Lord Brougham to provide the formal leadership they circularized individuals and organizations concerned with a wide range of social problems soliciting support for a congress the following year. The field of social issues was divided into five "departments": law-amendment, education, crime, public health, and the relations of production and other miscellaneous questions lumped together under the head of "social economy." Chairmen and committees specialized in each of these areas were set up as the effective working nucleus of the movement. The response was spectacular: "among the great majority . . . of those whose aid was solicited in establishing a point of union for social reformers . . . there was a ready recognition of the need for such an institution and a hearty support both in advice and labour." The appeal was particularly successful among the chambers of commerce and the churches. Great emphasis was placed on a commitment to a free flow of opinion within the Association: "it was distinctly stated that its object was to elicit truth, not to propound dogmas, and that in every department any argument coming within the limits of the subjects for discussion, and temperately and fairly urged, would be listened to with respect."

Quite explicitly, the rationale for the Association in the minds of its most active promoters was the need to cut a way through the complexity of social problems towards relevant and effective action. There was a problem of understanding as well as a problem of action:

Do we not find that each of the social problems we have been in any way at pains to unravel strikes its roots into the substance of the nation, ramifying through a hundred secret crevices into classes apparently the most removed from its influence? Surely the investigators of the many intricate questions which spring from the necessities of society have no less need of mutual instruction and help than the exponents of the laws of the material universe.[9]

[9]   NAPSS, *Transactions*, 1857.

Similarly, in Lord Brougham's ópening presidential address two role models are held out to the future social scientist: that of the philosopher generating new understandings of the close-woven mesh of the social network, and that of the engineer of social change performing a service function for legislators. But already in Brougham's case the priorities are clear. For him the Association was an outgrowth of the earlier Society for Promoting the Amendment of the Law, and its utility was above all that of a lever of legislation. In 1845, Brougham pointed out, he had introduced nine bills to parliament, six of which had become law:

> Two of the six were suggested by the Society and another, the most important of the whole . . . I never should have succeeded in carrying but for the Society's correspondence with all the county court judges and their almost unanimous testimony in favour of the change.

The Association was to function in the same way on a more extended territory. By comparison with this opportunity and need to "aid legislation, by preparing measures, by explaining them, by recommending them to the community, or it may be by stimulating the Legislature to adopt them," the problem of the strictly intellectual development of social science received scant attention. Of 873 papers presented to the Association in its first ten years only 37 devote as much as one paragraph to evaluating the theoretical significance of the social problem being discussed: there is not one that fails to indicate an appropriate measure of reform.

Consensus and Political Action

To see more clearly why the promotion of social science was not conducive to the growth of sociology we need to look at its intellectual dimension more closely. The first thing that strikes us, as with the statisticians, is the orientation to consensus. This was fundamental but not naïve. Again and again in the presidential addresses, in 72 out of 162 cases, the idea of an implicit consensus underlying apparent discord is appealed to. It was that belief that held the Association together. It was not that differences of judgment and principle would be obliterated by mutual discussion but that in the process of discussion some minimum basis for agreement, and therefore action, could be expected to emerge. As Brougham put it: "it is of incalculable importance that these points on which [men] are agreed should be separated from the rest, and the measures approved, regarding which no material difference exists." Conversely, he hoped to see measures brought forward and "so modified by mutual concession on the controverted grounds, as that what all approve should be adopted." Considering that the Association included both the temperance societies and the brewing organizations in its Social Economy section, that both Church of England and noncomformist ministers were active in the Education section, that in its discussions of strikes both the chambers of commerce and working men were involved, Brougham's optimism was remarkable. It rested on the belief that society was essentially in good order. Its ills, though urgent, could be righted by direct and relatively superficial action. That being so the divergence of theories would hardly prevent mutual agreement on what the action should be. In any event, "the wide difference between the various theories of electricity and magnetism is altogether disregarded by those who would frame the mechanism of the telegraph." More important was the conviction "that there is less diversity of opinion than might be supposed even upon general subjects"—a perfectly well-founded conviction with reference to the stratum of public persons in English society in the 1850's. Where disputes did occur, it followed that: "ignorance or misinformation, or inattentive, and therefore inaccurate, observation, or careless reflection and hasty declaration, is the cause of most of these differences." The work of the social scientist was clearly indicated and it did not include any serious theoretical activity.

Closely linked to this restricted image of the social scientist was a special image of society. The most frequently used units of social analysis in the *Transactions* of the Association are those of the state, the individual (moral or immoral) and occasionally, the classes. What is missing is any developed concept of the social system, any extended or general analysis of structured interactions between individuals or classes, any theory of the social basis of the state. Where there *is* a model of society it is typically an administrative one suffused with moral judgment. Hastings uses the analogy of a properly run school for delinquents in a representative example:

> In a well-regulated reformatory school may be seen the effect of moral and religious discipline, combined with good sanitary conditions, and a proper union of industrial and intellectual education, upon wayward, ignorant and hardened natures. Such an institution is a type of the great work before us, for there is nothing done in a reformatory school which might not, with proper appliances, be effected for society at large.[10]

Time and again the terms of analysis are the custodial state standing face to face with individuals in need of help, correction or regeneration. The data to be analyzed is that of institutional provision on the one hand, crude rates of mortality, drunkenness, literacy or crime on the other. Society, seen thus, was directly accessible as the social scientists' laboratory. As one president of NAPSS was to put it: "what experiment is to physical research an act of legislation is to social inquiry." Confidence in this over-political understanding of society had to be broken before sociology could develop further.

The Collapse of Consensus

The break was made in the 1880's. The crisis in which NAPSS was then embroiled was a different aspect of that broader intellectual crisis in which the statisticians and political economy as a whole were caught up by the inability of Victorian social science to make sense of the economic experiences of the 1870's. But for the Association the crisis was much more directly political. To see why, one must understand just what function NAPSS had had in the political process in the previous quarter-century. Whereas the statistical movement had been from the first strongly oriented to the executive and its members had become increasingly associated with particular executive departments, NAPSS

[10]   NAPSS, *Transactions*, 1857.

had been more intimately and generally involved with government. It had served as a functional substitute for a party system.

Called into being by a parliamentary elite, the work it was assigned was just that processing of issues into measures typically handled by parties. Its structure allowed it at once to scan organized public opinion and to derive from public opinion the legislative proposals most likely to obtain wide support. It flourished in that period of nineteenth-century English history when, for a very wide range of issues, the party system had been dismantled. In the era of party decomposition precipitated by Sir Robert Peel, parliament ceased to provide an effective institutional framework for determining social policy issues. The class of public persons found itself enjoying a broad consensus as to the desirability of social amelioration within the structure of the existing society, but denied adequate access to the legislature by the collapse of organized party conflict. The Association filled the gap. Proposals had to be evaluated and effective measures initiated. The system of parliamentary parties being no longer capable of the work, it was done elsewhere.

The Association declined, therefore, when meaningful and socially structured party cleavage on questions of social policy reappeared. One of its last great efforts was a special Temperance Congress in 1885. Here were brought together representatives of all the interested organizations. The assumption, as in the 1850's was that men of good will would hammer out some minimum position for reform. But between the brewers and vintners and the United Kingdom Alliance no such position existed. The Congress was a bitter experience. And in making temperance a party issue in 1885 (which previous party-politicians had carefully refused to do), Gladstone simply confirmed that for this particular issue the Association had ceased to be viable.

The same thing was happening on a dozen fronts. In the 1870's the Council of the Association could regularly claim that between Congresses it had "made many representations to Government or to Parliament," typically with success. A decade later it was difficult to find proposals with enough support among the Association's membership even to be passed to government in its name.

And it was still more difficult to win a sympathetic response to proposals from an increasingly partisan parliament. The debates at the Congresses became more rancorous. In 1884 Professor Leone Levi did for NAPSS what Giffen had done for the Statistical Society—produced a statistical demonstration of the long run improvement in the condition of the working classes. But NAPSS was not the Statistical Society, and the discussion that followed took a different direction. Mr. H. J. Pettifer, for example, stood and said that he:

> Would have been pleased if they had had a little less figures, because no one knew better than the readers of the papers that it was possible to make figures prove anything. It had been said that this was a question of humanity, but it was a question of the workmen of England first, and he would like to see it argued by a different class of people from those who would do so that day. The writers of the papers had been talking of the working classes as though they were some new-found race, or extinct animal. The best way to have dealt with the question, and to have arrived at the truth, would have been to have called a meeting in the town hall, where the working man could have spoken for himself. Everyone might take it for granted that the working classes were better-off now than they were twenty-seven years ago, but ought they not to be? The question was, were they as much better off as they ought to be?[11]

Pettifer was the secretary of a London's Workman's Association. He and others like him, increasingly articulate, introduced a tone and a perspective into social politics which was not compatible with the image of social science embodied in NAPSS. The members and the constituent organizations of the Association began to go their own way, creating their own ties with this or that political party, marking out their own peculiar and restricted spheres of interest and influence.

The attempt to work up an applied sociology, a sociology of description and experiment, of report, discussion and legislation, had, despite its sense of the complexity of social issues, assumed an underlying consensus about the nature of society and of the social problem. By 1885 it was clear that that consensus no longer

[11]   NAPSS, *Transactions*, 1884.

existed. Not science but a parliamentary majority in an increasingly rigid party system had become the critical lever of reform. Of course the ameliorist impulse as a basis for social inquiry and social action did not die with the decline of the Association. It was a powerful element in the motivation of Booth and Rowntree as of Mrs. Webb, and some of the most representative of recent British sociology; the work of Marshall, Titmuss, and Townsend, for example, is strongly informed by it. But after 1885 it was no longer possible to take the structure of the scene of action for granted. As in the 1830's so after 1885 disagreement about the meaning of social experience was too manifest to be ignored.

In some ways the very success of the ameliorist movement aggravated the general perplexity. An outstanding product of the movement was the Charity Organisation Society, and the vehemence with which the C.O.S. and its supporters reiterated the traditional moral sociology, "that character is nine-tenths of life," in the face of intensified social disorder in the 1880's, exacerbated the doubts of others. By reaction they were driven back to first principles—and to the possibility of new first principles. What was bad for the science of social reform was, if anything, good for sociology. The turmoil of policies and ideas precipitated in the 1880's opened a door to new kinds of speculation. In its heyday NAPSS had found an alternative to analytical sociology in easy access to social experiment via legislation. Loss of access created the context in which sociological theory, the hitherto missing complement to rigorous empirical inquiry and an orientation to problems, was worth developing. Economic deregulation was followed at once by intellectual ferment. It produced a large scale and wide ranging effort to redefine society. Some, like the statisticians, directed their energies toward a more meticulous search for facts. Others found new modes of political action. Yet others tried to grasp the meaning of their experience by working out a more comprehensive theory of social organization.

5

SOCIAL EVOLUTION

THE STRIKING THING about the development of British sociology is the continuity of its principal traditions. The pattern of work of the 1960's flows from that of the 1830's. But the years of long-run malaise in the economy from 1873 to 1885 were a period of critical intensification. The experience of those years produced empirical inquiry of a new quality and scale—an extraordinary series of Royal Commissions and government investigations culminating in the Poor Law Commission of 1905, as well as the work of Booth, Rowntree, Bowley, Chiozza Money, and Beveridge. It produced a more critical focusing of the ameliorist instinct on questions of the mutual articulation of social institutions. And it produced a great flowering of social theory. Strands of thought which had lurked below the surface of English intellectual life for a generation or more suddenly become visible and important. The influence and relevance of Comte, LePlay, and Herbert Spencer begins to be felt.

Comte

The importance of Comte is hard to determine. It raises again the broader question of what appraisal one is to make of the many strands of positivism in English thought, strands into which Comte's Positivism was subtly woven. During his lifetime he was known in England to only a small band of enthusiasts. Harriet Martineau's short version of the *Positive Philosophy* came out in 1853 but sold slowly. Most discussion of Comte was critical and in 1870 he was known mainly through the negative reactions to him of Mill and Spencer. His English followers, Harrison, Bridges, Lewes, and others, remained an isolated, slightly incoherent group within the broad ameliorist tradition. Positivism in their hands was an educational movement, moralistic, utopian, and diffuse.

But Comte spoke with an appealing voice to men oppressed by a sense of the fragmentation of knowledge and by their own inability to focus knowledge effectively for purposes of social action. And it was in that way that British intellectuals discovered him after 1873. Harriet Martineau had been quite explicit about the relevance of Comte twenty years earlier:

> My strongest inducement to this enterprise was my deep conviction of the need of this book in my own country, in a form which renders it accessible to the largest number of intelligent readers. We are living in a remarkable time, when the conflict of opinions renders a firm foundation of knowledge indispensable, not only to our intellectual, moral and social progress; but to our holding such ground as we have gained from former ages. . . . In close connection with this was another of my reasons. The supreme dread of every one who cares for the good of the nation or race is that men should be adrift for want of an anchorage for their convictions. I believe that no one questions that a very large proportion of our people are now so adrift. . . . The work of M. Comte is unquestionably the greatest single effort that has been made to obviate this kind of danger.[1]

A generation later the "uncertainty and depression" she had sensed were widely felt and widely visible. The appetite for intellectual synthesis and perspective was proportionately greater. The second edition of *Positive Philosophy* which appeared in 1873 sold well. In 1878 the Irish Comtist John Kells Ingram became president of the Economics and Statistics Section of the British Association. It was he who from that position opened the public debate on the rival merits of economic science and sociology which became so heated in the next few years. Ingram's speech is reprinted in this volume and it will be seen that his conception of sociology—synthetic, comparative, historical and generalizing— was authentically Comtist. Thirty years later Harrison and Bridges,

[1]   H. Martineau, ed., A. Comte, *Positive Philosophy*, Introduction.

the leaders of the Comtist movement, were prominent in the group that founded the Sociological Society and set its early course. Three avowed Comtists were chairmen of the Society in its first decade. The first volume of the *Sociological Review* carried a long evaluation by Hobhouse of Comte's Law of the Three Stages. The idea of a continuing tradition running from Comte by way of Tylor, Hobhouse, and Ginsberg to the work of the present is quite widely held among contemporary British sociologists.[2]

But the debt to Comte remains difficult to specify. There is force to the argument, used by both Mill and Spencer, that much that was intellectually new about sociology in the 1870's sprang from the common scientific (positivist?) culture of the age in which Comte, too, was a participant. The demand for a science of society was rampant. To articulate the spirit of the age did not give one property rights in it. This was especially true, the critics urged, of the positive method, the method of inverse deduction. According to Mill this was "not a recent invention of M. Comte, but a simple adherence to the traditions of all the great scientific minds whose discoveries have made the human race what it is." In other words, he, Mill, had not necessarily been influenced by Comte because he advocated the same method for sociology. Spencer went to great pains to make the same point.[3]

Comte was seen to have done three things. He had defined a subject matter. He had demonstrated a method of analysis. And he had set out a program of moral education and political action. The tendency of British social scientists was to absorb the subject matter and the method while repudiating the program and thus to deny that they had been influenced by Comte. Resistance to admitting the influence of Comte was rooted, for Mill and Spencer as for most others, in revulsion from his politics. This was the "supremely important" divergence for Spencer. Appealing to the spirit of the age made it possible to agree with Comte that sociology should

2   Cf. R. Fletcher, *Auguste Comte and the Making of Sociology*, (Auguste Comte Memorial Lecture) London, 1966.
3   H. Spencer, "Reasons for dissenting from . . . M. Comte," *Essays*, vol. 2. J. S. Mill, *Auguste Comte and Positivism*, and cf. F. Harrison, *On Society*.

adopt his version of the positive method (in other words that it should cease to take for granted the assumptions about human nature at the heart of political economy), and that its commitment should be to grasp laws of social organization by means of historical and cross-cultural comparisons. It made it possible to agree that the most fundamental laws of social organization were laws of evolution. And all this without being contaminated by the Religion of Humanity.

The obverse of this is easy to see. Just because Comte's most articulate interpreters, both friendly and critical, made so much of the religious and political extension of sociology, it was easy to lose sight of the broader debt to him. Comte's peculiar contribution, the argument went, had been to confound the building of sociology with the building of a new social and ethical order. While recognizing the nobility of Comte's secular religion, British social scientists tended to find Comte's "positive polity" a nightmare. The objection was often inflated to become a question of alternative *analytical* theories of evolution. It was a cardinal difference in Spencer's eyes that Comte saw evolution as tending toward a society, "in which government is developed to the greatest extent," whereas, he, like Adam Smith and Karl Marx, held "that form of society towards which we are progressing, to be one in which government will be reduced to the smallest amount possible."

In a narrow sense, then, Comte's influence was small. Few of those who turned to sociology in the last quarter of the nineteenth century followed Comte along all three of the paths he had opened. Positivist Societies sprang up in several cities in the 1880's. But in London organized Positivism, especially in its religious form, was a fragile growth. Individual Positivists were active and influential in the wider movement toward a theoretical sociology. But they never managed to diffuse the Positive Religion. Their efforts to promote popular education remained small scale and sectarian. Their political interventions, in favor of trade unionism, against imperialist wars and the policy of coercion in Ireland, were marginal to the main thrust of events. As a social movement Positivism was certainly not a synthetic enterprise. Comte's most devoted followers came to feel that he had not been given his due. In 1884 Harrison admitted that he was "in dread" lest the Comtist tradition should perish for want of young men to carry it on. In 1918 S. H. Swinny, president of the English Positivist Committee, could not but admit that "the chief sociologists since (Comte's) time have pursued the study from rather different standpoints"—the standpoints he had in mind were those of Spencer and LePlay.

On a broader view, however, all the pioneers of British sociology were positivists however much they might dissociate themselves from Comte. And it was largely by reaction to Comte that they matured their own conceptions of sociology. To Mill, Spencer, and Hobhouse the points at which they departed from Comte were critical. But they could hardly have arrived at those points unless their own thinking had been dialectically engaged with his. When all allowances are made for the spirit of the age— for Spencer's point that "all men of science have been more or less consistently 'positivists' "—certain central emphases of British sociology, emphases which distinguish it from that which was developing in Germany, France, and the United States at the same time, have plainer origins in the work of Comte than anywhere else. Among them would be: great concern with problems of "historical filiation": the conception of sociology as a science with the ultimate objective of enabling men to master their own destiny —ameliorism writ large; stress on the evolution of mind as both the prime mover of evolution in general and the immediate means of man's eventual leap into freedom—an idea common to both Tylor and Hobhouse; a prevailing image of society as a consensus of interdependent elements in shifting equilibrium rather than a Spencerian organism; use of the social system, rather than Spencer's major institutions, as the primary focus of sociological inquiry; use, too, of the distinction between statics and dynamics as analytically separate dimensions of social organization—a distinction Spencer was to repudiate (wisely, I think) as a definite obstacle to an understanding of social process; and of course fascination with the law of the three stages, both as a typology of belief systems and as a theory of the structure of evolution. So if Harrison was right to be alarmed at the shortage of recruits to organized Positivism in 1884, he was perhaps also right to sense that, "Positivist principles are leavening and impressing public opinion. . . . Positivism is in the air."

But the greatest contribution of Comte to British sociology, as of LePlay, was probably that he provided a counterweight, an alternative conception of a possible sociology, to be invoked against the oppressive genius of Herbert Spencer. We shall see this relationship in action shortly. First we should note the influence of LePlay.

LePlay

Frederic Harrison had visited Comte in Paris in 1855. Mill had corresponded with him at length. The continuities were direct and personal. In the case of LePlay the links are weaker. His own visits to England were successful but his reputation was as a social reformer and adviser to Napoleon III, not as a sociologist. By the time Patrick Geddes turned to sociology, or Charles Booth became interested in new methods of social research, LePlay himself was dead. But whereas Comte's influence was for years encapsulated in a small intellectual community, LePlay had become a recognized authority in the whole field of social science represented by the National Association well before the sense of intellectual and policy crisis became overwhelming in the 1880's. His relevance in that crisis was easily seen because he was known as a familiar and respectable participant in the business of scientific ameliorism. Like the English ameliorists his primary concern was social suffering and moral disorder. Like them he had concluded in true positivist style that "a social science was necessary for the cure of the ill" and that "that science should be built not upon a priori conception but upon systematically observed facts and upon an inductive method." But unlike the typical ameliorist he had actually constructed a social science of this order. He had seen the need to combine observation with conceptualization at a fairly high level of generality before proceeding to measures. And he had thus managed to derive specific policy proposals, and a system of policy priorities, from a body of attractively concrete, empirical, and middle-range social theory.

Observation of many different occupational milieus had led LePlay to the view that individual behavior had to be understood in terms of its institutional contexts—specifically in terms of the mode of family life different individuals experienced. The deregulation of modern societies he saw as primarily an effect of the disruption of the family as an agent of moral education and as a base for stable social relationships. Social peace, the great object to be obtained, depended on individual happiness. Happiness in turn was a matter of bread and morale. The type of family emerging from the industrial revolution was incapable of providing either. The family rather than the individual was the important unit of social analysis and object of social action. Reform was to be directed to encouraging the growth of a type of family which would restabilize society by providing moral anchorage for the individual as well as being a viable nexus of material life. But the family had to be adapted to its setting to perform these functions. As physical environment and the relationships of work varied, LePlay's observations suggested, so did the capacity of any one type of family to integrate the individual with a wider social order.

LePlay was thus led to a primitive typology of industrial and preindustrial societies based on the transformation of critical social institutions. Industrialization—cities and factory work—entailed constraints of place and work that disintegrated the traditional patriarchal family and tended to replace it with an atomized, excessively volatile family form in which neither economic nor socializing functions could develop with any real salience for the individual. But, LePlay found, in certain environments a third type, the stem family, was proving equally viable under conditions of industrialism. And it was conducive, as the atomized family was not, to the moral integration of industrial society as a whole. In this form the family became economically viable, able for instance to maintain a limited number of members through a limited number of vicissitudes—those of infancy and old age, say—and it could thus begin to function again as a point of moral orientation for the individual. The challenge was to re-constitute the family. But this meant reconstituting the influences of work and place as well as acting directly on the family through welfare legislation.

In short, LePlay offered the ameliorist something that had not emerged in England—a sociological theory of social reform. The reforms he proposed were strictly derived from a generalized analysis of the integration and malintegration of social institu-tions. In the chaos of proposals and interpretations of the 1880's he was seen to hold out a recipe for social order which was itself both scientific and practical . . . as well as being essentially con-servative. Given this entrée to the heart of social controversy in England it is not very surprising that his influence should have been great. We can trace it in the methods no less than in the ideology of later British sociology.

The ideological appeal was straightforward. As Cardinal Manning said, looking back on his great mediating work in the dock strike of 1889, "whatever I may have done in this matter, has been due to the counsels and teaching of my illustrious master, LePlay." LePlay's sociology contained a prescription for class peace. If his account of social organization was correct, the rooted belief of political economy in a natural social harmony, the re-sistance to socialist arguments about the structured incompatibility of class interests, could be maintained. In the thirty years before 1914 many British intellectuals came to see the new sociology and the new liberalism—the liberalism of free education, un-employment insurance, town-planning, old-age pensions, guaran-teed minimum wages and a managed labor market—as theory and practice of a last stand against socialism.[4]

Sociologists under the influence of LePlay, men such as Bran-ford and Geddes, were particularly clear about this. To them the sociology of LePlay opened up a "third alternative" to both the anomie of disordered capitalism and the tyrannies of socialism.

---

[4]   B. Semmel, *Imperialism and Social Reform* provides striking con-firmation of this view; and cf., P. Abrams, "The Failure of Social Reform in Britain 1918-1920," *Past and Present*, 1961, or for a direct statement, V. Branford, *The Coal Crisis and the Future.*

They used LePlay's analysis of the conditions of social well-being to urge men to turn away from class conflict and to summon them to collaboration in a great effort to rebuild their common physical and moral environment—the environment of work, place, and family. Eighty years earlier arithmetic had been the social scientist's alternative to politics: now it was town planning. Once again sociology was turned into a social movement too quickly for its own good. Instead of working at the careful analysis of interactions between social institutions the heirs of LePlay devoted their energies to rhapsodic adumbrations of the "third alternative" in Branford's series of studies on *The Making of the Future.*

More serious and permanently fruitful was LePlay's contribution to British sociological method. His own research had been based on a combination of the field survey of urban districts and intensive case studies of selected family units. The rationale for this was simple. The family was the decisive social-structural matrix of well-being or suffering. Only through close scrutiny of families in their relation to other elements of social structure could the extent of suffering be assessed, its causes identified and realistic remedies specified. A standardized data frame was constructed and used in over 300 family monographs completed by LePlay to lay bare what he took to be the critical structural linkages. The major categories of data he sought were ecological and economic. His object was to specify in great detail the mode of existence of different families—meals and menus, clothing and furniture, household routines and division of tasks, religious practices and recreation, and above all family income and the fluctuations of income through the year as related to expenditure and fluctuations of consumption. The intention was to establish relationships between modes of life thus defined and the constraints and opportunities provided by locality and occupation, the community and the market.

The anticipation of Booth is quite startling. Booth of course adopted different statistical techniques from those of LePlay. And he did not attempt to follow LePlay in some of his more adventurous exercises—the effort to establish indicators of status crystallization between economic and social standing for example.

But the influence of LePlay in determining Booth's main strategy, as in the shift of attention from the individual to the family, or the meticulous analysis of household budgets, was direct, powerful and acknowledged. It was, LePlay's first English biographer could rule in 1898,[5] "chiefly through his working class budgets that LePlay is known in this country." That would not have been true twenty years earlier.

By way of Booth the LePlay method was fed into the main stream of British social research after 1890. In that whole body of research, running out only in the 1930's, the work which comes closest to the style and spirit of LePlay is probably Seebohm Rowntree's study of the rural poor, *How the Labourer Lives*. It is not just that the weaving together of household-budget data and family case histories is done with rare skill. In this book Rowntree achieved what he hardly attempted in the better-known York studies, a real integration of the case studies, including variations in the moral and material quality of life of different families, with the influences of the ecological and economic setting of rural work. But there is no need to seize on a single work. The whole survey tradition of British sociology in the early twentieth century reveals LePlay, as well as the British statistical movement, standing behind Booth. Among the many varieties of empirical social research which had been successfully practiced by 1930 the style of British sociology stands out as distinctively narrow.[6] Family budgets are everywhere, of course. But there is also an almost complete concentration on surveys of territorial groups—primarily working class groups: family and community provide the structure of interpretation; and there is a strong tendency to implicit ecological determinism—the Howarth and Wilson survey of 1907, *West Ham*, is a good example; so is Sherwells' earlier study of Soho.

[5]   Dorothy Herbertson, *The Life of Frédéric Le Play*.
[6]   An interesting contrast can be made between the range of research procedures discussed in the report commissioned from A. F. Wells on British social surveys in 1934 and that found in the students manual put out by the Community Research Committee of the University of Chicago in 1929: Wells, *The Local Social Survey in Great Britain*, V. M. Palmer, *Field Studies in Sociology*.

The influence of LePlay on British survey research was brought to bear more directly, but less usefully, by Patrick Geddes. From Comte, Huxley, and LePlay, Geddes concocted a curious brand of evolutionary ecological determinism. We shall look at this later on. What is immediately important is the use he made of LePlay's type of social survey as an instrument of this social philosophy. Within the Sociological Society in its first years Geddes was the most active proponent of the social survey and it was largely through his efforts that the Society, reconstituted as the Sociological Institute with its headquarters named LePlay House, became after 1919 the promotional center for a certain kind of survey work. Trained as a biologist, a passionate ameliorist, first made aware of sociology by reading Comte and attending meetings of the London Comtist Church, Geddes found in LePlay's survey techniques a means of access to the root principles of the organic integration of society. He expanded the concept of the survey to take in all possible interactions, past as well as present, of place, work, and family in any given territory. In Geddes' hands the holistic conception of the survey became the principal tool of a synthetic sociology just as a narrower definition of the survey became the distinctive strategy of piecemeal empiricism in the tradition of Booth.

Geddes' own comment on Booth is revealing: "The qualities and defects of each community are to be judged, not simply by a contemporary survey, but primarily by a geographic and historic one. For lack of this it is that Mr. Booth's vastest of civic monographs—his *Life and Labour of the People in London*—despite its admirable intention and spirit, its manifold collaboration, its accurate and laborious detail, its mapping of every house, has thrown after all so little light upon the foggy labyrinth." It is worth remembering that Booth himself was finally bemused by the mountain of facts he had assembled: "I have at times doubted," he was to write, "whether the prolongation of this work has had any other basis than an inability on my part to come to a conclusion." As Geddes saw it Booth went on gathering facts because he had no way of knowing what the facts he gathered meant. Or as his most recent biographers put it: "It was his inability to construct a sufficiently elaborate and clearly defined framework of analysis that led him to accumulate vast numbers of facts that, far from "speaking for themselves," obstructed the development of a better understanding of their significance."[7]

It was Geddes' belief that LePlay provided just the organizing framework that Booth lacked. The conception of family and community as dynamic protagonists in the historically structured process of ecological-economic interaction both showed one the meaning of facts and indicated what sort of facts the survey researcher should seek. An important shift of emphasis followed. Studies in the Booth tradition are studies of this or that social condition—typically, poverty. Family and community are taken, following LePlay, as the appropriate context for the study of such conditions. The survey tradition launched by Geddes is primarily a study of regions. These surveys were considered sociological as distinct from merely social because their object was to demonstrate the structural reality of region or community and its inner institutional organization. "A regional survey," according to what became official LePlay House doctrine, "is a complete and scientific study of a region from every point of view, all the departments of the study being viewed in relation to one another . . . and all contributing to an understanding of the spirit of the place and its potentialities and providing a basis for definite plans for its future development." In such a survey "the essential thing is to bring out the connection between the various features of the life and work of the community studied." The great danger for survey research on this model was the tendency to degenerate into parish-pump eclecticism. What was needed was a great deal of hard methodological work to develop models of survey design which would provide tools adequate to the job LePlay and Geddes had envisaged. Unfortunately, Geddes himself was not the man for such work. Local surveys proliferated, but their value, except as a means of community self-education, became increasingly doubtful.

In 1955 Ruth Glass, now Director of the University of London Centre for Urban Studies, wrote a report for *Current Sociology*

[7]   T. S. and M. B. Simey, *Charles Booth—Social Scientist;* cf., the comments of R. Glass, *Current Sociology*, 4, 1955, and J. W. Burrow, *Evolution and Society.*

on the state of urban sociology in Britain. She found the LePlay tradition as represented by the surveys of Geddes and his followers thoroughly impoverished—eclectic, diffuse, and disorganized. Of the many surveys that had been undertaken she found only one that embodied a disciplined conception of the structure of urbanism. For the rest, planning surveys proceeded town by town with little in the way of integrating theory or method, while sociologists seemed reluctant to use survey methods at all. She explained the popular success of the LePlay-Geddes school, and the resulting weakness of urban sociology in Britain, by suggesting that LePlay had contrived to appeal to a deep-seated theme of British middle-class culture—a rooted antipathy to cities, an insistence that the good society was rural and provincial, built on the small community. I am not sure about this. Geddes, Abercrombie, and the other pioneers of the Town Planning movement influenced by LePlay were not hostile to cities as such, but only to the type of city that had been produced by failing to control the forces of the market during the early period of industrialization.

What is more certain is that the image of the sociologist held out by LePlay was unacademic, if not antiacademic. And this did appeal to his British followers. LePlay repeatedly urged social scientists to live rather than write. So intimate was the connection of social analysis and social action that painstaking academic craftsmanship was easily seen as a dissipation of energies. "It is useless," LePlay ruled, "to sum up knowledge in a book . . . social science is truly transmitted only by the scholar who lives it for the earnest men who listen to him." Sociology was essentially an extramural activity—Branford was to call it just that in the 1920's —and LePlay's willingness to cut out the academic middleman appealed strongly to the activist temperament of men like Geddes.

But there were curious side effects. After 1900 a decisive factor in slowing down the growth of sociology in Britain was the refusal of the older universities to recognize sociology as a possible university discipline. In part this was because the integrating perspective of sociology was easily mistaken for an undisciplined eclecticism. Universities that were willing to teach economics, history, biology, geography, even certain sorts of specialized anthropology and psychology, had to be convinced that there was a middle ground between their established departments where unresolved problems could be effectively dealt with. But conversely, the most vociferous advocates of sociology from 1890 onward had continuously decried the universities as bastions of specialization, idle and impractical academicism, and general unenlightenment. In Geddes' writings there is a persistent current of invective against the English universities. It is perhaps not surprising if many university people came to agree with him that sociology was not the sort of thing that universities did.

Meanwhile Geddes himself tried to give expression to LePlay's belief in direct education in sociology through an endless series of summer schools, traveling exhibitions, and conferences. The tours and field surveys sponsored by the Sociological Society were part of the same enterprise. LePlay had hoped to create a new agency of applied sociology in the *Unions de la Paix Sociale*. The Outlook Tower and the Edinburgh Social Union were Geddes' counterpart.

The Outlook Tower, the world's first sociological laboratory, as Charles A. Ellwood was to call it, with its collection of maps, photographs, projections, demonstrations by means of *camera obscura* and ad hoc lectures, was the most brilliant of Geddes' many attempts at an action sociology—an immediate presentation of the sociological dimension of cities, city problems, and town planning. The Social Union was a cross-class effort at voluntary social improvement by collective direct action—the clearing of slum courtyards, for example. These were Geddes' most representative achievements.

In the spirit of LePlay Geddes adopted for himself the motto "by living we learn." And the influence of LePlay must in part explain why Geddes, whose charisma for his own generation is still easily seen, left no work by which his achievement as a sociologist can be adequately judged or his impact understood.

Herbert Spencer

Comte and LePlay are dwarfed at once as influences in British sociology when we turn our eyes to Herbert Spencer. But

Spencer, the sociologist who first made a systematic analysis of the unintended consequences of social action, was himself a victim of the process he studied. Confronted with Spencer's conception of sociology many British intellectuals of the 1880's felt themselves drowning in their own thought world. Comte and LePlay were the straws they clutched at. Modern British sociology was built, more than anything else, as a defense against Spencer. It is in this sense that his influence was decisive.

Spencer's importance springs from the simple, central feature of his sociology. He managed to combine evolution and Adam Smith. Comte and LePlay had also made theories of evolution fundamental to their understanding of society. But Spencer did so in a way that made the nature of social evolution an imperative theoretical and empirical issue for all his contemporaries. He did so in a way that made his sociology the apotheosis of political economy. The device that worked the trick was natural selection. Any account of Spencer's importance for British sociology has to begin from there. By incorporating natural selection, or as he renamed it, the survival of the fittest, into his sociology he was able to give an account of social organization which gripped and interpreted critical processes of social change more cogently than could be done by any of the other attempts at a general sociology made in his age. But the price was to arrive at policy conclusions (in fact Spencer started from them) which many of his contemporaries refused to contemplate.

The building of his sociology began with Malthus and Lamarck—with the conception of social systems as self-regulating and with the idea of evolution as the key to understanding the causes of social phenomena. His appetite for causes was boundless and his approach to causality entirely positivistic. The theory of social evolution allowed him to find causes for everything while preserving the self-regulating view of social systems. These rudiments of a sociology were first put together in 1851 in *Social Statics*, where Spencer treats social evolution as a development from simple to complex existence, "all organic development is a change from a state of homogeneity to a state of hetereogeneity." Six years later he had moved on to a first effort to spell out the immediate dynamics of this process. In the essay *Progress: Its Law and Cause*, there is not only a reassertion of the general law of evolution but a more concrete formulation of it. Evolution is now seen as an advance "from homogeneity of structure to heterogeneity of structure" an advance effected by the continuous differentiation of functions. And at the same time he introduces an empirical generalization which he claims will reveal the cause that gives evolution its character. This is the proposition: "Every active force produces more than one change—every cause produces more than one effect." A corollary of this proposition in turn is that throughout the past there must have been "an ever-growing complication of things"—a movement in other words towards ever greater heterogeneity. Spencer's example is the growth of industrial organization through division of labor.

Already we can see that between Spencer's evolutionism and his functionalism there is symbiosis not contradiction. Society is conceived as an organism of functionally interdependent parts evolving through structural differentiation as functional forces act on one another. What Spencer needed at this point was a stricter account of how the momentum of evolution was maintained. It was also desirable to introduce some principle of economy into the analysis in order to show how the process of ever-growing complication could proceed indefinitely without producing chaos. This was where the idea of natural selection came in. The theme of adaptation of the fit to changing conditions and elimination of the unfit through their failure to adapt provided just the organizing device that Spencer required. It makes its appearance triumphantly in *First Principles* and again in *The Study of Sociology*.

From this basis Spencer struck out in many directions. Using the principle of natural selection Spencer achieved what is often supposed to be impossible, a structural-functional sociology of change. The biological analogy, used as an analogy, was very important here. It allowed Spencer to see how a society, just because like an organism it was integrated by the functional interdependence of its parts, was susceptible to the laws of evolution. His great advance on other theories of social evolution was his ability, thanks to the mechanism of natural selection, to deal concretely with elements of social structure. Indeed, only by doing so could he spell out the dynamics of social evolution through natural selection. Thus he is constantly taking up problems such as the relationship between structure and growth or trying to evaluate, say, the functionality of given types of trade unionism at particular levels of industrialization. The organization of *Principles of Sociology* in terms of institutions, and of structural and functional differentiation springing from the interaction of institutions, reveals the same bearing. His social system is a structure of mutually dependent institutions exerting force on one another in the course of their several efforts to survive and grow. Society is an unstable equilibrium of structured forces moved into ever new forms of organization as the more powerful (Spencer sometimes but not always avoided the trap of saying more functionally important) forces institutionalize their aggression on the less powerful. Hence capital displaces feudal tenure only to find itself face to face with the proletariat it has created. Hence the differentiation of priestly from royal functions paves the way for domination by ecclesiastical institutions which in turn opens the door to the differentiation of new professional functions—those of doctor and teacher for example—and new modes of social structure which eventually appropriate earlier priestly functions and begin to displace the churches.

The imagery of force, conquest, and movement is subtly interwoven with that of balance, order and integration. The unintended balance of social cohesion tomorrow is struck by the collision of forces today. In every case the balance is a product in part of mutual adaptation, in part of the elimination of the less fit —the "non-adaptation of constitution to conditions." Not only was Spencer the most ambitious of evolutionary theorists; he also went as far toward structural-functionalism as anyone could without knowing where he was going. Social systems are dynamic and self-regulating. Integrated by the structuring of their functions, they are moved by the functional interaction of their structures.

Spencer's thought developed in other directions, too. By extending his early notion of single causes having multiple effects he arrived at a brilliant sociology of unanticipated consequences. This is presented forcefully in *The Study of Sociology*. "How," Spencer asks, "can any man, and how more especially can any man of scientific culture, think that special results of special political acts can be calculated, when he contemplates the incalculable complexity of the influences under which each individual and . . . each society develops, lives and decays?" Behind the simplest event stands a pyramiding structure of influences "too involved to be traced beyond its first meshes." By way of illustration he devotes two pages to enumerating the "enormous complication of causes which determine so simple a thing as the rise or fall of a farthing per pound in cotton some months hence." And then the argument is stood on its head. If the slightest effects presuppose such mountains of causes, how much more likely is any simple action to produce unanticipated than intended results. Many reasons for this are adduced. There is, for example, the problem of institutional self-interest:

> Not only has a society as a whole a power of growth and development, but each institution set up in it has the like—draws to itself units of the society and nutriment for them, and tends ever to mutiply and ramify. Indeed, the instinct of self-preservation in each institution soon becomes dominant over everything else; and maintains it when it performs some quite other function than that intended, or no function at all. See, for instance, what has come of the "Society of Jesus" Loyola set up; or see what grew out of the company of traders who got a footing on the coast of Hindostan.[8]

Turn where one will, similar lessons emerge; there is a multitude of unperceived obstacles in the way of achieving any "special result" embedded in every social structure. It is in this connection that Spencer introduces his famous metaphor of the wrought-iron plate—every effort to hammer it flat making it more warped. Every example, every case examined, leads back to the same conclusion: "that in proportion as an aggregate is complex, the effects wrought by an incident force become more multitudinous, confused and incalculable, and that therefore a society is of all kinds

[8]   H. Spencer, *The Study of Sociology*, p. 52.

of aggregate the kind most difficult to affect in an intended way and not in unintended ways."[9]

Spencer also produced a brief but effective analysis of social facts. His motive for doing so was to calm those of his critics who felt that the deterministic implications of his account of social evolution were incompatible with individual free will. He began with a discussion of the levels of generality of different types of facts about individuals—distinguishing between the biographical, the quasi-biographical and the sociological. The last category includes all the "facts of growth, development, structure, and function." Facts in this category admit of a high degree of prevision. He then introduces the example of marriage. The explanation of the marriages of different individuals is a matter of biography. But the explanation of the marriage rates manifested in different societies is a problem of sociology, it being "a truth statistically established, that in each community, while its conditions remain the same, there is a uniform rate of marriage."[10] His treatment of marriage rates and birth rates is a quite striking anticipation of Durkheim's analysis in *Suicide*. And it leads him to an easy resolution of his critics' problem: "While everyone holds that in the matter of marriage, his will is, in the ordinary sense of the word, free; yet he is obliged to recognize the fact that his will, and the wills of others, are so far determined . . . as to produce these average social results; and that no such social results would be produced did they not fulfil their wills." The individual in short, appears as one "whose will is a factor in social evolution, and yet as one whose will is a product of all antecedent influences, social included."

The main tendency of Spencer's empirical sociology, however, flowed directly from his confidence in evolution as the matrix of social causality. Attention had to be turned to a massive enterprise in comparative history. As societies develop from simple to complex a vast proliferation of species and genera is produced by the working out of the plexus of social forces in different ways. The business of the sociologist is to identify types and levels of de-

9   *Ibid.*, p. 43.
10   *Ibid.*, p. 81.

velopment by an orderly, inductive and comparative examination of historical data. The critical test for any particular sociological account of evolution was itself historical: do we in fact find patterns of evolution conforming to the laws which, whether derived empirically or from biological analogy, are held to structure the evolutionary process? If not what alternative generalizations do the observed patterns suggest? To agree or disagree with Spencer was to have one's attention forcibly directed to the problem of laying bare the content of social evolution. Whatever one felt about Spencer the temptation to follow him in grandiose exercises in comparative history was powerful. Two things distinguish Spencer from most of those who trod in his footsteps, however. His own treatment of historical materials is always highly dynamic. Although he uses a conception of stages of growth as an organizing framework, his analysis throughout the *Principles of Sociology* tends to be in terms of particular interactions of structure and function in this or that concrete institutional setting. What Spencer is doing is trying to work his way through the labyrinth of social causes. He was not primarily interested in formal sociology and never used his own theory of the stages of social development very rigorously. What he did see clearly was the need for a substantial, well-ordered data base as a first prerequisite for historical sociology. This was the purpose of the successive volumes of his *Descriptive Sociology*, "a cyclopaedia of social facts—representing the constitution of every type and grade of human society, past and present, stationary and progressive." Whatever judgment may be made of Spencer's own contributions to this undertaking, the work carried on by his trustees has produced at least one classic in the genre, Reuben Levy's *Social Structure of Islam*.

In many ways, then, the contemporaneity of Spencer, like his achievement, is astounding. *The Study of Sociology,* with its treatment of social institutions as ossified social forces, of history as a process of mutual aggression and defense among forces and institutions, its coordination of structure and function, its analysis of the nature of social facts, its masterly working out of the flow of unanticipated consequences, its conception of functional differentiation as the defining attribute of modernity, its elaborate account of the intellectual hazards of sociological inquiry, is perhaps the most successful textbook of general sociology yet produced in Britain. But because it is also a sustained polemic against ameliorism it was virtually unusable in Britain for three-quarters of a century.

There is no need here to examine the logic of Spencer's sociology. Much of it could, I think, be rescued from the criticisms usually made of it. What concerns us is rather the impact of what was taken to be its distinctive content. For this purpose we must distinguish between Spencer's understanding of society and what he sought to do with it. He believed that his sociology led ineluctably to a particular orientation to social action. Much of the reaction against him was shaped by the fact that his readers shared that belief. What made the negative intellectual influence of Spencer so compelling was the seemingly tight relationship between his account of social evolution and his evaluative analysis of the present. Spencer was understood to have held that the survival of the fittest was the primary mechanism of social evolution, that the resulting tendency of evolution was beneficent, no greater rate of progress being attainable, and that the great purpose of sociology was therefore to impress upon men the fatuity of efforts to accelerate the improvement of their condition by legislative measures. Spencer *had* said all of these things and he spent a great part of his later years modifying or disavowing them. But it was too late. In an essay of 1886 he maintained the diminishing importance of natural selection as compared with functional adaptation and voluntaristic intervention as a factor in evolution. In the case of the highest creatures, he now argued, "survival of the fittest is greatly interfered with." In advanced societies in particular the transmission of modifications of structure induced by modifications of function displaces natural selection as the "chief factor" in evolution.[11] But such statements could not undo the impact of *First Principles* or *The Study of Sociology*.

In his great and distinctive works his position appeared to be clear. On the one hand, "my ultimate purpose, lying behind all

11   "The Factors of Organic Evolution," *Essays*, 2:462.

proximate purposes, has been that of finding for the principles of
right and wrong in conduct at large a scientific basis." Most of
his readers conceded that he had moved scientifically enough
toward this end. On the other hand science seemed to have led
him to a philosophy of inaction, to a massive attack on ameliorism
both as a social theory and as a way of life. Again it is important
to see Spencer did *not* believe he had justified passivity but only
a willingness to postpone action until it could be derived from a
sociologically adequate analysis of social structure and social
causation. On the other hand he certainly did set himself implac-
ably against the ameliorist impulse, above all in its main form,
the impulse to protect the poor from the consequences of their
own ineptitude by legislative reconstruction of their lives. "I have
contended," he wrote in a postscript to *The Study of Sociology*,
"that policies, legislative and other, which, while hindering the
survival of the fittest, further the propagation of the unfit, work
grave mischiefs." And in the body of the book he is still more
explicit: "Fostering the good-for-nothing at the expense of the
good, is an extreme cruelty. It is a deliberate stirring-up of miseries
for future generations. There is no greater curse to posterity than
that of bequeathing to them an increasing population of imbeciles
and idlers and criminals." This aspect of Spencer's thought was to
provide a basis for the most vigorous branch of applied sociology
in Britain in the first twenty years of the next century—Eugenics.
Meanwhile he left no doubt what he thought about the evolutionary standing of the socially dependent: "the whole effort of nature
is to get rid of such, to clear the world of them, and make room for
better. . . . If they are not sufficiently complete to live, they die, and
it is best they should die."

But Spencer went beyond this particular objection to "maudlin
philanthropy," and advanced a general case against the sociological assumptions of the ameliorists. For him the argument for
abstaining from measures of reform turned on the extreme difficulty of knowing what any given measure would do; its dysfunc-
tions would almost certainly outweigh the benefits. Among the
mistaken tendencies of his time he gave pride of place to what he
called the "must-do-something" impulse. This impulse, which he

found rampant all around him, rested in his view on two errors: a simplistic view of the causes of social phenomena and a simplistic view of what legislation could achieve. The purpose of sociology was, by demonstrating the extreme difficulty of producing intended effects and the impossibility of improving the pace of evolution, to educate men out of the "must-do-something" impulse. The study of sociology, "scientifically carried on by tracing back proximate causes to remote ones, and tracing down primary effects to secondary and tertiary effects which multiply as they diffuse, will dissipate the current illusion that social evils admit of radical cures."

Section after section of the *Principles of Sociology* is dragged to the same conclusion. His analysis of professional institutions ends thus:

Though as we have seen, the process of evolution exemplified in the genesis of the professions is similar in character to the process exemplified in the genesis of political and ecclesiastical institutions and everywhere else; and though the first inquiry rationally to be made respecting any proposed measure should be whether or not it falls within the lines of this evolution, and what must be the effects of running counter to the normal course of things; yet not only is no such question ever entertained but one who raised it would be laughed down in any popular assemblage and smiled at as a dreamer in the House of Commons; the only course thought wise in either the cultured or the uncultured gathering being that of trying to estimate immediate benefits and costs. Nor will any argument or any accumulation of evidence suffice to change this attitude until there has arisen a different type of mind and a different quality of culture. The politician will spend his energies in rectifying some evils and making more—in forming, reforming, and again reforming—in passing acts to amend acts that were before amended; while social reformers will continue to think that they have only to cut up society and re-arrange it after their ideal pattern and its parts will joint together again and work as intended! [12]

His censure was distributed impartially to politicians, administrators, and reformers. What it did was to drive a wedge through all the patterns of nineteenth-century thought at which we have

[12]   H. Spencer, *The Principles of Sociology*, vol. 3, part 7, pp. 217–18.

so far looked. It split apart the ideas of social science and social action, pulverizing the linkages which statisticians and ameliorists alike had taken for granted. To Spencer, "a fly seated on the surface of the body has about as good a conception of its internal structure, as one of those schemers has of the social organisation in which he is embedded." Confronted with the proposition that a scientific sociology required the acceptance of almost all forms of present social suffering what was the conscientious "schemer" to do? Spencer had not only revived Adam Smith. He had turned the Invisible Hand into an Invisible Fist. And now he invited his contemporaries to watch quietly as it did its malignant work.

6

CRISIS AND SYNTHESIS,

1875-90

THE INTENSIFICATION of intellectual dilemmas to a point of crisis in the last quarter of the nineteenth century has been mentioned several times. Now that some of the tools and traditions of social thought with which Victorian Englishmen entered that crisis have been identified we must look more directly at the crisis itself. In it new syntheses were struck. New lines of inquiry were opened up. New methods of work were attempted. The character of twentieth-century British sociology was set.

Primarily it was a crisis of economic experience. A decade of violent oscillations of trade was followed by a long run downward movement of prices and profits after a peak year in 1873. In this situation men turned critically and anxiously to political economy for guidance. And they found it wanting. The centenary celebration of the publication of *The Wealth of Nations* in 1876 was from all accounts a dismal affair. As early as 1870 Cairnes had detected, "signs of belief that political economy has ceased to be a fruitful speculation . . . it is not denied that the science has done some good; only it is thought that its task is pretty well fulfilled." Jevons noted "an ignorant dislike and impatience of political economy" in the atmosphere of the 1870's. Another writer remarked "a widespread tendency to look on its teaching with suspicion." The president of the economic section of NAPSS in 1878 opened his address with the blunt observation: "Political economy at the present hour is undergoing a crisis." He went on to describe the nature of the crisis with striking lucidity:

When the cholera or the yellow fever visits a country, there is a rush for help and advice to its physicians. . . . In the war of classes political economy is absent. The man who thinks he has suffered wrong and seeks redress from law calls in his lawyer, and submits with entire obedience to his counsels. But who sends for a professional economist in a strike? . . . and should the dangers of the hour ever impel him to demand the aid of economical instructors, what will he find? Discordant opinions, theory and counter-theory, unintelligible language which sounds as jargon, grand deductions of which he does not understand a word, and all this on matters which belong to his everyday life, and which he feels his untutored common sense can judge as well as his scientific but incomprehensible instructor. . . . The prosperity and happiness of nations depend on the processes which political economy has for its mission to explain . . . and yet with sorrow be it said, chaos and weakened authority prevail in it to a degree unequalled in any other branch of human knowledge.[1]

The difficulty was not to choose between conflicting interpretations; it was to save the scientific credibility of any interpretation. "Political economy is not refuted and thrust aside: it has simply become discredited."

As the applied mode of political economy, statistics shared in this general discrediting. The heated discussions of the 1880's on the degree to which statistics could qualify as a science have already been mentioned. In 1877 G. J. Shaw-LeFevre, the president of the London Statistical Society, felt obliged to use his presidential address to remind his colleagues of the "great abuse" of statistical method which "so frequently takes place [and] brings the method into contempt." His own conclusion was that statistics was merely a special method of scientific investigation and subject as such to the common rules of scientific method. It was a tool available to a great variety of sciences ranging from physics to sociology. His warning was by no means premature. The previous year a group of eminent natural scientists had tried to persuade the British Association to disband its Statistics and Economics Section on the ground that neither activity had any serious scientific standing.

1   NAPSS, *Transactions*, 1878.

Francis Galton, who was increasingly influential in all fields of social inquiry from 1875 to the end of the century, was active in this campaign. He submitted a memorandum to the Association pointing out that in a large sample of papers read to Section F, "not a single memoir treats of the mathematical theory of Statistics," and that "few of the subjects treated of fall within the meaning of the word 'scientific.' " He further objected that because of the subject matter of the papers presented to Section F, "it attracts much more than its share of persons of both sexes who have had no scientific training," and accordingly, its discussions are apt to become even less scientific than they would otherwise have been." Giffen, replying for the Statistical Society, reiterated the old belief that "there is a scientific order traceable" in social life even if little progress had so far been made in tracing it. In any event, the Statistical Society would be happy to help the Association make Section F unpopular by applying "rigorously most stringent rules against the admission of unscientific papers." Science and substance were felt to be pulling in opposite directions and the professional or semiprofessional statistician was plainly invited to choose.

Beyond Political Economy

The abuse of statistics that Shaw-Lefevre had in mind in 1877 was the habit of prematurely inferring causes from statistical demonstrations of conditions. An aggravation of the habit was the tendency to assume single-cause explanations for social phenomena and then to conduct research in a way that precluded the discovery of causes other than the one that had been at first assumed. Like Spencer he was struck both by the multiplicity of causes involved in any social event and by the unwillingness of most social scientists to recognize that multiplicity. Precisely for this reason, he concluded, the study of social statistics ought in future to be conducted within the framework of a general science of social causality—namely sociology. The most powerful statement of this new view, Shaw-Lefevre subsequently recognized, was that made in 1878 by the president of Section F, J. K. Ingram.

Since political economy was on its deathbed, it was widely agreed that sociology was a likely heir. But no sooner was the case for sociology made than it became clear that there was ample disagreement about what sociology was. In particular there was disagreement about what particular methodological features of sociology gave it its superiority over political economy. The confusion was aggravated by the determination with which the most enthusiastic advocates of sociology insisted that their subject was at the same time scientific in a higher degree than political economy *and* in the true line of descent from Adam Smith—Ricardo being named most frequently as the man who had bastardized the succession.

Thus, for Shaw-Lefevre, viewing sociology from the vantage point of statistics, the function of sociology as distinct from either statistics or social science was to provide a new encompassing ideology to take the place of the exhausted tradition of political economy. Sociology he saw as offering an alternative comprehensive theory of society within which deductive positivistic reasoning about social problems and the statistical mobilization of social information could be carried on. "The science of Sociology," he ruled, "is essentially a deductive science."

Ingram, a theoretical political economist powerfully influenced by Comte, when talking to the less specialized audience of the British Association also invoked sociology to destool political economy in its incoherent senility—his immediate object was to persuade the Association to turn Section F into a Sociology Section. But for him the distinctive methodological merit of sociology was its inductive style: "this method, in which inductive research preponderates, and deduction takes a secondary place as a means of verification, is the really normal and fruitful method of sociological inquiry." The ingenuity with which he, like Shaw-Lefevre traced the roots of true sociology to the *Wealth of Nations,* and the amount of energy he devoted to doing so, are impressive.

Although critics were to make a great deal of it, the debate over methods was largely an unreal one. Shaw-Lefevre was objecting to a simple-minded inductivism in a great deal of mid-nineteenth-century statistical work, work which had more and more obviously skimped critical problems of causality. Ingram was objecting to an equally naïve deductivism, the type of which he found in Senior's attempt "to deduce all the phenomena of the industrial life of communities from four propositions" about human nature. But both of them advocated a mode of inquiry and reasoning in which disciplined observation of social phenomena was contained by, and mediated between, both induction from data and deduction from principles. And what made sociology compelling for Ingram was its fusion of method and subject matter. The method of inverse deduction was inescapable for sociology because of its unique ability to handle problems of historical transformation. More than anything else the inability to offer an adequate account of historical change had discredited political economy. The method of sociology, therefore, must be the historical method. As British pioneers of this method he cited Spencer, but also the ethnologists Maine, Tylor, and Lubbock. Maine, for example, had achieved an understanding of the social functions of property altogether beyond the ken of political economy. The historical method had led him to perceive the mutual adaptation of structure and function in property relations at different stages of social evolution and thus to demolish once and for all propositions about the naturalness of any particular type of property system.

Ingram's intention, as he admitted, was to launch a nation-wide debate on the merits of sociology. He can hardly have been disappointed with the result. His argument was taken up and defended or rebutted in a dozen periodicals and in all leading intellectual societies during the next two years. It became a point of reference for public lectures, conference papers, and essays. For the next decade echoes of it reverberate everywhere in the writings of economists, statisticians, anthropologists, reformers, and philosophers. By the end of that decade a new consciousness —a sociological consciousness—had emerged.

Much of the reaction was hostile. Jevons damned all critics and clung to political economy. A more usual response was to recognize the present defects of political economy and statistics but still maintain their viability in principle. For many this meant taking up a strongly methodological definition of science, shelving questions of theory and turning eagerly to improvements of technique. Other writers retaliated more aggressively. One strategy was to dismiss sociology as utopian: "the enthronement of a science of society, possessing the splendour and the supremacy here attributed to sociology, and reverentially obeyed by all mortals, must be reserved for the millenium." More effective was to point out the prevailing disarray among sociologists: "and then who is to be authorised to speak in the name of sociology and issue its decrees? Shall it be Comte, or Herbert Spencer, or [some] other expounder of what society ought to be?"[2]

When, in 1885, Henry Sidgwick came to occupy the position from which Ingram had launched his attack seven years before, he used the latter argument to prove that no science of sociology existed. As representative sociologists he selected Comte, Spencer, and Schaeffle, and went on to show that on each important matter of substance on which all three men had written all three disagreed:

> With equal confidence, history is represented as leading up, now to the naïve and unqualified individualism of Spencer, now to the carefully guarded and elaborated socialism of Schaeffle, now to Comte's dream of securing seven-roomed houses for all working men. . . . Guidance, truly, is here enough and to spare; but how is the bewildered statesman to select his guidance when his sociological doctors exhibit this portentous disagreement?[3]

He enlarged greatly on this theme and concluded by begging his audience "that our Association will take no step calculated to foster delusions of this kind."

Sidgwick's argument is worth attention because in the next two generations it became the orthodox basis for resistance to sociology—above all for academic resistance. The style, elevated contempt, was to become as familiar as the content. "Mr. Ingram and his friends," according to Sidgwick, were putting the cart before the horse. Nobody would deny that sociology as they en-

2   *Ibid.*
3   British Association for the Advancement of Science, *Proceedings,* 1885.

visaged it would be a wonderful tool of understanding and action if it existed. The question was whether it existed. And of course it did not—yet. Certainly:

> If we could ascertain from the past history of human society the fundamental laws of social evolution as a whole, so that we could accurately forecast the main features of the future state with which our present social world is pregnant . . . the science which gave this foresight would be of the highest value. . . . What has to be proved is that this supremely important knowledge is within our grasp; that the sociology which professes this prevision is really an established science.[4]

For the present, "It would certainly seem that the science which allows (such) discrepancies in its chief expositors must still be in its infancy." Was it not likely, in fact, that sociology was not so much science as politics? "I do not doubt that our sociologists are sincere," Sidgwick allowed, but on a close examination of sociological accounts of evolution it looked suspiciously as though each sociologist had stumbled on those laws of evolution best suited to his own personal feeling and experience.

In sum: "There is no reason to despair of the progress of general sociology, but I do not think that its development can be really promoted by shutting our eyes to its present very rudimentary conditions." Sociology was a possible science, but before making ambitious demands for academic recognition, sociologists should produce some solid knowledge. They must "offer us something better than a mixture of vague and variously applied physiological analogies, imperfectly verified historical generalisations, and unwarranted political predictions." And meanwhile, those who felt the need for a disciplined understanding or treatment of social problems—the political economists or ameliorists—had a clear course before them: "It is our business to carry on our more limited and empirical studies of society in as scientific a manner as possible."

By 1890 the fields of statistics, social science, and sociology had been separated and defined. The distinctions between them as well as the peculiar intellectual problems of each were widely

4   *Ibid.*

recognized. There were of course individuals with feet in more than one camp. Shaw-Lefevre was president of NAPSS as well as of the Statistical Society. The historian Oscar Browning was active in the educational section of NAPSS as well as an advocate of sociology. Galton combined statistics with sociology. But the predominant pattern was one of fragmentation, if not of conflict. And that in itself was one reason why the appeal of sociology, despite the disapproval of Sidgwick, Jevons, and other eminent men, continued to grow. The root problem, the problem of finding meaning in social experience and of proceeding from meaning to effective action was being exacerbated not eased by the flow of debate. The break-up of NAPSS and the increasing scientism of the statisticians deepened the crisis still further. And then of course Spencer had ruled that even if sociology existed its lesson was one of virtual inaction in the face of present social problems.

The New Generation

It was in this atmosphere that Geddes and Hobhouse, Rowntree and the Webbs pieced together their sense of vocation. Each of them was to testify to the splintering of thought that characterized the decade and to find in the falling apart of social theory and social action a peculiarly cogent source of his own movement toward sociology. Each felt the urgent need for an account of society which revealed the connectedness of conditions and institutions. The best approach to such an account was that of the socialists, especially of the Marxian socialists such as Hyndman. And it was seen that even if the socialists were wrong they had to be answered with arguments as sociological as their own—arguments which were also presented in terms of the interconnections of poverty and wealth, work and the market, law and welfare. Booth for one saw clearly that the appeal of socialism was that it made the fragmented experience of individuals meaningful by translating it into a language of social process and social organization. Because political economy and piecemeal statistical inquiries deliberately eschewed such an organic conception of society they were powerless to meet the socialist challenge.

William Booth, the founder of the Salvation Army, certainly

exaggerated when he announced in 1890 that "the Social Problem has scarcely been studied at all scientifically." What he meant was that none of the many studies had related the social problem to social organization. There were plenty of head counting exercises. What was missing was treatment of the social *process* of poverty, of "the evolution, or rather the degradation . . . of the multitudes who struggle and sink . . . in the midst of . . . unparalleled wealth." By science he meant not facts but understanding. The general effect of the years of crisis was to diffuse a mood of concern coupled with helplessness. As they had done earlier in the century, British intellectuals turned instinctively in this predicament to the pursuit of more and better empirical information. But they now also saw the need to structure their information into new kinds of knowledge. One possibility was socialism; another was sociology; there were many others.

The first and perhaps the most influential product of this new dilemma of relevance to sociology was the work of Charles Booth. Booth rightly has a volume to himself in this series of studies. All that need be done here is to see that he did begin his work with the explicit intention of contributing new knowledge as well as new information. The conclusion to the first part of his London survey, presented as a paper to the Statistical Society in 1887, makes this quite clear:

> It is the sense of helplessness that tries everyone; the wage earners, as I have said, are helpless to regulate or obtain the value of their work; the manufacturer or dealer can only work within the limits of competition; the rich are helpless to relieve want without stimulating its sources; the legislature is helpless because the limits of successful interference by change of law are closely circumscribed. . . . To relieve this sense of helplessness, the problems of human life must be better stated. The *a priori* reasoning of political economy, orthodox and unorthodox alike, fails from want of reality. At its base are a series of assumptions very imperfectly connected with the observed facts of life. We need to begin with a true picture of the modern industrial organism, the interchange of service, the exercise of faculty, the demands and satisfaction of desire. It is the possibility of such a picture as this that I wish to suggest, and it is as a contribution to it that I have written this paper.[5]

5   *Journal of the Royal Statistical Society,* 1887.

Booth was to lose his sense of direction later as facts accumulated around him. And he was to be widely regarded as the man who had done more than anyone to reestablish the utility of statistical empiricism. It is worth remembering therefore that this was not quite what he had intended when he set to work in the 1880's.

Booth was 47 when his poverty studies began to appear. To see the full impact of the intellectual crisis that moved him we must turn to the generation that was in its 20's: the generation of Hobhouse. For them the tension of experience and received ideas was acute. Their inherited tools of thought included a variety of highly optimistic and rationalistic theories of social man. From the bland materialism of Bentham to the blander idealism of Green these theories all culminated in an axiom of progress. But their own immediate experience of history was an experience of contradiction, unreason, suffering, disorder and conflict, an experience which made the idea of history deeply problematic. A mainspring of the intellectual momentum to pursue sociology in the face of all criticism for this generation was the question "Whence have we come and whither are we tending?"—and the fact that it was often asked in just this limp rhetorical form should not conceal either its urgency or its centrality. Hobhouse caught the intellectual predicament of his contemporaries very aptly in his image of Condorcet lying in prison rethinking the theory of progress while awaiting the guillotine. The ameliorist impulse was strong in them and tended to grow stronger with every socialist demonstration; that was the very reason why work like Booth's was not enough for them. Booth's findings indeed, aggravated their problem. They wanted a sociology which, in addition to revealing the principles of social organization, would indicate strategies of improvement. Hobhouse's own account of his intellectual formation specifies clearly the environment in which his whole generation had to make their way:

As an undergraduate at Oxford (1883-87) I was greatly interested in questions of social reform, but in probing them I came upon real or apparent difficulties, sociological and philosophical. I rather innocently took Herbert Spencer's evolutionary theories as the last word of science, and though attracted by T. H. Green's social and ethical outlook

I could not see in his metaphysics a valid philosophical solution. . . . It occurred to me, however, that Green's "Spiritual Principle" might represent an "empirical" rather than a "metaphysical" truth, that it might be identified with the Comtist conception of Humanity . . . and that the development of this principle might represent the true line of evolution.[6]

What Hobhouse had discovered was that one could accept Spencer's general understanding of the nature of scientific sociology without having to come to Spencer's own disagreeable political conclusions. Amid the mob of would-be reformers, "often at cross purposes, sometimes coming into violent conflict, at best with no clear sense of any common cause," the need for the distancing effect, the perspective, of social theory was evident: "the prophylactic that we need . . . is an articulate social philosophy." The social philosophy that Hobhouse and his contemporaries were looking for had, however, to do three things: it had to demonstrate the meaning of history, to unravel the structure of present social problems, and to specify strategies of amelioration.

The effort of Hobhouse himself to work out such a philosophy was not merely representative; it was decisive for British sociology as a whole. Whatever others might have done in the way of spelling out new methods of empirical research, or deriving policy proposals from surveys of poverty or a priori accounts of social evolution, it was Hobhouse who made possible a convergence of ameliorism and sociology by finding a way to stand Herbert Spencer on his head. He contrived an evolutionary sociology which endorsed reformism without requiring society to progress in any particular direction. Hobhouse recognized four roots of sociology —politics, the philosophy of history, natural science, especially biology, and the array of special social studies developed during the nineteenth century. The relevance of politics in the sense of "the passion for improving mankind," was obvious enough. More specifically, contemporary Liberal politics, the "old cause of social good against class interests," pointed toward the need for systematic social theory and the coordinated analysis of social phe-

6   L. T. Hobhouse, "The Philosophy of Development," in *Contemporary British Philosophy*, ed. J. H. Muirhead (London, 1924).

nomena. Like Rowntree, Hobhouse saw the new sociology and the new liberalism as sides of a single coin. The philosophy of history had likewise brought men to the brink of sociology by forcing them to recognize the social complexity of progress. The natural sciences, first mathematics and now biology, provided the models in terms of which social process could be conceptualized. And the proliferation of special social sciences—political economy, social history, demography, anthropology, comparative religion and jurisprudence—had revealed within each specialization the need for an over-arching and synthetic general sociology: "If we take any aspect of social life and think of it as forming the subject of an investigation entirely separated from other investigations, we see at once how futile this attempt must be."[7] The specialized studies were integral to sociology, but the cumulation of material in discrete fields was merely a preliminary to science: "The problem before us as sociologists is to bring together in vital connection the enquiries which hitherto have been pursued apart. The nature of the subject itself demands this synthesis." In short, Hobhouse had a Platonic idea of sociology fairly clearly in mind. The problem was to realize it.

Survival of the Fittest

The immediate difficulty was Herbert Spencer—or rather, Darwin as mediated by Spencer to his contemporaries. In seeking a philosophy of history that would resolve the anomalies of experience, the generation of the 1880's had seized eagerly on the tools provided by biology, the most potent of contemporary natural sciences and the only one which was itself historical. The problem was reconceptualized as a problem of evolutionary process. And the main line of social interpretation built directly on the substance as well as the method of biology—closely following Spencer in seeing progress as the survival of the fittest, and the mechanism of progress as the struggle for existence. On this basis the special social sciences of eugenics, social biology and social medicine

[7]   L. T. Hobhouse, *Social Evolution and Political Theory.*

developed powerfully. Drawing on the tradition of vital statistics, finding connections with demography and reinforced by the statistical innovations, ingenuity, and financial support of Galton, these specialisms quickly generated a sweeping analysis of the condition of Britain based to all appearances on meticulous and extensive empirical work, a sound philosophy of history and a scientific method—but also, so it seemed, thoroughly illiberal in its political tendency. As with Spencer, this was a stumbling block.

A true amalgam of statistics and biology, eugenics as developed by Galton was the science of the average effects of the laws of heredity. The line of influence from Malthus through Darwin and Spencer to Galton and Pearson was acknowledged. Working in this tradition the eugenicist claimed at once to be rooted in science and to have escaped from the ameliorist nightmare of not knowing where or how to attack the social environment. The publication of Galton's *Hereditary Genius* in 1869, followed by *Inquiries into Human Faculty* in 1883 and *Natural Inheritance* in 1889, was seen to have established on an impeccable statistical basis the case for treating biological transmission as the primary factor in social welfare. It was also a factor directly susceptible to human control. Accepting natural selection as the true mechanism of progress, it was proposed to ease the working of that mechanism by both positive and negative means—by facilitating the birth of the fit and by discouraging the birth or survival of the unfit. As Galton put it: "Eugenics cooperates with the workings of Nature by securing that humanity shall be represented by the fittest races. What Nature does blindly, slowly, and ruthlessly, man may do providently, quickly, and kindly." Pearson habitually made the same point more concretely. Heredity accounted for nine-tenths of a man's capacity and efforts to improve either men or society by environmental changes were footling if not positively malignant:

Selection of parentage is the sole effective process known to science by which a race can continuously progress. . . . Where the battle is to the capable and the thrifty, where the dull and idle have no chance to propagate their kind, there the nation will progress, even if the land be sterile, the environment unfriendly and educational facilities small.

Give educational facilities to all, limit hours of labour to eight-a-day—providing leisure to watch two football matches a week—give a minimum wage with free medical advice, and yet you will find that the unemployables, the degenerates and the physical and mental weaklings increase rather than decrease.[8]

Misplaced compassion, according to Pearson, "the maudlin sentiment," prevented men, even fifty years after the *Origin of Species* was published, from seeing the beneficial character of differential mortality rates between classes: "the great function of eliminating the weeds is maintained in the garden of human life by the hand of death." What we should see in the high death rates of the poor is merely nature removing "the weaker stock before it has had any, or its full quotum, of offspring."

The sociology of men like Hobhouse and Geddes developed in direct reaction to this sort of social biology. In each of Hobhouse's seven major works we find long critical discussions of the biological treatment of society and specifically of eugenics. Sociology stood in a dialectical relationship to the tradition of Darwin and Spencer. Only when and if the errors of that tradition had been demonstrated would sociology, embodying a true understanding of social evolution, come into its own. Conversely, it was the errors of the social-biological tradition that made efforts to develop sociology so imperative. The force of the ameliorist impulse here can hardly be overstated. The intellectual calling of sociology for Hobhouse was twofold. It was to show first, that "the biological conditions of human development are not such as to present any insuperable barrier to progress," and second, that "we may expect to find progress, if anywhere, rather in social than in racial modification." And it was for this reason that he saw the work of Darwin as having "cut across the normal and natural development of sociological investigation," just as Henry Drummond ruled in his best-selling essay *The Ascent of Man,* that "the first step in the reconstruction of sociology will be to escape from the shadow of Darwin."

[8]   Karl Pearson, *The Groundwork of Eugenics.*

Naturally, the eugenicists were not all as callous as some sociologists thought them. There were great differences between them both in matters of theory and on questions of social policy. But Hobhouse was right to sense that however subtle Galton's own thought might be, social biology lent itself easily to the rhetoric of political reaction. The equation of fitness to survive and social success was made almost instinctively. Galton himself had maintained that "the men who achieve eminence and those who are naturally capable, are, to a large extent, identical." Starting from the biologists' assumption that the "best was that which survived," one was led by a natural chain of logical errors to the happy position, as Hobhouse put it, "of being able to verify the existence of a soul of goodness in things evil":

Was there acute industrial competition? It was the process by which the fittest came to the top. Were the losers in the struggle left to welter in dire poverty? They would the sooner die out. Were housing conditions a disgrace to civilization? They were the natural environment of an unfit class, and the means whereby such a class prepared the way for its own extinction. Was infant mortality excessive? It weeded out the sickly and the weaklings. Was there pestilence or famine? So many more of the unfit would perish. Did tuberculosis claim a heavy toll? The tubercular germs are great selectors, skilled at probing the weak spots of living tissue. Were there war and rumors of wars? War alone would give to the conquering race its due, the inheritance of the earth.[9]

This was a caricature, but it was one to which eugenicists often lent color. The first issue of the *Eugenics Review* went out of its way to endorse the view that social welfare legislation was "penalizing the fit for the sake of the unfit." And then there was Pearson's unflagging campaign to disseminate "the conception of the destruction of the less fit as a beneficent factor of human growth." In sum, given the defining properties of sociology as Hobhouse understood them, the science had to be built around a theory of evolution, but, imperatively, it had to be evolution without Spencer.

9   Hobhouse, *Social Evolution and Political Theory.*

From Evolution to Progress

Hobhouse managed this by introducing the concept of orthogenic development. Here his early interest in Green, and through Green, Hegel, was important. His first work was epistemological; he approached the problem of evolution from the standpoint of a primary concern with the development of the human mind and the evolutionary movement of ideas. And he found in the evolution of mind the principle that separated the subject matter of sociology from that of biology and made them distinct sciences. *Mind in Evolution* which he published in 1901 is an evolutionary study of animal psychology. It culminates in the emergence of the self-conscious intelligence and in the conclusion that with the coming of self-consciousness the laws of evolution binding on less developed forms of life are relaxed. Man participates in his own destiny. Evolution becomes increasingly purposive. The object of the book is to establish an empirical basis for the proposition that mind is the organizing principle of evolution even in the simplest forms of life. When self-conscious intelligence is least developed life has indeed the character of a relatively unorganized Darwinian struggle. But a primary adaptation to the struggle is increasing self-consciousness, the elaboration of mind and with it the introduction of a higher principle of organization into the evolutionary process. There is a qualitative transformation of that process when human intelligence reaches the point of postulating social goals and purposes and of coordinating efforts and resources in order to reach them. At that point evolution finally gives way to the higher mode of organization, development. Sociology may be seen as the peculiar form of self-consciousness which marks the transition from evolution to development.

Hobhouse is very careful to avoid any suggestion of teleology. The final stage of social evolution may well be a stage of collaborative movement toward a shared standard of development. But this standard is itself produced organically in a largely unintended manner through the earlier interaction of partial purposes and uninformed will. The whole presentation is thoroughly dialectical —not least in that the present, though it has distinctive possibilities of development, is and must be open-ended. On the one hand "we have reached a point at which it is becoming possible to solve the problems of social life by the deliberate application of rational methods of control." But the critical word is possible:

> Up to this point civilisation still moves in large measure through conflict, though the social systems, the principles, the purposes that conflict are wider and give more scope for internal development. As civilised societies become more highly organised and their ideas more comprehensive, the onward movement in each becomes more sure and its orbit more vast. And yet, to this day, how great a proportion of the energies of the best and ablest men is spent in combating one another.[10]

Whether and when men will seize the opportunity increasingly available to them through the evolution of mind depends on many factors—not least on the speed with which they come to understand their situation sociologically instead of biologically or politically. In *Mind in Evolution,* however, Hobhouse had at least cleared the stage for sociology:

> In orthogenic evolution we find a constant development of Mind in scope and accordingly in power. Slow at first, the development gathers speed with growth, and finally settles into the steady movement of a germ unfolding under the direction of an intelligent knowledge of its powers and of its life conditions. The goal of the movement, as far as we can foresee as present, is the mastery by the human mind of the conditions, internal as well as external, of its life and growth. The primitive intelligence is useful to the organism and a more elastic method of adjusting itself to its environment. As the mental powers develop, the tables are turned, and the mind adjusts its environment to its own needs. . . . With the mastery of external nature, applied science has made us all familiar. But the last enemy that man shall overcome is himself. The internal conditions of life, the physiological basis of mental activity, the sociological laws that operate for the most part unconsciously, are parts of the environment which the self-conscious intelligence has [yet] to master, and it is on this mastery that the

10   L. T. Hobhouse, *Mind in Evolution,* p. 339.

regnum hominis will rest. The development in its highest stage is beyond doubt purposive.[11]

From this point the development of sociology and the development
of society might, one might hope, go hand in hand.

Hobhouse's first step forward from this position completed the
drawing together of the roots of sociology as he understood them.
From his earliest works he was clear that sociology could not and
should not be value free. Sociological analysis, developing from
political philosophy, presupposed an evaluation of goals and a
commitment to policies. The sociologist should perceive his own
values clearly, make them explicit and understand their relationship to his investigations of social structure. A main part of the
work of the sociologist was to specify the structural conditions
under which different potentialities of history, different values,
might be realized. For this purpose a rigorous distinction of values
and conditions is necessary:

> A theory of the end, purpose or value of social life is one thing,
> and a theory of its actual conditions another. Dealing with the same
> subject-matter they are intimately related but must never be confused.
> . . . Both enquiries are not only legitimate but necessary to the full
> understanding of social life and . . . the question of supreme interest is
> the relation between their respective results.[12]

But because the subject matter of sociology is society in evolution these important distinctions are difficult to maintain. The
temptation to confuse evolution with progress is strong. Dealing
in the comparative analysis of social institutions at different stages
of evolution, the sociologist can hardly resist the inclination to
extrapolate tendencies of institutional development. The border-
line between legitimate and illegitimate extrapolation is often
obscure. The difficulty of seizing the appropriate level of generalization is great. Hobhouse proposes a dialectical confrontation of
evolution and progress as a means of escape from these difficulties. This idea is worked out in all his early writings—nowhere
more clearly than at the end of his inaugural lecture as Britain's

11   *Ibid.*
12   *Sociological Review*, 1907, Editorial article.

first professor of sociology in 1907. "It is necessary" at the outset, he there argues, "for us to distinguish from evolution in general, the kind of evolution that we hold to be good and desirable," and we may call the latter "progress," by contrast with the former which generates parasites and cancers no less than music and liberalism. The next thing is to form "a coherent conception of what progress means for us." The method of the sociologist is to maintain a dynamic polarity between this conception and the empirical analysis of institutions:

> The ethical conception of progress once formed, we have to con-
> front it with the facts; we have to ask ourselves how the various combi-
> nations that we find in experience, arrange themselves in relation to it,
> whether they can be placed along the line of advance, or fall on some
> side path or blind alley. We have to ask ourselves how the movement
> of history comports itself, whether we find that civilisation, or any
> particular form of civilisation, does in fact move in this direction as
> the ages pass, and if so, we have to ask what are the conditions on
> which this advance depends. If, again, we can assign them, we have
> finally to determine the point at which we ourselves stand, and the
> conditions of subsequent advance. Thus for the completion of our task
> we need both a science and a philosophy, and it is only through the
> union of the two that we can bring the certainty and precision of sys-
> tematic thought to bear on the problems of practical life.[13]

The ideal sociologist will be both a social philosopher and a social scientist, continuously testing his science against his philosophy and his philosophy against his science. Much of the criticism of Hobhouse springs from a misunderstanding of his sense of this dual role. The business of the sociologist is to establish relationships between the actual movement of society and the attainment of possible goals, to evaluate change in relation to development. Now in principle the criteria of development may be specified in any way one pleases. Objective indicators can be derived to measure degrees of approximation to one's criteria. Typically these criteria will reflect the sociologist's own concep-

---

[13]   L. T. Hobhouse, "The Roots of Modern Sociology," inaugural lecture at the London School of Economics, reprinted in *Sociology and Philosophy* (London, 1966).

tions of value. It is best that they should do so explicitly. Hobhouse for one specifies development in terms of his own ulterior understanding of the rational good. But what matters to the sociologist as scientist is that he should self-consciously use a yardstick of development, not that it should be any particular yardstick.

First, then, one specifies theoretically derived indicators of development—organizational scope or efficiency, democratic pluralism or whatever it may be. Then one introduces objective measures of actual social change—levels of material culture, say, or literacy or urbanism. And one's empirical work takes the form of a comparative analysis of institutions at different objective levels designed to determine degrees of correlation between change and development in different institutional settings. Finally one is in a position to talk fairly concretely and at varying levels of generality about the social conditions for development—fully aware, of course, of the provisional status of one's definition of development. There are, as Hobhouse himself was painfully aware, many problems about such a strategy. But in advocating and implementing it Hobhouse can be said to have opened a door through which the sociologist could proceed to an increasingly specific multivariate investigation of the structural conditions for the realization of different types of social purpose. When the sociology of development was revived in the 1950's there was hardly a backward glance to Hobhouse. But he was a true precursor and it is the discontinuity that is curious.

The Uses of Anthropology

Several writers have recorded the exhilaration with which they read or listened to Hobhouse and contemplated the sociological task he set. Most sociologists of the Edwardian period had traveled the same path as Hobhouse, and much of their most characteristic work—work on the institutional correlates of social development in different types of social system—conformed to the blueprint he had drawn. Geddes began his career in the laboratory of T. H. Huxley; found Huxley's influence "determinant for life"; spent a decade working as a biologist and distancing himself from political economy with the help of Spencer and Comte, and from Spencer with the help of Comte and LePlay; began his intellectual migration with *The Evolution of Sex;* and emerged as a sociologist with *Cities in Evolution.* Westermarck, having immersed himself in the writings of Darwin, saw the need for an evolutionary treatment of the institutional development of sexual behavior and from there, maintaining the mechanism of natural selection and repudiating the idea of stages of development, he proceeded to *The History of Human Marriage* and *The Origin and Development of Moral Ideas.* Hobhouse himself, having cleared his mind on the fundamental problems of sociological method, embarked on his major empirical work, *The Material Culture and Social Institutions of the Simpler Peoples*—an essay in correlation. There were important differences of emphasis, interpretation, and direction among sociological writers, but in the early years of the new century it was easy to believe that a school of developmental sociology was emerging in Britain and that its subject matter and functions were those articulated by Hobhouse.

An important resource in the development of this school was the mass of historical ad comparative data already assembled in the fields of comparative jurisprudence and social anthropology. These were, of course, among the special social sciences which Hobhouse wanted sociology to synthesize. Developmental sociology built enthusiastically on a body of evolutionary anthropological and ethnographic work dating from the 1860's: Maine's *Ancient Law,* Wake's *Evolution of Morality,* Lubbock's *Prehistoric Times* and *The Origin of Civilization,* McLennan's *Primitive Marriage,* Tylor's *Early History of Mankind* and *Primitive Culture.* Here was the evidence that gave preliminary support to the broad reconstruction of social theory which men like Hobhouse felt to be necessary. Maine and Tylor in their different ways had already shown how a historical and comparative method could be used to support theories of social organization critical of political economy. Now empirical and theoretical synthesis was needed. It was in this sense that sociology could be intellectually differentiated from anthropology—it carried the science of social development to a higher level of generality. Westermarck, Hobhouse, and

Geddes all recognized this relationship; so did Lubbock and Tylor.

The history of British social anthropology as an evolutionary science has been written recently by John Burrow.[14] There is no need here to note more than a few lines of influence within the general relationship of the two fields. Observe first how closely anthropologists and sociologists agreed in defining the functions of their subjects. Both were developmental sciences, specifying the conditions of social progress and pointing the way toward progressive social action. The thesis worked out in *Primitive Culture* culminates in the proposition, "the science of culture is essentially a reformer's science." For Tylor the contribution of social science to reform lay primarily in its power to reveal "the survival of savage thought in modern civilisation," the persistence of primitive institutions at higher stages of development—with a view, naturally, to their elimination. Lubbock shared these ideas but usually expressed them less precisely. He may, however, have been more directly influential than Tylor because, like Galton, he was willing to give time to oganizations; he had been president of the Anthropological Institute when it was founded in 1871, and as Lord Avebury he was president of the Royal Statistical Society in 1900 and of the Sociological Society in 1904—in each role he seems to have had clear ideas about what the organization should do.

At a rather different level there were more immediate influences. Westermarck came to England and chose to work there so that he should have closer contact with Tylor, Lubbock, and Marett; his method of work, especially in his Moroccan studies, was directly shaped by the anthropologists, and his views on the origins of social institutions closely followed those of Tylor. Hobhouse recognized Tylor as the pioneer of the technique of statistical correlation in comparative evolutionary studies which he adopted in his own empirical work. He was referring to Tylor's paper on "A Method of Investigating the Development of Institutions" read to the Anthropological Institute in 1888. But neither

14   J. W. Burrow, *Evolution and Society* (Cambridge, 1966).

he nor Tylor did anything about the suggestion made by Galton, who was president of the Anthropological Institute that year, that this "most valuable" innovation would be still further improved by the use of simple tests of statistical significance. And finally, whether or not we accept the claim that the curious emphasis on community studies in British sociology can be traced to the charisma of the ethnologists' method of research, it is certain that anthropological influence lies behind the central place given to Comparative Institutions courses in the earliest sociology syllabuses in Britain—how else was the budding sociologist to generalize about development?

Before leaving this topic we should note two ways in which the convergence of some anthropologists and sociologists was also a divergence from others. Tylor and Hobhouse both represent a move away from unilinear evolutionism and from Spencer's version of the comparative method, the more or less indiscriminate amassing of cases, the "slips-of-paper" method described by Spencer in his *Autobiography* and by the Webbs in *Methods of Social Study*. The difficulties of this method were those of confusion and arbitrariness, of sinking beneath "the facts, so multitudinous in their numbers, so different in their kinds, so varied in their sources," or of creating order on the basis of what was really no more than an intuitive, or even an alphabetical, classification. For both Tylor and Hobhouse the problem of classification remained pressing, but at least statistical ordering and correlation indicated the possibility of a more rigorous comparative analysis. Galton did not miss the chance to point out how useful Tylor's method would be to Spencer. Tylor himself was clear that the "treatment of social phenomena by numerical classification" was an imperative development if serious standards of information were to be preserved in the face of an encompassing eclecticism: "In statistical investigation the future of anthropology lies. As soon as this is systematically applied, principles of social development become visible." While holding to the idea of the comparative method, then, both Tylor and Hobhouse, and Westermarck and Geddes in slightly different ways, departed from the mainstream of British social anthropology—a tradition which was to reach its apogee only in 1900 with the appearance of the complete edition of J. G. Frazer's *The Golden Bough*. On the other hand they did not go far enough, as we shall see, to effect a union with the tradition of statistics.

7

SOCIOLOGY

.

WE HAVE TRACED the complicated intellectual parentage of British sociology. What of the child itself? If there had ever been a single central tradition of social inquiry in Britain it was pulverized, as we have seen, in the critical years after 1873. Hobhouse might offer sociology as a new synthesis in the 1890's, but it was open to question whether there could really be anything more than a desperate piecing together of intellectual interests whose real tendency was to fly off in a dozen different directions. Apart from anything else there was a problem of manpower. The British educational system, unlike the German, did not encourage the production of any large surplus of free, institutionally unattached intellectuals. In a sense it was, at the highest levels especially, severely vocational. There was by no means an indefinite number of "Oxford classicists primarily interested in religion and folklore," as Burrow puts it. The supply of potential recruits to sociology was strictly limited. The role had to compete for a small number of actors with many others which seemed to offer, often more directly, the same advantages. If ameliorism was one's real commitment, politics was open and in the process of redefinition; government was sponsoring the ad hoc statistical investigation of social problems on an unprecedented scale; the whole structure of political conflict was shifting and energies devoted to hammering out new political ideologies and programs seemed assured of quick returns. The skills of the economist and statistician continued in demand even if their peculiar philosophy was in disrepute. Indeed, the growth of government, starting with the creation of

101

the research-oriented Labour Department in 1893, made for an increasing need for these skills. If the problem of relating right action to evolution gripped one's imagination at a more general level one was likely to be led, unless prepared to tolerate a full-blown moral relativism, into the morass of utilitarian ethics and thence to one or another of the new modes of logical analysis. And if the study of social structures was really one's vocation, it was far better to go off with A. C. Haddon to the Torres Straits and do some unequivocally substantive work than frustrate oneself in semantic disputes or doubtfully satisfactory secondary analysis in London—everyone agreed that the really solid parts of Westermarck's work were those that sprang directly from his own field experience in Morocco.

Then again there were academic positions in anthropology which there were not in sociology. Was one a biologist interested in social evolution? The academic limits of biology had already expanded to allow that interest to be pursued as far as one wanted from one's own distinctive technical base—and the main thrust of discussion has been set by Galton's brilliant demonstrations of the genetic factors in the sociology of achievement. After Galton's death there was the Eugenics Laboratory and then the London University Department of Social Biology and later still units of the Medical Research Council, all encouraging the specialized development of eugenic and demographic studies. The great problem, therefore, was not whether Hobhouse was right to define sociology as he did and urge the need for it, but whether, in a highly competitive market, he would be able to find enough followers to promote this new division of labor. In 1874 in one of the classics of British sociology, *English Men of Science: their Nature and Nurture*, Galton had demonstrated the tendency of the educational and occupational systems to obstruct the recruitment of natural scientists. Everything he said was doubly true for the recruitment of sociologists thirty years later.

The problem is very apparent in the early history of the Sociological Society. The men who took the decisive part in institutionalizing sociology in the Edwardian period—Victor Branford and J. Martin White, Geddes and Hobhouse, Galton and Frederic

Harrison—were one of three things: wealthy amateurs with careers elsewhere, academic deviants, or very old men.

Victor Branford, a banker and chartered accountant, had attended Geddes' Summer Schools in Edinburgh in the 1890's and had fallen under his spell. He was for a time a Fellow of the Royal Statistical Society but resigned soon after presenting a paper on "The Calculation of National Resources" in which he extended the concept of resources in a thoroughly Comtist manner to include a whole range of psychic and cultural energies. The paper was altogether at odds with almost everything the Society had experienced and must have bewildered or irritated many of the listeners. Thereafter Branford devoted his energies, and his money, to publicizing Geddes, and through Geddes the LePlay school of sociology.

J. Martin White came from a substantial Dundee family and his interest in sociology was largely formed by his early friendship with Geddes and Branford—in other words it was both ameliorist and synthetic. Experience of Parliament suggested to him that M.P.'s and government officials needed to be trained in sociology and it was for that purpose that he endowed the teaching of sociology at the newly organized University of London. Hobhouse and Westermarck both owed their Chairs to White's benefaction. And so did Patrick Geddes. Having refused, or failed to get, a series of orthodox academic positions—largely because he would not recognize the established boundaries of the academic disciplines —Geddes ended up for thirty years as Professor of Botany at University College, Dundee. The appointment had been endowed by White and was carefully designed to allow Geddes to spend nine months of the year elsewhere, and in nonbotanical activities. As for Hobhouse, he came to London in 1902 in a state of deep dissatisfaction, having tried and abandoned two conventional careers. Finding himself at odds with both the professional and political style of his fellow Oxford philosophers, he had worked for six years as a journalist on the *Manchester Guardian*. But that work, though strenuous, failed to satisfy either his nagging concern with the ethical implications of evolution or his appetite for active involvement in social reform. He arrived in London with no clear future in mind. He was peculiarly available for new roles. And he was quickly drawn into the enterprise on which Branford and Martin White were already embarked, the formation of a Sociological Society.

Branford and White, Geddes and Hobhouse shared a common interest in discovering the nature of sociology and, once discovered, in promoting it. The approach of Galton and Harrison was rather different. Both were very old and eminent. And both by 1903 had become patriarchs of their own private churches. Harrison had always treated Positivism as a religion. Galton took to referring to eugenics as a new religion only when he began advocating it to the Sociological Society. For each of them the Society represented an opportunity to disseminate a specialized perspective. Each saw clearly how sociology should develop and brought to the Society, in addition to his own powerful personality, an enthusiastic group of followers—in Galton's case, an army of young lecturers in biology. The function of the Society for them was essentially strategic; as Galton put it, "The first and main point is to secure the general intellectual acceptance of Eugenics. . . . Then let its principles work into the heart of the nation."

If we turn from these men to the larger group of leading but distinctively less active members of the early Sociological Society some contrasts become very clear. First, unlike either the Statistical Society or NAPSS the sociologists had little success in mustering celebrities—the galaxy of peers, politicians and civil servants is missing. The Eugenics Education Society did much better in that respect. But second, we find a high level of intensive commitment to professions often competing with sociology. Oscar Browning, who made the formal proposal that launched the Society in June 1903, was a historian and busy at the endless task of reforming Cambridge history. Halford Mackinder had devoted his life to developing geography as an autonomous social science; though willing to "represent" geography among the sociologists, he was not prepared to jeopardise a subject just gaining recognition by diffusing its identity. A. C. Haddon was in the same position in relation to anthropology—at best a watchful friend of sociology. C. S. Loch was already caught up in defending the

Charity Organisation Society against newer views of the proper treatment of poverty. And James Bryce was rising fast in the hierarchy of Liberal Party politics. Graham Wallas decided after a few years that psychological explanations of the questions he was interested in were both more concrete and more satisfactory than sociological ones. In any case he was preoccupied with the problems of the London School of Economics. Even the Statistical Society in its first years had faced the danger of perishing for want of people who would really work in a technically specialized way at the new craft. As Galton showed, government appointments were a critical factor in helping statistics over that hurdle. Eighty years later there were only J. Martin White and Victor Branford to do for sociology what the Whig peers had done for statistics.

Mackinder was perhaps a critical figure. Early in the development of the L.S.E. he had taken part in a program of social science lectures organized by the Webbs, and he became director of the school in 1903. Of the same generation as the Webbs and Hobhouse, he had hammered out a personal synthesis in response to the common crisis, a synthesis of which the center was the idea of geography as a social science. The purpose of geography for him was to make clear "the interaction of man in society and so much of his environment as varies locally." In his strict environmentalism as well as in his specific interest in the environmental effect of cities, he was akin to Geddes. But unlike Geddes he was prepared to delimit his sphere of interest and to develop a specialization—which no doubt had a good deal to do with his ability to persuade Oxford to create a school of geography by the end of the century. Like Geddes, too, he used extramural activity as a means to change the established universities, traveling an average of 10,000 miles a year at the height of his campaign. Had he become deeply involved in the work of the Sociological Society he might have provided a badly needed counterweight to Geddes, an element of discipline and substantive focus which in the event was lacking. A serious urban sociology might have resulted. The work of R. E. Dickinson and others suggests that this was always a possibility. In fact Mackinder became increasingly detached from sociology. His active support was critical in establishing the teaching of sociology at the L.S.E. But after geography his main commitment was to steering the School on its still precarious course. And by 1908, powerfully moved by the great issues of Ireland, tariff reform, and social policy, he turned to party politics.

The problem for sociology was one of making its way, while still itself formless and undefined, in an environment of compelling distractions. Many people who were sympathetic to the idea of sociology were simply too engaged elsewhere to contribute much to the actuality. Sidney and Beatrice Webb are the obvious cases. Above all they thought of themselves as social scientists. But the L.S.E., government work, the Fabian Society and the Labour Party were all of more central concern to them than was the cultivation of sociology. During the critical years they were wholly caught up in the business of the Poor Law Commission. And then there was W. H. Beveridge, deriving his conception of sociology from Huxley, passionately and actively concerned with questions of town planning and social insurance, who became a member of the Council of the Sociological Society in its early years and contributed a paper on unemployment. His study, *Unemployment, a Problem of Industry,* ranks among the best pieces of analytical and empirical sociology produced in Britain between Rowntree's *Poverty* and Bowley's *Livelihood and Poverty,* and his gradual withdrawal from the activities of the Sociological Society was a grave loss. If the balance between theoretical and empirical work, and between macro- and microsociology was to be held in the shaping of the new subject, men like Beveridge were vital. But Beveridge was an expert on unemployment and when the Liberal government established a national system of Labour Exchanges he was the obvious man to become director. There were several such cases—Shena Potter, later Lady Simon of Wythenshawe, is another—and it becomes hard to resist the conclusion that the slow and patchy growth of sociology was a small price that had to be paid for comparatively rapid and early social reform. The ameliorist and the social-scientific instincts now tended to be forced apart. What was good for social reform was bad for sociology.

More remarkable is the virtual noninvolvement in the Sociological Society of Booth and Rowntree—especially when contrasted with their rather closer connection with the Statistical Society. Indeed, the only effective link between the two societies was Sir Edward Brabrook, the statistician-historian of friendly societies, insurance organizations, and cooperation. Rowntree's seduction into politics and administration has already been mentioned. But his lack of enthusiasm for sociology may have had other sources too. He shared with Booth a distaste for sociological synthesis in the grand manner. The information he sought concerned narrowly defined social phenomena and problems. Booth had revealed a method of generating such information superior to anything previously available. For both of them the habit of ad hoc compartmentalized analysis rooted in the statistical tradition and reinforced by the structure of government was strong. Throughout *Poverty* Rowntree shies away from the temptation to discuss the social structure as a whole, insists on the adequacy of a narrow perspective, firmly refuses to think about the causes of poverty at the level of the social system.

Theory-Building or Data Gathering

There was a problem of definition aggravating the problem of competing roles here. In 1903 it was not clear what sociology was, but it was loosely associated for most people with the system-building of Comte and Spencer. If a further definition was to emerge it would do so largely through association with the sort of work actually done by those who now identified themselves, or allowed themselves to be identified, as sociologists. But those most concerned to appropriate that identity were in the tradition of Comte and Spencer. They tended to insist on building sociology from the roof down, on proceeding from the general to the particular. Men like Rowntree, concerned very definitely with the particular, had no reason to be hostile to sociology. But neither had they any reason to connect themselves with it. The prevailing pattern of opportunities as well as prevailing definitions tended to discourage them. And of course the noninvolvement of such men invited the development of a vicious circle. It was likely from the start that sociology, far from providing the over-arching and integrating discipline Hobhouse proposed, would turn out to be yet another discrete fragment in an already over-fragmented situation. The danger for sociology, as Hobhouse saw very clearly by 1908, was that by too eager pursuit of the general and the synthetic it would produce a new and peculiarly divisive specialism. How far was the danger averted?

By 1890 it was seen that the flow of energy unleashed by the crisis of economic life had to be caught and organized in new institutional forms—new patterns of party politics, new machinery of government, new educational arrangements, new shape and division among the fields of intellectual activity. Whether one of the emerging fields would be called sociology, whether that would be the common focus for a wide range of the new enterprises as Hobhouse and a few other concerned and active people hoped, was an open question. Like the L.S.E. and the Labour Representation Committee, the Eugenics Education Society and the Ministry of Health, the Sociological Society in its first ten years was an experiment in creating new structure. An initial difficulty, we have already seen, was the extreme divergence among the would-be builders of sociology as to the boundaries and content of the field. More than anything else that divergence is apparent in the three volumes of *Sociological Papers* which were the Society's first publications. By the end of 1907 Hobhouse, at least, was clear that sociology could hope to move toward integration only in a tentative, open-ended way: "It is clear that the definition which is to satisfy everybody must come not at the beginning but at the end of discovery. We must know what we are investigating only in the sense that we must have a rough and provisional outline of the field of work. If this imperfect and broken knowledge be ruled out, it remains that we can only know what we are looking for when we have found it."

To Branford and White, whose commitment as secretary and treasurer was essential to the Society's success, a major purpose in founding the Sociological Society was to provide a London platform for Patrick Geddes. For Hobhouse it was "to build up the great comparative Science which alone can put the theory of social evolution on a firm basis." For Bryce it was to provide a base of scientific knowledge for the use of those "practical men" anxious to "ascertain the grounds and methods upon which they can most effectually benefit their fellow men." If these purposes were to be aggregated into a single science the Society would have to develop internal division of labor as well as explicit lines of coordination. But the former was much more easily generated than the latter. By 1909 the Society had organized itself into four working committees: Eugenics, Civics, Education, and Social Economy (which as it had done with NAPSS meant the whole array of otherwise unclassified practical issues of social reform). The two first were by far the most active of these committees, being dominated by Galton and Geddes respectively. It is significant that the divisions recognized were traditional divisions of policy-related subject matter. And that there was no provision for sociology as Hobhouse understood it, or for what Branford was to call organized "research of synthesis." What there was instead was the *Sociological Review* with Hobhouse as editor. His first editorial, reprinted here, reads as a desperate plea for centripetal movement in the face of overwhelming centrifugal force.[1]

In addition, J. Martin White, as well as carrying the deficits of the Society, had begun to endow the subject academically. As a first step he financed a course of lectures in 1904; Westermarck lectured on general sociology, A. C. Haddon on ethnology, and Hobhouse on comparative ethics. In 1907 he went on to found a department of Sociology in the University of London, in effect at the School of Economics, with Hobhouse and Westermarck as joint professors. Branford maintained that in endowing sociology it had been "the hope and intention of the benefactor that an

---

1   The second theme developed by Hobhouse is that of the relationship of fact and value in social science. In this connection a comparison with Max Weber's introductory editorial to the *Archiv fur Sozialwissenschaft und Sozialpolitik* is interesting. Hobhouse and Weber take identical positions but Hobhouse presents his case rather less dogmatically. Much of Weber's article, however, is about the difficulty of social scientists' obtaining any effective access to political life. Hobhouse has the opposite problem.

academic Department of Sociology might grow up in active co-operation with the Society."

For a time, with Hobhouse as both editor and professor, that seemed possible. But in his inaugural lecture, already quoted, Hobhouse had given a very pure, theoretically oriented, account of the nature of sociology—an account which, while it reflected the content of the *Sociological Review* fairly well, bore little relation to the sort of work the other active members of the Society were trying to promote in its committees. In 1911 Hobhouse resigned as editor, partly through overwork, but partly too, "on account of criticism that . . . his general line of editorial policy tended to depart from the scope and aims of the Society." The criticism was not unfounded. The tendency of the journal while Hobhouse edited it was represented by C. L. Tupper on "Comparative Politics," A. E. Zimmern on "Was Greek Civilisation based on Slave Labour," Laurence Gomme on "Sociology as the basis of Inquiry into Primitive Culture," Westermarck on "Suicide: A Chapter in Comparative Ethics," R. R. Marret on "Comparative Religion," Hobhouse himself on "The Law of the Three Stages."

When the new Department of Sociology produced its first syllabus in 1909 the implicit divergence of academic sociology from the work of the Sociological Society was again suggested. The establishment of a *separate* Department of Social Science and Administration three years later confirmed it. The Director of this new Department, E. J. Urwick, was active in the Sociological Society and provided continuity with the older ameliorist tradition of NAPSS. The bulk of the material dealing directly with social policy problems that appeared in the *Sociological Review* in its first four years was contributed by him—mostly in the form of short expository and evaluative notes on government publications, the Census of Production of 1908, the Registrar General's Annual Report, and on the reports of a host of departmental committees, special advisory groups, congresses, and the like. The topics he wrote on in 1910 included industrial statistics, birth and marriage rates, preventable disease, continuation schools for young workers, civic education for girls, imprisonment for debt, the training of probation officers, statistics on the cost of living, school meals, town planning, trade boards for sweated industries, starvation, and the employment of married women. He also delivered a sweeping and considered attack on the pretensions and the very idea of a general sociology: "the claim of the general Sociologist," he argued, "is invalid at every point."

Understandable as it was, the separate institutionalization of sociology and social administration was a misfortune for both fields. Many of the more active recruits to social science, C. R. Atlee and R. H. Tawney, for example, when forced to choose, chose the latter. And the already precarious integration of theory and practice, and of the analysis of social systems and the documentation of social problems, was made still harder. Yet it was clear by 1910 that this was to be the pattern of development. The new School of Social Science established at the University of Liverpool in 1909 was oriented almost exclusively to training for social administration. Accordingly, "the general courses of study have been devised to meet the needs of those preparing for regular (social) work, especially the younger workers in local societies, candidates for the ministry, the junior clergy, and those connected with the administration of relief." The sociology syllabus at the L.S.E., by contrast, offered an introduction to evolutionary philosophy and comparative anthropology:

As the subject of Sociology has been so recently introduced, it is thought desirable to indicate the scope of the subject as set forth in the following Syllabus.

1. Sociology in its relations to Biology and Psychology. The principle of evolution applied to Social Phenomena.
2. Forms of Family Structure:—Maternal and Paternal Descent. Power of the Head of the Family. Joint and Individual property. Regulation of Marriage. Position of Women.
3. The Forms of Social Structure:—The Clan and the Tribe. Monarchy, Feudalism, the City State. The Modern State. Federal Government.
4. The Development of Social Control:—The Blood Feud. Retaliation. Compensation. Primitive Courts and Processes. The Oath and the Ordeal. Growth of Public Justice and Rational

Procedure. Individual and Collective Responsibility. Punishment and Prevention of Crime.
5. Religious and other beliefs and their bearing on social relations. Influence of Magic. Animism. Ancestor-worship, Polytheism, the World Religions, on Social Morality. Antithesis of Temporal and Spiritual Powers.

In dealing with this subject in the Examination candidates will be allowed a choice of questions.[2]

One can see why members of the Sociological Society might have felt that Hobhouse, far from leading them to a new mastery of the real world, was luring them back into the old ivory tower.

The picture I have drawn is a little exaggerated. The would-be sociologist intent on discovering all he could of the subject in 1909 or 1910 could have heard 40 lectures by Hobhouse on *Social Evolution*, 36 by Westermarck on *Social Rights and Duties, Social Institutions*, and *Early Customs and Institutions*, all at the School of Economics, a course by Geddes on *Evolution in Mind, Morals and Society* and another by J. W. Slaughter, Chairman of the Eugenics Education Society, on *Psychological Factors in Social Relationships*, both sponsored by the University Extension Board, two further courses by Geddes within the University on *Town and Country in Development, Deterioration and Renewal* and *The Philosophy of Occupations*. And if he had made his way to the School of Sociology organized by C. S. Loch, Geddes, and others at the headquarters of the Charity Organisation Society he could also have heard a course by Urwick on *Social Progress*. In addition he could have taken a class in social statistics with A. L. Bowley and a couple of years later he could have heard him lecture on *The Measurement of Social Phenomena*. Then he could have gone to the home of Lady Emily Lutyens to hear the Eugenics Education Society debate the problem of *Eugenics and The Poor Law*, or to meetings of the Sociological Society (which by now had almost 400 members) to hear R. H. Tawney on *The Theory of Pauperism* or F. G. D'aeth on *Present Tendencies in Class Differentiation*. D'aeth argued that economic and ecological dif-

[2]   *Sociological Review*, 1912.

ferentiation were producing a class structure based on life style instead of on kinship, characterized by bridges instead of barriers between classes and organized in the form of two primary socio-economic classes and seven subformations—social mobility being largely a function of fluctuations arising from economic growth in the supply of vacant statuses at different levels. He would, however, have needed influential friends in order to have heard Lord George Hamilton analyzing the statistics gathered by the Royal Commission on the Poor Law at the annual meeting of the Royal Statistical Society. With luck he could have won a J. Martin White Sociological Scholarship to help him in his studies. He could, in fact, have pieced together a quite comprehensive sociological education. But if he had concluded that a coordinated sociological tradition was developing in Britain he would have been mistaken.

The real momentum in all this work was divisive. To see this clearly it is necessary to take a step back and follow the lines of influence springing from the work of Geddes, Galton, Hobhouse, and Booth in the mid-1890's through the first perceived crisis of the Sociological Society in 1911, to the recognition in the 1920's that peaceful coexistence between divergent modes of social science and not an integrated sociology was the best that could be expected in the immediate future.

Civics

Geddes' first contribution to social analysis was an attempt to devise categories of statistical classification which would permit higher levels of comparability in cross-cultural studies.[3] In place of the ethnocentric, economically based and institutional categories used in almost all British statistical work he proposed a comprehensive system of functional categories derived from a Comtist conception of social organization. Neither the biologists nor the political economists to whom he offered this idea were impressed. If, however, we examine the frameworks of analysis

[3]   Geddes, "The Classification of Statistics," *Nature* 24, 1881 and cf., B. Gross, *The State of the Nation* (New York, 1966) ; R. Bauer, *Social Indicators* (M.I.T., 1966).

recently developed by Gross, Bauer, and Biderman for the purpose of "social systems accounting" it becomes clear that Geddes had brilliantly anticipated a style of sociological work which would be seriously developed only in the 1960's. The effect of indifference, meanwhile, was to drive Geddes into more marked eccentricity. His next work, while renewing the appeal for a broader, analytically integrated conception of social science data, was also a sweeping attack on the mental habits of economists, "reincarnated metaphysicians," and an attempt to establish biological man in interaction with his environment in the place of economic man as the focus of social inquiry.[4] Here we see for the first time Geddes' peculiar fusion of Spencer, Comte and LePlay. Economic production is treated as an adaptive system coordinating the environment with human functions. From a sociological perspective the criterion for judging economic behavior and institutions ceases to be their relation to the production of wealth and becomes their functionality in enabling or preventing men's adapting their environment to their wants. From this point of view the institutions of urbanism emerged as a particularly problematic object for sociological study.

The temptation to see Geddes as a precursor of contemporary sociology on the basis of this early work is very strong. But now he began to strike off on his own eccentric course. A great deal of the difficulty people later experienced in coming to terms with Geddes as a sociologist turned on his ubiquitous use of diagrammatic "thinking machines." Developed during a period of temporary blindness, the machines were designed to allow him to manipulate large sets of concepts without reading or writing. They did this only too well. Geddes acquired an extraordinary ability to cover vast ranges of subject matter in a very small compass. But the machines also eliminated, from Geddes' own mind at least, the need for conventional verbal expositions of the logical relations between concepts. It thus became quite easy for those who heard or read him to conclude that he was talking nonsense. He was the

[4]   Geddes, "An Analysis of the Principles of Economics," Royal Society of Edinburgh, *Proceedings* 12, 1884.

only member of the Sociological Society whose lectures were regularly printed not in the form he had delivered them in but "in abstract."

When he came to London in 1903 it was with a view to persuading British sociologists to accept the city as their distinctive unit of empirical study. Its aptness for this purpose was threefold: it was the territorial context of the most pressing social problems: it allowed one to treat social problems sociologically—in terms of adaptive interactions between men and their environment: and it therefore provided an ideal framework for the concrete specification of sociology as a synthetic science. Massive empirical work on social process and organization was necessary to underpin and develop the theoretical superstructure of sociology. Nowhere could the hypotheses derived from that superstructure be so effectively scrutinized and refined as in the investigation of cities. Mixed up with this was a crusading zeal to develop community life, and to plan and rebuild. One problem for Geddes was that by 1903, although he insisted on the need for surveys and inquiries, he knew too well where he wanted to go. And this was certainly a factor in his failure to articulate a technically specific research method.

The method he advocated was the method of survey derived from LePlay and Demolins. The unit to be surveyed could be specified in terms of extent and structure at various levels—the city, the village, the community, the neighborhood. Geddes' particular contribution was to direct attention to two larger units, the region and the conurbation. But once determined the object to be surveyed had to be examined organically. It was on this score that Geddes and Branford objected to the work of Booth. Enormous improvement on the fractured surveys of government agencies and earlier political economists as it was, Booth's study was itself an attempt to understand an organism by minute examination of selected detached parts—as though one were to try to analyze an individual by knowing everything about his blood cells. What one needed was first of all an account of the structure of the whole organism, then a specification of its critical elements, then, through the use of appropriate indicators, statistics that would reveal the elements in interaction. Particularly important for Geddes was the need for surveys to have a historical dimension, to reveal the community acting on itself through time. Only such a perspective could make clear the capacity of the community for development. Communities could not be developed according to a single blueprint, but only according to their peculiar, historically structured, capacities. There is a true line of influence, winding and subterranean no doubt, from Geddes' *Chelsea, Past and Possible* to such distinctive products of modern British town-planning as Sir William Holford's *Plan for Cambridge.*

But neither Geddes nor Branford ever went much beyond indicating the most general outlines of the method of sociological surveys. LePlay's "place, work and family" was broadened to a general recommendation that surveys should be organized in terms of a historical treatment of geographical, economic, and anthropological data with a continuing effort to see the community under investigation as the product of interactions through time of variables in these three categories. And that was about all. From 1905 to 1947 first Geddes and Branford and then LePlay House issued a host of pamphlets, articles, and studies advocating the sociological survey. But nowhere is there a rigorous specification of the principles of survey design. In 1908 Geddes saw clearly enough what had to be done to develop urban sociology in Britain. The sociologist's conception of the city (that of LePlay and Geddes that is) had to be transposed into a disciplined research method. And the method had to result in surveys which would not only reveal the distinctive structure of urbanism in each locality but do so in a way that led directly from survey to planning by indicating the conditions governing development in each area and the relative meaningfulness (in Max Weber's sense) of different policy options. But in the event this was not what he chose to do. Instead he plunged as an active propagandist into the town planning movement.

In its first six years he lectured the Sociological Society regularly on the need for sociological surveys of cities, on the appropriateness of the city as an empirical focus for general sociology, and on the importance of linking surveys and plans in a tight analytical chain. He persuaded the Society to establish its cities committee to study these problems and in particular to deal with questions of survey design. Meanwhile he was preparing his own survey and plan of Dunfermline—published as *City Development*—helping to promote the great town planning conference which followed the passing of Britain's first Town Planning Act in 1909, mounting Civic Exhibitions, and addressing endless groups of school teachers, architects, and local politicians on the need to preserve local individuality. He did not change his view of the importance of developing survey methods but his experience in these years seems to have convinced him that a more urgent task was that of sensitizing public opinion, including the opinion of planning officials and local authorities, to the rudimentary idea of the city, region, or village as a social structure. After that one might introduce the idea of the possible relevance of surveys to the business of planning. That would be the time to perfect survey techniques. Meanwhile he set himself to arouse a sense of locality. And increasingly he saw that the survey, in addition to being a preliminary to planning, could serve that end. Working on a local survey, however naïve and unscientific, might do more than anything else to develop civic involvement.

The Cities Committee was accordingly put to work to stimulate local community surveys on a do-it-yourself basis. As many local residents as possible were to participate in these surveys. And the bridge between survey and plan was to be the exhibition. The educational purpose was often more evident than the analytical. In the handbook to survey methods published by LePlay House in 1924 the tendency is evident: "The problem in hand is not merely the practical one of the improvement of the environment, but the more fundamental question of how to direct the attention of men and women . . . to the natural conditions and social possibilities of the world around them in their own neighbourhood." It did not follow that surveys conducted for this sort of motive—very evident in another handbook of the period, *Social Survey: A Guide to Good Citizenship*—would necessarily be naïve in conception or unscientific in their execution. Some of them, such as Hilda Jennings' *Brynmawr*, or Ford's survey of Southampton were quite the opposite. But taken as a whole the rich crop of surveys, mostly village surveys, which resulted from the proselytizing of

Geddes and Branford suffered very badly from the lack of a clear substantive focus and a well-defined methodological paradigm. And as Branford in particular came to insist that this type of work was par excellence, sociology, it had unfortunate effects. Many social scientists investigating more limited topics by more traditional methods and anxious to establish the significance and reliability of their findings felt the need to dissociate their work from that of the Geddes school.[5]

Geddes' campaign was in some ways very successful. He added great momentum to the town-planning movement and he was instrumental in the setting up of departments of town planning at both Liverpool and London. His direct influence on pioneers in this field such as Unwin, Mears, and Abercrombie was considerable. The idea of survey-before-plan became an axiom of British town planning—often with unhappy effects for the pace of development. But paradoxically it was just as sociology that the typical planning survey was likely to be defective. Geological and geographical data, information on land use and institutional facilities, on economic demands and resources, on transportation and occupational patterns, could be and usually was easily mobilized in these surveys. But while Geddes' belief in the comprehensive survey was to this extent respected, he had indicated no techniques by which the all-important thing, the culture of a city, could be reliably gauged or the sociological conditions for enhancing or modifying it specified. Whatever else the British planning survey became, it did not typically become a work of sociology.[6]

[5]   Usually this was done quite discreetly. D. Caradoc Jones' introduction to the *Social Survey of Merseyside* provides a representative example.
[6]   This has been less true since 1946, however—largely because Ruth Glass and a few others have begun to deal with the methodological problems of urban sociology which Geddes raised but then abandoned. The total failure of Geddes and his immediate circle to deal with this problem is quickly apparent if one contrasts Branford's optimistic paper distinguishing sociological from merely social surveys in the *Sociological Review* for 1912 with his thoroughly woolly treatment of the same issue in 1929. Geddes' own paper in the same year "Social Evolution—How to Advance It," in which the primary method of research turns out to be "living," is equally an admission of defeat in relation to his earlier aspirations.

According to Branford, Geddes first derived from Comte, Spencer, and LePlay a general framework for sociology in the form of "a unifying theory of social evolution," and then went on to claim "for sociology an observational and concrete basis in the study of cities." Many of the early sociologists were keen to follow Geddes in this direction. R. H. Tawney, reviewing the Howarth and Wilson survey *West Ham* in 1908, made very much the comment Geddes himself had made on Booth, pleading:

> That future investigators should not confine themselves to an analysis of industrial evils, but should give a far fuller account of the geographical, economic and historical circumstances under which particular towns have grown up. We want not only a pathology, but a history and a morphology of urban life and conditions, in order to understand more fully the broad economic causes which are normally operative. The sort of questions which one would like to see treated at greater length are: Why do particular industries settle in particular localities? What has caused a very rapid increase in population at particular moments? What function does West Ham perform in the general economy of the Thames valley and of Southern England? What are the commercial causes which make for home work and casual labour as distinct from the evils produced and the remedies suggested? Generalization is very dangerous; yet is it not worth the risk?[7]

But neither Geddes nor anyone else had shown how these desirable tasks were to be executed.

In many ways Geddes saw what a mature sociology would be. He saw, for example, that it would have to destroy the disciplinary boundaries of the existing sciences. This posture, which made it so difficult for sociology to gain acceptance in ancient universities in 1910, is, of course, just what makes sociology widely attractive today. The perception of the interdisciplinary nature of the most compelling social problems has, as it were, caught up with the universities. The most fashionable social science is now being done in groups studying "Technology and Society," "Science and Public Policy," "Urban Affairs," and the like—groups which are productive just because they bring disciplines together in the way Geddes tried to do when he staged a Sociological Society seminar on "The Coal Crisis and the Future" in 1926. Geddes' sense that

[7]   *Sociological Review*, 1908.

the true subject matter of sociology would be found in the common territory of other sciences is now entirely professional. Yet forty years ago the proposition that "Geography, Economics and Anthropology are so intimately related . . . that it can hardly be much longer before all their separate cultivators realise their co-operation and union within the field of Sociology," was enough to make a man ridiculous.

In the last analysis Geddes' achievement was negative. In focusing empirical sociology on questions of the structure of regions, cities, and communities he created an opportunity for the rapid growth of a sociology peculiarly appropriate to the world's most highly urbanized nation. Such a sociology might have incorporated the work of Booth and others and at the same time have escaped from the ultimately unanalytical empiricism of that work. But he threw the opportunity away. His failure to devise an adequate method for urban sociology and his premature diversion into planning propaganda and educational projects were critical. They discredited urban sociology among sociologists and they established an essentially nonsociological use of the social survey among planners.

Eugenics

For Geddes the issues of social policy resolved themselves into problems of reconstituting the environment of individual life. This was not, as he saw it, a position at odds with the teachings of Eugenics. He hoped sociology would be "Civics and Eugenics in association." Admittedly there was a type of "crudely Darwinian eugenist," with whom the sociologist was bound to quarrel, since it was evident that "many of those whom [such] eugenists are apt to think of and to tabulate as degenerates in type and stock are really but deteriorates, and this in correspondence to their depressive environment." For the sociologist there could be no doubt that these types and stocks were ones which "slum culture has proved most sensitive or adaptive to its evils" and which, "should correspondingly no less respond to better conditions, and thus rise above the average as they now fall below." Geddes treated the divergence of the two schools as superficial. It was in fact to be of fundamental importance. What he did not recognize was that by 1914 rather large numbers of the more articulate eugenicists were of the "crudely Darwinian" type. The difference of emphasis in the interpretation of social problems thus tended to grow into a radical disagreement. For environmental sociologists such as Geddes the disturbing phenomena of British society were phenomena of waste—of an environment failing to make the most of its human resources. For the heirs of Galton the problem was one of the overproduction of essentially unusable human material. The resulting controversy was to drive a wedge between the would-be sociologists of Edwardian Britain. Yet ironically it was to be from efforts to resolve this controversy that a line of research would finally grow to provide a basis for the rebirth of British sociology in the late 1930's.

After biding his time for fifteen years Galton decided in 1904 that the world was ready for eugenics, and having read six papers to the Sociological Society outlining the nature and aims of the field, he endowed a Research Fellowship in the University of London. From this developed the Eugenics Laboratory. Simultaneously he promoted the Eugenics Education Society and a program of lectures—analogous in function to the LePlay House social surveys—to stimulate local consciousness. At the same time Karl Pearson was emerging as the champion of the parallel science of biometrics and the development of general genetics by biologists such as Bateson at Cambridge contributed to the same movement. When Pearson became head of the Eugenics Laboratory considerable integration of diverse approaches to a common problem —the problem of "the influences that improve the inborn qualities of a race"—had been achieved. The purpose of eugenics, according to Galton, was "to bring to bear as many influences as could reasonably be employed so as to enable the useful classes in the community to contribute more than their proportion to the next generation." Such a statement of aims was widely approved.

Nevertheless, there were important differences. Galton himself had always been rather guarded, seeking to establish the importance of heredity without diminishing the importance of environment. This was especially so when he was dealing with the famous, as in *English Men of Science* and *Noteworthy Families*. Pearson, by contrast, early concluded that all the available evidence pointed to the preponderant influence of heredity: "With our present knowledge," he declared in 1909, "we can safely affirm that not only physical but psychical characters, and not only psychical characters but morbid and pathological constitutions, are largely, and probably in absolutely equal degree, the product of inheritance." And he went on to dismiss efforts to modify personality by environmental action. On the other hand, some of the eugenicists more closely involved in the Sociological Society, Dr. C. W. Saleeby for example, seemed to advocate little more than that attention should be paid to questions of marriage, parenthood, and inheritance as well as to education, community, and work. Where, then, was the common ground of eugenics? For Galton there were two critical unifying elements. The first was substantive: "the great fact upon which Eugenics is based, that able fathers produce able children in a much larger proportion than the generality." The second was methodological—for unlike civics, eugenics developed at the outset a rigorous and distinctive research method—involving the application of statistical principles of probability to large masses of objectively classified data. In both respects the possibility of eugenics being perceived as a polemical departure from the main tendency of sociology was real.

Galton's greatness in relation to most of his followers is manifested in his inconsistency. Having established the "great fact" of eugenics in *Natural Inheritance* he adhered strictly to it. His best known presentation of it, made in three separate contexts, was that in which, following the earlier work of statisticians such as Farr and Newmarch, he assigned cash values to the lives of members of different social classes on the basis of their inherited capacity for socially useful activity—the infant son of a laborer being worth five pounds while the offspring of parents of the "highest class" were valued at many thousands. One version of this analysis is printed below. But in *Noteworthy Families* he confronted the question of the relative contribution of innate ability and favorable environment to personal achievement and concluded that as one moved to higher levels of success the tendency for achievement to "become an equal measure *both* of Ability and of Favourableness of Environment" would steadily increase. The purpose to which he put this analysis was to sustain the equation of high success and high ability. It was a long time before eugenicists came to see the equal viability of the obverse equation—high achievement with highly favorable environment—although it had been latent in Galton's work all along. It was not that they necessarily wished to deny that relationship but that the data that most concerned them, as they saw it, made the relationship of inherited ability to achievement infinitely more salient. Their problem was to integrate into a general social analysis the Registrar-General's statistics of births, marriages, and deaths.

Eugenicists, too, were caught up in the general ideological crisis of the late century. Seeking to account for the facts of economic and social disorder on the basis of specifically biological training, they brought the principles of genetics to bear on contemporary vital statistics and discovered, as a more or less imminent danger, the prospect of race degeneration. Eugenics, when its history is written, will have to be treated in close relation to political economy. By discovering a systematic reversal of the laws of social organization, specifically the law of natural selection, eugenics afforded an ideologically generalized interpretation of the condition of Britain in which the assumptions of political economy were maintained intact. Dr. Saleeby was right to sense that many self-styled eugenicists were in the first instance antisocialists. Eugenics culminated in demands not for a new social order but for the reconstitution of the old order at a higher level of efficiency. By the end of the century there was a veritable cult of national efficiency, and the criterion of efficiency was ubiquitously used in social analysis. Much of Rowntree's impact turned on the way he had pegged poverty to criteria of physical efficiency —and concluded his analysis by confronting his readers with the prospect of a stunted and inefficient people.

It is striking to see how far this last extension of political economy drew on the statistical resources generated by political economy in an earlier phase. Eugenics did not spring inductively from social statistics, but its arguments were always given a statistical point of reference. Fertility had been declining since the mid-1870's and a class differential within the general pattern had become increasingly apparent. Conversely, working-class infant mortality was also steadily declining. With a readiness typical of the habit of reasoning of political economy the most alarming projections were made in the most mechanical manner from these figures. The justification for extreme rigidity was found in Galton's law of ancestral heritage. It became commonplace to envisage the future of Britain in terms of a grotesque proliferation of degenerates alongside an ever-diminishing minority of the capable, intelligent, and fit. One unintended consequence of the flood of statistics of poverty, crime, intemperance, and mental disorder in the 1890's and after was to lend color to these projections. Figures created a more cogent sense of the extent of these social ills, the numbers of the socially dependent, than most middle-class Victorians had had before. And this easily produced the illusion of a *growth* of dependence. In a more direct way, too, the work of Booth, Rowntree, and government inquiries such as the Royal Commission on the Feeble-Minded became the raw-material of eugenics. Galton used Booth's figures with considerable effect to support his own thesis that contemporary social organization was permitting the growth of a hereditary class of failures. General Maurice seized on Rowntree's findings to scare his colleagues with the prospect of an army increasingly incapable of combat. The chain of reasoning was nicely illustrated by Karl Pearson in his Huxley lecture of 1903:

We are ceasing as a nation to breed intelligence as we did fifty to a hundred years ago. The mentally better stock in the nation is not reproducing itself at the same rate as it did of old; the less able and the less energetic are more fertile than the better stocks. No scheme of wider or more thorough education will bring up, in the scale of intelligence, hereditary weakness to the level of hereditary strength. The only remedy, if one be possible at all, is to alter the relative fertility of the good and bad stocks in the community.[8]

8   Pearson, *The Groundwork of Eugenics.*

Or as another writer put it: "the lesson to be drawn from these figures is that ever-increasing numbers of weakly children have had their lives artificially preserved by medical science, who would otherwise have died in early infancy." Such children would of course grow up, marry, and "beget fresh generations of weaklings." Clearly, "a race which thus counteracts the working of selection does so only at the risk of immediate peril . . . it has entered on the path which leads to degeneracy and bankruptcy."

But the importance of eugenics lay in its methods as much as its substance. Thanks to Galton the science was committed to a rigorous empirical method. And its propositions were thus open to empirical scrutiny and verification. For this reason it was dialectically fruitful in a way which Geddes' embryonic urban sociology was not. Already in 1911 Pearson was involved in vehement controversy with J. M. Keynes and others. The argument was ultimately about the merits of the eugenic interpretation of social problems. But immediately it was about the adequacy of Pearson's research method—both data-gathering and statistical analysis—to the investigation of cause-effect relationships among social variables. Increasingly those who resisted the eugenicist's conclusions were encouraged to show that the eugenicist's own methodology, properly applied, would not support those conclusions. Thus, in the history of British sociology we have to turn our attention slightly off-center to discover lines of work which had both sufficient ideological momentum and sufficiently exact empirical content to sustain the kind of disputes from which a cumulative science could spring.

Starting from an interest in the phenomenon of regression Galton had opened up an entirely new style of statistical analysis. His contributions to developing the use of frequency curves, of principles for the determination of error, of methods of correlation, and specifically of correlation coefficients, need no discussion here. A memoir in the *Journal* of the Royal Statistical Society recognizes him as "the parent of modern statistical methods." What is directly relevant is that he made the application of these tools to the data of vital statistics the indispensable method of eugenics. His Herbert Spencer lecture of 1907, "Probability, the

Foundation of Eugenics," was in effect a short lesson in statistical techniques. "Eugenics," he ruled, "seeks for quantitative results. It is not contented with such vague words as 'much' or 'little,' but endeavours to determine 'how much' or 'how little' in precise and trustworthy figures." Or as Pearson put it, more aggressively: "We depart from the old sociology, in that we desert verbal discussion for statistical facts." In doing so they indicated the methods which unregenerate environmentalists would need to use if they were to retrieve their own views from the eugenicists' attack. Critics like Keynes and Marshall and Hobhouse met the successive publications of the Eugenics Laboratory on their own ground; their objections took the form of appeals for more careful sampling, more discriminating classification, more adequate empirical data, more sophisticated mathematical analysis. The conclusion reached by Keynes after the first round of his debate with Pearson over the latter's study, *The Influence of Parental Alcoholism,* is representative: "The methods of 'the trained anthropometrical statistician' need applying with much more care and caution than is here exhibited before they are suited to the complex phenomena" under analysis. At the end of the battle the position as he saw it was this: Pearson's data was too partial and his analysis too limited to support the case he had tried to make. On the other hand, "a large mass of general experience makes it exceedingly probable . . . that alcoholic homes exert in general an evil environmental influence upon children." But as between this probability and others there was at present no way of determining relative influences. Pearson had opened up the problem of tracing and weighing influences in specific social settings very forcefully: the immediate outstanding problem was to devise a method— statistical or experimental—that would be adequate to the task. The ideological temperature of the debate ensured that such work of methodological refinement and development would indeed be carried on.

In the same years we find a number of other sociological encounters with eugenics having similar results. Thus, at the British Association meetings of 1908 the president of the Anthropological section had maintained the view that "ability was inherited, that in the United Kingdom the present differences in class were due to differences of ability, and that the presence of the middle and upper classes represented an evolutionary process of natural selection from the artizan and labouring class." The eugenic implications of such a view were obvious. "The legislator must . . . as far as possible conform to the principles of the stock breeder." It was in reaction to this statement that F. G. D'aeth of the newly formed Social Science department at Liverpool wrote the paper on class differentiation that has already been mentioned. His purpose was not to depart radically from a eugenic point of view but merely to indicate the existence of certain socially structured constraints on ability and having done that to call for research designed to evaluate, the "importance of ability and its influence in determining the construction of society . . . its forms, its distribution in a people and the laws of its production and transmission."

But in the long run the Sociological Society, having largely detached itself from statistical work, was a less important arena for the confrontation with eugenics than the Royal Statistical Society. Civil-servant statisticians such as Arthur Newsholme and T. H. C. Stevenson were particularly active in contributing to the long series of papers in which the data of vital statistics were continually reworked between 1890 and 1940. Their orientation, though not theoretical, was palpably environmentalist. This was already plain in Newsholme's paper "Vital Statistics of Artisans' Dwellings" in 1891, in *The Prevention of Tuberculosis* which he published in 1909 and in *The Declining Birth Rate* of 1911. In contrast to the typically aggressive posture of many eugenicists, from Karl Pearson to Leonard Darwin, these critics, while matching the eugenicists in statistical competence, adopted a pacific manner: "It is not certain," we find Newsholme writing after demonstrating that it was highly uncertain, "that the average inherent mental and physical qualities of the majority of the wage-earning classes are not equal to those of the rest of the population." And again: "Continued family success may be due in at least a high proportion of the total cases to the favourable environment of the children of the able, to their possession of all the means of training for success." Conversely, of course, unfavorable environment might possibly account for the persistent lack of success of the children of laborers. Here were the beginnings of a controversial tradition, stiffened by meticulous statistical work, in which the distinctive problems and research styles of modern British sociology were finally cultivated. *The Population Question* by Alexander Carr-Saunders was a critical landmark in its development. And a generation later the tradition was producing studies such as Gray and Moshinsky on "Ability and Opportunity in English Education," a statistical study of the question, "To what extent does the existing machinery of social selection adjust educational opportunity to individual ability?"; Glass and Gray on "Opportunity and the Older Universities," a demonstration of the systematic working of particular selection mechanisms to frustrate the concurrence of ability and achievement; and Titmuss on "Poverty and Population," a compelling mobilization of demographic statistics to reveal the calamitous impact of poverty on national efficiency, intelligence, and mortality. The line forward from such studies is obvious enough. By reaction and in the long run eugenics had generated an authentic sociology of social waste.

Meanwhile in the short run it provoked a withdrawal on the part of those who had appropriated the role of sociologist from both Darwinism and statistics. By 1914 the gulf between the Sociological Society and the Royal Statistical Society was cavernous. There were four hundred members of the one, eight hundred of the other, but among active participants only four people belonged to both. And who could say to which of them sociology belonged? The great event of 1909 was the publication of the *Report* of the Royal Commission on the Poor Law. Every learned society concerned with social questions discussed it. But Lord George Hamilton's analysis of the Commission's statistics could no more have been read before the Sociological Society than R. H. Tawney's "The Theory of Pauperism"—as essay in the sociology of knowledge seeking to explain the persistence of Poor Law ideology—could have appeared in the *Journal of the Statistical Society*. The process of institutionalization had driven a wedge down the middle of British social science. The activity of the Sociological Society was acquiring its own coherence by 1914

—but at the price of a visible narrowing of range, a deeper commitment to the Comte-LePlay-Geddes manner of work. D'aeth's suggestion was not followed up. In 1914, however, the *Sociological Review* published an article by Gustave Spiller, "Darwinism and Sociology," on the heritage of Darwin. The article was written in strong language: "the theory of heredity is only strong so long as it is not analysed," "our whole thought relating to human problems is today vitiated by the unwarranted assumption of mental heredity," "the statistical method which Karl Pearson's school pursues does not seem to have yielded as yet any striking results." But there is no real analytical confrontation. Spiller advocates an environmental treatment of human variations rooted in the concept of culture. But essentially the article is an ideological repudiation: "With the Darwinian incubus removed, Sociology may breathe freely at last." Thereafter, for two decades the members of the Sociological Society went their own way. In 1929 the Sociological Society was formally amalgamated with LePlay House, Geddes' and Branford's institute of applied sociology, of "surveys for service" as Geddes put it. And a decade later Lancelot Hogben, resigning from what seemed to him a failed experiment, his Chair of Social Biology at the London School of Economics, found it still true that "the study of population is the only branch of social research with its own logical technique for the detection and coordination of factual data."[9]

Social Philosophy

The splintering of British sociology is apparent in a different way if we turn back to the work of Hobhouse. Hobhouse was in a difficult position. Both his own intellectual inclinations and the terms of reference of his appointment urged him to concentrate his energies on the more abstract philosophical themes of sociology. At the same time he was deeply involved in a wide range of practical social problems and the prevailing interest of his students also lay in that direction. But then again two aims of

[9]   L. Hogben, ed., *Political Arithmetic.*

the Martin White benefaction were "to aid in establishing the *academic* status of Sociology in the Universities" and "to promote the application of *scientific* method to sociological studies" (my italics). What balance was he to strike? In 1906 he had published *Morals in Evolution,* extending and making more concrete his conception of the qualitative transformation of evolution with the emergence of mind, the creation of culture and social tradition as the effective context of development, and thence, the growing possibility of self-conscious purposive social action. This work was widely regarded as a decisive landmark for British sociology. In it he first set out and applied the strategy of research which he considered sociologists should use if they were resolve the central problem—the problem of the extent to which evolution (empirically observed social change) and progress (movement toward the rational good) were in fact coordinated in different settings. This was the strategy of a "morphology of social institutions" realized in *The Material Culture and Social Institutions of the Simpler Peoples.* The interest and value of this work today, as of most of Hobhouse's later writing, lies in treating it as a contribution to an empirical sociology of the conditions of development (movement toward any goal) within particular cultures of different types. For Hobhouse himself its importance was as a first step toward a general synthesis of moral philosophy and social analysis. And it was always toward such a synthesis that he himself tried to move on.

Inevitably, he moved away from the work of the Sociological Society, eugenicists, statisticians, and social reformers alike. Not from any strong polemical sense but because the way he was building his subject led him to specialize in inquiries which easily seemed more remote from other work than Hobhouse meant them to be. Nevertheless by 1910 adverse comments, both on the abstraction of British sociology and on its fragmentation, were beginning to be heard. Writing in the *Revue Internationale de Sociologie* in October of that year R. Maunier accused British sociologists of "misty thinking" and found that the product of that process was "an anomalous body of beliefs and practices which is neither an art nor a science." At the same time Geddes delivered the first of a number of attacks on the academic detachment of "the sociologist," who, he found, typically "shrinks from [the] great opportunity of social interpretation" offered him by the immediate structure and organization of his own society. Rather, "he is absorbed in his study, apart even from his own immediate kind, save for his learned society's meeting, and there he is commonly occupied with older questions, with less immediate and pressing issues . . . with the abstract philosophy of the State, or busy amid masses of fresh concrete observations." In 1911 a self-critical debate developed within the Sociological Society as objections of this type mounted. "Much of the criticism," J. A. Hobson noted, "consists in charging the Sociological Society with not concerning itself directly and sufficiently with the Art of Social Reform." His own view was that "the Society is engaged in developing the Science rather than the Art of Society," and that it might therefore: "be a better economy of our resources in the earlier stages of collecting and stating laws of social forms and forces not to concern ourselves too closely or too clearly with the practical uses to which the knowledge may be put when it is got." Branford, surveying the debate as a whole, was pessimistic about the prospects of realizing the original intentions of the society. There was, he now felt, little chance "of putting before sociologists a common enterprise in which each participant would feel that he was contributing something to one great social purpose." It was in this atmosphere that Hobhouse surrendered to the demand that a new editor be found for the *Sociological Review*.[10]

In 1904 Hobhouse had seen sociology as "a number of specialisms . . . suffering from the want of coordination." He had earlier given his support to the statement of aims the Sociological Society had set for itself at its foundation. Much of that statement, indeed, reads as though Hobhouse himself had written it. His own work was intended to be above all a contribution to coordination. Looking back one can see how a theoretical political sociology could have grown out of it and provided a frame of reference for more practical social investigations. Clearly specified hypotheses

10   That this was what happened seems clear from Branford's obituary article on Hobhouse, *Sociological Review*, October, 1929.

about the conditions for social development might have given regional surveys a discipline and perspective they urgently needed. Rooting the theory of development in the problems of particular regions and communities would have provided a substance and empirical focus that it increasingly lacked. It was nobody's fault that there were too few people and too many obstacles, theoretical and methodological, for such an integration to be effected quickly. But neither did it help that within a decade of the experiment being launched people working toward coordination from different bases had come to view one another as sectarian. In 1913 *La Science Sociale*, the journal of the direct heirs of LePlay, launched a "service de vulgarisation"—a program of study guides, research materials, and other means of winning popular acceptance for a sociological understanding of social phenomena. Welcoming this development enthusiastically the *Sociological Review* could not refrain from noting that such a program would be deeply offensive "to the highly scientific and superior sociologist of these islands." Nor, when writing his obituary of J. Martin White fifteen years later, could Branford refrain from recording White's "disappointment" at "the drifting apart of the University Department and the Society" or his many unsuccessful efforts to bring the two into closer association.

Meanwhile, what of the "superior sociologist" himself? For a decade after his appointment at the L.S.E. Hobhouse seems to have marked time. There is little movement of thought beyond *Morals in Evolution* in the books he wrote in the next few years— only clearer statements of earlier positions. His teaching seems to have combined excitement and obscurity in a curious blend. In the accounts of his lectures testimony to his brilliance is finely balanced by admissions of the extreme difficulty of following him. J. A. Hobson in his memoir of Hobhouse published a number of statements by former students who had taken the Sociology course in its early days. The following is representative:

> The lectures covered a wide field of thought and fact and theory— they were above the heads of the larger proportion of his audience. . . . Professor Hobhouse led us through new subjects—psychology, theories of heredity, types of social organisation, theories of society, theories

of progress. I remember struggling to understand his extraordinarily eloquent disquisition on Hegel. They were subjects linked with others, a new subject emerging—sociology. We were a generation with our minds on concrete problems. . . . Yet Professor Hobhouse's conception of society had a definite influence on his students—even if they were incapable of following it and understanding it in its entirety. It gave them a setting for their efforts in thinking out their particular social problems and showed them the interrelation and complexity of social subjects.[11]

For whatever reason Hobhouse, according to Victor Branford, had become quite seriously dissatisfied with his own approach to sociology by 1914. "He was wont," Branford writes, "to speak despondently about his own lectures on sociology, complaining of his failure to get the field of studies and research clear," and going so far on one occasion "as to indicate some thought of resigning the chair." How deep this discontent may have been, or what its roots were, need not be discussed here. There were in any case periods of counteracting confidence and purpose—one such was the time he spent at Columbia in 1911. And by 1916 he had found his lasting sense of direction.

The turning point is said to have been the writing of a general article on Sociology for the *Encyclopaedia of Religion and Ethics*. In it the elements of sociology are surveyed and ordered more clearly and comprehensively than in any other of his writings. Its effect on Hobhouse himself, to quote Branford once more, "was transformative . . . a veritable regeneration of his mental powers followed." The article has recently been republished in the anthology of Hobhouse's writing, *Sociology and Philosophy*. It is easy to read it as a piece of intellectual map-making, a necessary prelude so far as its author was concerned to the four volumes culminating in *Social Development* which he went on to write in the next eight years and which constituted in his eyes his definitive treatment of the principles of sociology.

It would be going beyond the prescribed boundaries of the present book to give close attention to the encyclopedia article or the works that followed from it. But some points must be men-

[11]   J. A. Hobson and M. Ginsberg, *L. T. Hobhouse: A Memoir.*

tioned briefly. One feature of the article is the attempt Hobhouse makes to introduce a middle level of generality into sociological analysis. While still treating the investigation of total social systems, and beyond that of society as such, as the ultimate purposes of sociology he also advocates the comparative examination of specific social functions as the best means of working concretely toward such purposes. Kin, community, and association are suggested as the major modes of structural formation between which such functional comparisons might proceed. Then there is the attempt he makes to integrate force and self-interest as organizing principles of social structure. And finally there is the attempt to specify objective criteria of development:

> Structures which maintain themselves in continual process, through the interaction of their parts and by dealings with their physical or social environment, may be said to differ from one another in one or more of three principal points, and it is by such differences that we measure their development. These points are (a) the efficiency of their operation, (b) their scale or scope, (c) the basis or principle of their organization.[12]

The criterion of efficiency raises much the same difficulties as have been found in Professor Parsons' notion of societal goals, and Hobhouse is not really successful in settling them. He comes near to doing so several times in *Social Development* by making efficiency a measure of the capacity of government to realize its objectives in critical situations—which leads him on to a subtle discussion of the relationship between efficiency and the process of social differentiation—but he never quite breaks out of the functionalist circle.

Most important from the point of view of the immediate development of British sociology was the way he specified the task of the sociologist both in the article and again in *Social Development*. I quote the decisive paragraph:

> Ultimately, then, sociology is a synthesis of the social studies. In the meantime the immediate task of the sociologist is humbler and yet

---

[12]   L. T. Hobhouse, "Sociology," in *Encyclopaedia of Religion and Ethics* (London, 1916), reprinted in *Sociology and Philosophy* (London, 1966), pp. 23–56.

difficult enough. Having in mind the inter-connection of social relations, it is his business to discuss and expose the central conceptions from which a synthesis may proceed, to analyse the general character of society, examine the action of social development and distinguish the permanent factors on which society rests and from which social changes proceed. In a wider sense sociology may be taken to cover the whole body of sociological specialisms. In a narrower sense it is itself a specialism, having as its object the discovery of the connecting links between other specialisms. In this sense the problem of sociology is the investigation of the general character of social relations and the nature and determining conditions of social development.[13]

The ordering of these tasks and the way they are formulated is revealing. The first thing is the study of conceptions, the last thing is empirical work on the conditions of social development. Connecting links between the social sciences could be found either at a high level of abstraction or in the immediate conjunction of geographic, economic, and anthropological variables in particular social settings. So far as Hobhouse was concerned his whole training had defined the former level as the one that really mattered. The sequence of inquiry represented by *The Metaphysical Theory of the State* (1918), *The Rational Good* (1921), *The Elements of Social Justice* (1922), and *Social Development* (1924) followed naturally from the general statement of sociological priorities he had achieved in 1916. Conversely there were no more studies following on from *The Material Culture and Social Institutions of the Simpler Peoples*—the option of an early move toward an empirical sociology of development was not taken up. Much of the importance of Hobhouse in the history of sociology resides in the insight on which he so often insisted that: "A theory of the End, Purpose, or Value of social life is one thing and a theory of its actual conditions another. Dealing with the same subject-matter they are intimately related, but must never be confused." But his own substantive contribution to sociology was limited by the belief that went with this insight, not so much that "both inquiries are not only legitimate but necessary to the full understanding of social life," as that, "the question of supreme interest is the relation between their respective results." Convinced that their relation

13   *Ibid.*

could be more than merely strategic he devoted the great part of his energies to studies which increasingly obscured the fruitfulness of his own first steps toward a theory of "actual conditions."

The Tradition of Booth

The final strand of the tattered fabric of sociology in Edwardian Britain was that which is often called the "tradition of Booth." What strikes one here is how discontinuous that tradition actually was. We have already seen that to the group which increasingly dominated the Sociological Society Booth's type of work was inadequate. Nor did his brand of survey take root in the Statistical Society. There were several reasons for this, of which the sheer cost of such research was among the more important. Then, too, the growth of data-generating government departments and special government inquiries increasingly discouraged private initiative. Government surveys and government statistics were not only likely to be more comprehensive than anything an individual investigator could mobilize. They were also widely thought to be more impartial and more authoritative. Private surveys came to be regarded as problem-exposing pilot studies which it was hoped would lead to definitive government investigations. By the 1930's this had become a convention: Glass and Gray, for example, concluded their analysis of entrants to the ancient universities by asserting the need for "a Government enquiry" because, "if reform is wanted it must be preceeded by complete ascertainment of the facts, itself likely to be a lengthy task." In the face of "vested interests and flabby idealism" government facts would have a leverage private facts could not hope for.

As government developed the means for the descriptive scrutiny of discrete social problems the tendency to leave the task to government was reinforced. It must be remembered that Booth's own work was not essentially unlike the investigations already carried out by numerous administrative agencies. It differed in quantity rather than quality—it was a census focused on a particular area and a particular level of society. The questions Booth asked were "who?," "where?," "how much?"—direct questions uncomplicated by hypothesis. Government was ready and willing to do such work or to patronize it. The investigations of the Commission on the Poor Law—largely the work of Beatrice Webb under the influence of Booth are a case in point. In 1908 came the first Census of Production. In 1909 Urwick was advocating the use of the Board of Trade's annual *Abstract of Labour Statistics* as a sourcebook for sociologists: "It is doubtful whether any document published contains so much valuable sociological information in so small a compass." He went on to illustrate his point as follows:

In less than 300 octavo pages, it furnishes the details, not only of the earnings and occupations of the people, but of their consumption of food, their housing, their accidents and diseases, their thrift, their pauperism and a host of other important matters such as Trade Unionism, Cooperation, Profit-Sharing, and labour disputes. The volume issued in February last . . . contains also numerous comparative tables relating to the industrial progress of the nation.[14]

By 1914 statisticians and sociologists alike were beginning to complain of a surfeit of social information—most of it government-produced. The problem now was not to embark on new research but rather to find methods of sifting and evaluating the mass of data already available.

The main line of development from Booth is perhaps, then, to be found in the avalanche of blue books and official reports that marked the years from 1900 to 1914. And part of the price of having government carry on the burden of social investigation was the persistence of a rigorously empirical conception (in the manner of Sir Robert Boyle's "sooty empiricks") of social information. The favored strategy of such investigations was that of the Webbs—the strategy of sitting down open-minded and omnivorous in front of successive institutions and learning everything one could. The favored categories of classification were formal, quantitative, or derived from existing administrative arrangements—as Booth's had been. They were in any case almost invariably established a priori. As A. L. Bowley put it, speaking of

[14]   *Sociological Review*, 1909.

the census classification of industries when he set about introducing some analytical rationality into British social statistics in the spring of 1914: "It is evident that this classification lacks system and purpose, and it necessarily leads to curious results." With minor reservations his comment applies across the board to the Booth tradition as it was developed within British government.

There was, however, a meager and subsidiary line of development which was largely nongovernmental. To call it a tradition would be an overstatement. It consists in the transformation of the social survey from a descriptive to an analytical instrument. And in the period we are concerned with it was almost entirely the work of two men: Bowley and B. Seebohm Rowntree. Moved by the achievement of Booth they saw in the survey possibilities that Booth himself had not seen. The automatic coupling of Rowntree with Booth does less than justice to Rowntree, as does his own insistence that he was in his first York survey doing no more than repeating Booth's work in a provincial setting. In the general history of Britain Booth is rightly treated as the more important figure; the scale of his work, its relative originality and its impact on public opinion make any other judgment impossible. But in the history of social science the case is not so clear. Rowntree's innovations in survey methodology add up impressively. In the first place, of course, he did away with the middle-class administrator as middleman in the flow of information and went directly to the working-class families about whom he wished to know. Then he saw the need to use external and objectively specified criteria in classifying and evaluating incomes. Where Booth had used formal gradations of income and thus always left his conclusions about the incidence and meaning of poverty open to some dispute, Rowntree used the independently derived "physical efficiency" criterion and thereby gave his findings a higher cogency.

Not only were Rowntree's indicators of poverty autonomous but they had been established with remarkable care on the basis of a sampling of available physiological and dietetic knowledge. It was this that enabled Rowntree to be so unequivocal about the meaning of his findings. Setting his poverty line at the minimal "physical efficiency" level allowed him both to demonstrate the irreducible significance of current wage rates as an "immediate cause of poverty," and to make clear the stringent cultural deprivation imposed on even "comfortable" working class families by the desperate need to preserve the wage-earner's efficiency. In effect he was able to penetrate a syndrome of poverty where Booth had specified symptoms. The sense of pathology, or of social nexus and process, is very strong in *Poverty*, informing both the design of the survey and its analysis. This is most apparent in Rowntree's correlation of poverty and the life cycle, but it is evident, too, in the way he treats the relationship of poverty to health and diet, housing and education, pubs and friendly societies. His demonstration of the cyclical incidence of poverty was perhaps his greatest achievement—and one which has still to be fully assimilated to social policy. In this connection it is worth remembering that the Statistical Society which had received Booth's purely expository papers in the 1880's with enthusiasm gave a hostile reception to his efforts in 1891 to make a case for old age pensions. In Rowntree's study the connection of analysis and recommendation is much closer—he was able to evaluate very closely the extent to which old age pensions could deal with poverty and show it to be very slight. His understanding of the mutual involvement of family, life cycle, and poverty made him an early and determined advocate of the minimum wage and of a comprehensive system of social security. Booth seems to have become increasingly uncertain as to what measures of reform were appropriate in the light of his research: Rowntree became increasingly certain.

Finally, although Rowntree remained in the true line of political economy, statistics and official research to the extent of not overtly designing his survey in relation to a body of analytical hypotheses, it is clear that *Poverty* represents something more than the traditional effort to collect direct answers to direct questions. It is informed by a constant effort to conceptualize poverty in relation to a social system. We can see this not only in the way Rowntree treats the causes of poverty but in the argument he makes for taking family income rather than individual income as the proper unit of analysis, or in his evaluation "of the place which public-houses occupy in the social life of the working classes," or his discussion of gambling. Something should be said, too, of Rowntree's later sociological work between the publication of *Poverty* and the outbreak of the Great War. As Asa Briggs has pointed out, Rowntree became in a curious way a victim of the Whig interpretation of history. His research after 1901 was mainly concerned with the relationship between patterns of landholding and social welfare and conflict. It provided the basis for a central axis of the "new mandate" of Liberalism which Lloyd George hoped to use as means of restructuring British politics in the election of 1915. The strategic objective was to obliterate both Labour and the class war by detaching the rural poor from the working class through radical land-reform policies. The whole enterprise —the election, the land program and Rowntree's contribution to developing the role of the socially engaged social scientist—was obliterated by the world war: all have accordingly vanished from the historical record. Nevertheless *Land and Labour*, Rowntree's massive survey of Belgium, would repay study as a pioneering exercise in comparative sociology, just as *The Labourer and the Land*, read in conjunction with *The Land, the Report of the Land Enquiry Committee*, would prove instructive as an early model for the derivation of social policy proposals from social investigation.

The contribution of A. L. Bowley was rather different. His primary orientation was that of the social statistician, and like Urwick he was of the well-founded opinion that the analytically informed use of official statistics was for most purposes all one needed to achieve an adequate understanding of social organization and social problems. One of his earliest courses at the L.S.E. was devoted to the interpretation of government publications and a major objective of a great deal of his work was to demonstrate that the intensive survey—as carried out by Booth and Rowntree —was simply not necessary. Thus, in 1914 we find him writing:

> If we can define the task of sociological measurement, determine what are the facts which it is essential to know, and devise a means of ascertaining them, half the task is accomplished. In my experience it is neither a long nor expensive business to get the main rough measurements of quantities, though no obvious data are to hand. Official in-

formation, imperfect and badly adapted for sociological purposes as it often is, generally suffices to show the magnitude, nature and locality of a problem; common knowledge, obtainable by conversation with those who have lived in close contact with its circumstances, will place it in fair perspective; while a rapid investigation by sample will give an approximation to detailed measurements. Very often this is all that is wanted.[15]

The purpose of his own sample surveys—especially of the "five towns" poverty survey conducted with A. R. Burnett-Hurst in 1912—was not simply to demonstrate the viability of a new and cheaper research method, but to demonstrate how little new field research one needed to do if one was able to explore and mobilize the avalanche of available statistical materials in an intelligent way:

> If, for example, we know from the census account that in 5 per cent of the houses of a town there are more than two people to a room, if we ascertain that the worse houses are insanitary and small, and if we visit a few to find the actual accommodation, the age and sex of the inhabitants and their occupations, we have probably all the data we need for criticizing or suggesting a policy of reform, without measuring the rooms or making a house-to-house visitation. If the more intensive and extensive inquiry is necessary, the preliminary survey will have shown what is wanted and how it can be done.[16]

Bowley is primarily regarded as the pioneer of the sample survey—specifically of the random sample. No doubt this is correct. After 1918 we find a remarkably continuous and diffuse application of the method he had used in the research for *Livelihood and Poverty*, both in the descriptive investigation of social problems in different localities and in market research. It is arguable, however, that the contribution he made in examining problems of sociological classification was at least as important. This is a persistent and major theme in a great deal of his work. In *Livelihood and Poverty* there is extensive discussion of variations in family composition and the resulting difficulties in using

[15] A. L. Bowley, *The Nature and Purpose of the Measurement of Social Phenomena*, p. 11.
[16] *Ibid.*, p. 14.

family income as a measure of poverty. In *Has Poverty Diminished?* this problem of "the extraordinary variety of the working family" reappears and is treated more fully: "With only nine divisions by age or sex and a separation of earners from non-earners, there are more than three hundred and fifty categories of families." And conversely: "The conventional family, consisting of a man earning, his wife and three children dependent, and no other member, accounts for only 5% of the four thousand families reviewed." In *The Nature and Purpose of the Measurement of Social Phenomena* the issue of what categories of classification one can or should use is confronted directly. Having examined a wide range of institutional and a priori procedures of classification, including the French and British censuses, and observed the considerable difficulties all such procedures involve, Bowley there concludes by advocating a multidimensional classification as more truly sociological. Thus, for analyzing problems of social class structure he proposes an analytical grid derived from the combination of occupational or economic attributes on the one hand and of cultural or behavioral indicators of social interaction on the other. The anticipation of more recent approaches to stratification—that of Lipset and Zetterburg, say, or of Lockwood and Goldthorpe—is quite striking. His brief exploration of this possibility and of its uses in investigating social mobility is reprinted below.

What, then, did the Booth tradition amount to as an element in the making of British sociology by 1914? An enormous amount of social mapping had been done by official agencies. Essentially, however, this work was uncreative so far as research method or analytical perspective was concerned. The sequence of private inquiry, though markedly more creative, was attenuated. Since the completion of Booth's main study in 1891 the major steps forward had been *Poverty* ten years later in 1901 and *Livelihood and Poverty*, not actually published until 1915. A major effort at filling in would allow us to add H. H. Mann's *Life in an Agricultural Village* of 1904, the Howarth and Wilson survey *West Ham* in 1907, and *How the Casual Labourer Lives* by the Liverpool Statistical Society in 1909. Even so it is not much for a nation that prides itself on its cultivation of empirical survey research. In

1928 Eaton and Harrison reported 2,775 surveys completed in the United States since 1906: in 1935 A. F. Wells could find only 155 in Britain since 1891. The true situation in 1914 was in fact seen rather clearly by Bowley—who was, after all, involved equally in each of the branches of the Booth tradition:

> Private inquiries . . . are often directed to the study of isolated phenomena or to a special and badly-defined class, and are not arranged to fit into any general measurement of society. They very often serve their immediate purpose of proving the existence of some problem on a scale sufficiently large to call for attention; but they are uncorrelated with each other or with official statistics. The functions of private investigation, in the general task of the numerical description of a society, are to fill in the gaps left by official statistics, as a temporary expedient, to make estimates with a greater margin of uncertainty than is countenanced by the official mind, and above all to make intensive observations of those places and of those persons or households which official statistics show to be typical or to occupy a definite place in some scale, and so to interpret the meaning of the barren tables in terms of human significance.[17]

By and large this proposed division of labor was accepted. The critical problem for descriptive sociology on such a reading, however, lay not in the refinement of private research procedures but in the provision of a "central controlling statistical organization" or more generally, of "a better supply of intelligence," within government. This sense of priorities was also broadly accepted and its acceptance had curious effects. One was the marked failure to develop certain sorts of research technique. The questionnaire is a good example. Questionnaires had been in frequent and continual use ever since the 1830's, but for a full century there was hardly any effort to improve on the type of eclectic, open-ended, all-encompassing and structureless instrument distributed by the London Statistical Society in its early days: forty years later the questionnaire Galton distributed to the Fellows of the Royal Society was of that order: ninety years later the Webbs were employing the same means to gather information on Trade Unions. The elaboration of economical and analytically structured questionnaires had to wait on the development of market research.

[17]   *Ibid.*, p. 13.

8

LINES FORWARD

For both intellectual and institutional reasons British sociology was in a curiously fragmented condition by 1914. There were lines of growth which would be fruitfully developed in the next generation—the dialectics of the debate between eugenicists and environmental sociologists was perhaps the most important. But some of the countervailing tendencies, either toward arid polemicism, or away from social analysis and toward social action, would prove very strong in the immediate future. Contemplating the prospect that the *Minority Report* of the Poor Law Commission would not be accepted by government, Sidney Webb decided in 1910 that socialism, not sociology, would be the appropriate and necessary response—that it would be easier and more profitable to remake the political system than to spend further energy on the sociological education of the present incumbents. Such attitudes, and the fact that the judgments on which they rested were sound, were both cause and effect of the splintered state of British sociology.

We have traced in this essay the rise and collapse of the first effort to establish sociology in Britain. By 1914 there was a pervasive discomfort about the nature and definition of the subject. And this discomfort was both unprofitable and inhibiting for the future. The range of options, from Frederic Harrison's "science of the entire series of fundamental laws which apply to social phenomena," to the view of H. G. Wells that sociology could never exist as any sort of science and that its function was merely to provide the world with a choice of Utopias, was too wide. In the middle ground we find E. J. Urwick arguing (against Hobhouse no less than Harrison), that sociology should restrict itself to the "function of analysing and presenting the existing situation in as complete a form as possible and connecting any proposed future with the known schemes of purposes and values now in existence, without pressing any judgment as to the right or safest or most probable future movements." And there, too, we find A. L. Bowley wishing to appropriate the name sociology for the statistical effort to "define or delimitate classes, to specify attributes or characteristics of the members of these classes, to measure the prevalence or magnitude and variation of these attributes, and to discover relations and causal connexions," but unable to do so because the title had "already been chosen to include the knowledge of all group actions and relations, past and present, measurable or not." And then of course there was the school of Patrick Geddes.

These differences would have to work themselves out before a coherent sociological profession could begin to develop. But in 1914 the momentum was still divisive. Looking back on the whole history of sociology in Britain in 1929 Victor Branford was to insist that the disintegration of the field remarked by "most continental and American observers" was illusory. But only a little earlier we find the following in correspondence between Branford and Martin White:

Can we not all work together now as we did at the beginning of the movement? At the best we are few and of no great strength confronting a resistant world, which is anti-sociological when it is not unsociological; and leavened by a slender margin of thinkers, writers and publicists to whom we can appeal. By long years of labour we have increased that margin, I fear, by only an insignificant percentage. In view of the work still to do, we need surely more than ever to show a united front.[1]

Perhaps the front was not so much disunited as very wide and with the army scattered in small formations along its whole extent. There was, however, one spot where the gap between contingents was so great that they could easily be thought to be on opposing sides. This was the gap, again noted by Branford between "two schools, an academic one which pursues the science on the lines of Hobhouse, and an extra-mural one represented by the more characteristic work of the Sociological Society." The only essential difference between these schools according to Branford was one of method, the academic school proceeding by an "abstract and dialectial method" and adhering essentially to the tradition of moral philosophy, while the extramural school "proceeds by the method of observation in the concrete (and open air observation so far as possible)." There was thus no reason why they should not complement one another:

> The one concentrates on the study of "society" and its "principles" partly by the aid of specialized social studies but in the main by the light of ideas derived from philosophic tradition. The other also utilizing (and moreover systematically) the social specialisms, studies "societies", i.e., cities, towns, villages and the wider regional communities, in the living concrete, and by comparison and generalization of observed data works in the light of verifiable hypothesis towards a theory of societies in evolution, in degeneration and in regeneration.[2]

Ingeniously, therefore, Branford concluded that the best memorial to Hobhouse would be some "deliberate and organized efforts to bring the two schools into an effective working co-partnership." The only thing wrong with his analysis was that the extramural school, though occupying the center of the stage, was not a school of systematic empiricism at all. Either it was a school of prophecy, or by way of R. E. Dickinson, C. B. Fawcett, Patrick Abercrombie, and others, it was being absorbed in the new technical specialisms of urban geography and town planning. The rhetoric of "the movement" and the "united front" is revealing. Branford's description of the work of the extramural school simply does not reflect the kind of inspirational and impressionistic study which was increasingly filling the *Sociological Review* and being sponsored by LePlay House. Work of the "systematic" nature he attributes to the Sociological Society, represented here by J. A. Hobson's early exercise in electoral sociology, was to diminish, not grow, in the Society's publications in the years following 1910.

[2]   *Ibid.*

Where Branford was right was in sensing a latent hostility on the part of those who espoused academic criteria of science to the activities of his "extramural" school. The first effort to place sociology in the British university system had been made by Herbert Spencer in 1880. Martin White's success twenty years later had a great deal to do with the newness of the University of London and with the particular interests of the Webbs. But it is suggestive that of the available candidates it was Hobhouse, the philosopher, who was chosen. In any event it did not establish a precedent. In 1910 Urwick found that: "The disinclination to accept sociology as a science is very persistent. At our oldest universities there is a strong disposition to believe that the general treatment of social phenomena can never go beyond a philosophy of social life." Seventeen years later Harry Elmer Barnes, surveying what he called the "fate of sociology in England" from an American perspective, also singled out the ideology of the ancient universities as the peculiar cause of the backwardness of the discipline. And in 1938, when resigning from his Chair of Social Biology, Lancelot Hogben took the opportunity to inveigh against traditional academic attitudes in a manner which suggests that even at the L.S.E. they were felt as a heavy constraint: "We might have hoped," he writes in the introduction to *Political Arithmetic*, "that the substantial scholarship and English empirical common sense of the Webbs would have produced a more healthy attitude to social research." But alas:

> If the Webbs ever flattered themselves that they would find a following in the universities they failed to reckon with the Idol of Purity. The special province of the Idol of Purity is to protect its worshippers against dangerous thought. . . . The plain truth is that the academic value of social research in our universities is largely rated on a futility scale. A social enquiry which leads to the conclusion that something has to be done or might be done is said to be "tendentious"—the Idol of Purity ensures 'innocuous aimlessness' when social enquiry makes contact with the real world.[3]

For W. H. Beveridge, too, "the disappearance of social biology from the School of Economics was a symptom only of a larger

3   Hogben, ed., *Political Arithmetic*, Introduction.

defeat." Barnes offered a broader analysis, pointing to the problem of the diffusion of sociology among the set of special social sciences, history, political philosophy, and economics, already established in the older universities. But his central point is essentially the same: British education "is still primarily medieval or humanistic . . . the whole process is a dignified and seductive flight from reality." The orthodox academic mode of approach to natural as to social phenomena he found to be through "dialectic and metaphysics—Platonic rather than pragmatic and empirical." Normative and a priori social philosophy conformed to the mode; sociology did not.

Certainly British universities were slow to recognize the claims of sociology. But then as we have seen there was something of the self-fulfilling prophecy about the proposition that sociology as practiced extramurally was not an academic activity. In any event academic resistance to sociology was only part of the problem. Here we return to the root themes of this analysis. There can be no doubt that the resilience of political economy as an ideological system and its peculiar brand of uncritical deductive empiricism constituted an environment of ideas hard for sociology to penetrate. In his final *Report* as director of the L.S.E. Beveridge dwelt at length on the intellectual procedures of economists as an obstacle to the advance of sociology. J. M. Keynes, he pointed out, had compared himself to Einstein, but Einstein had worked from and to observation, Keynes from the definition of a concept to the logical derivates of a concept; and his method "had been accepted as adequate by practically all professional economists." But this was not the heart of the matter. Over and above all questions of the history of ideas at an intrinsic level, there was the weight with which the general institutional environment bore down on the infant science of society.

Beveridge touched on this more fundamental problem, too. He begged social scientists to develop a responsibility to their profession which could counteract the pull of politics and government. Throughout the period from 1834 a recurrent and insistent theme has been the diversion of the most promising sociologists early in their careers away from social analysis and research and toward administration, party politics, or one or another kind of institutional innovation. Beveridge himself was a conspicuous example. From its beginnings British social science had been oriented to policy, either in the form of statistics as a tool of more rational administration, or as a lever of social reform. The relative openness and malleability of the political system as such, particularly after 1900, encouraged a persistent migration of energies. It was only in this context that the intellectual difficulties of developing sociology became acute and academic demands for purity became both reasonable and fatal. Perhaps sociology was built slowly in Britain for the obverse of the reasons that the welfare state has been built slowly in America. At the best of times the social scientist is likely to be caught in the cross-fire of a concern to develop his science and a concern to promote social action. Potential British social scientists experiencing this dilemma found themselves in an almost unique situation: government and party politics were open to them, the universities were closed. It is hardly surprising that they succumbed readily to the lure of administrative opportunity. So sociology languished. Those like Harrison and Geddes, who would not pay either the low methodological price of access to government or the high substantive price of access to the universities, simply went into the wilderness.

In any event, the Edwardian sociologists had found no point of entry to the centers of British social and intellectual life. Nor could they create new centers. The synthetic enterprise begun in 1903 turned into a fissiparous growth of pseudosociological factions around three or four leading individuals. What remained for the future?

The most effective of the pre-1914 groupings was the school of eugenics developed by Galton and Pearson. Perhaps it is worth noting that this was the only variant of first-generation sociology to receive upper-class patronage. Not that the appeal of eugenics to a declining upper class—one faced with an ever more visible and demanding lower class—is hard to understand. And in the long run the combination of theory and method represented by eugenics and by social biology generally was to provide the point of departure for a rebirth of British sociology—as well as feeding into British social psychology. The distinctive themes and styles of contemporary British sociology spring in large part from the work of the eugenicists and the reactions to it: the demographic emphasis, the concern with questions of opportunity and ability, stratification, mobility, and social waste, the clustering of research around certain issues of educational sociology and the sociology of poverty, all have roots in the earlier attempt to build sociology directly on social biology.

But this was a long-run and unanticipated consequence of the failure to solve Hobson's problem of "the economy of our resources" in the eighty years before 1914. The immediate outcome was rather different. It was the effective fragmentation of empirical research, the science of social policy and social theory.

Social theory remained cramped, confused, and discouraged by the traditional organization of the universities. The ameliorist appetite for a policy science was being channeled more and more toward the Labour Party. Only at the level of empirical research could a continuing tradition be said to exist. And that tradition was statistical rather than sociological. There was to be little or no development of the Booth tradition beyond the work of Bowley until the 1950's. There were replications of Booth, and more or less imaginative applications of the Booth-Rowntree-Bowley method in surveys of a number of different localities. But there was no growth. If anything the later studies were less speculative as well as less emotionally engaged than those of the pioneers. The tendency was to move backward toward the criteria of research approved by the Statistical Society and by government departments.

A striking example is provided by the Webbs. Hogben had complained that the "idol of purity" enthroned in the universities would kill the social science the Webbs hoped to develop. But methodologically, by the time they came to write *Methods of Social Study*, the Webbs were themselves slaves to empirical purism. Much of that work reads like a parody of the worst features of the statistical tradition. Yet for a time it was orthodox doctrine in British social research:

The only right way in which to approach the subject-matter of sociology is not to focus the enquiry upon discovering the answer to some particular question in which you may be interested. On the contrary, you should choose a particular section of the social environment, or, more precisely, a particular social institution, and sit down patiently in front of it, exactly as if it were a form of energy or a kind of matter, the type-specimen of a plant or some species of animal, and go on working steadfastly to acquire all possible information about it, with the sole purpose of discovering every fact concerning its constitution and its activities, together with every ascertainable action and reaction between it and its environment.[4]

Another instance of the same tendency is the Howarth and Wilson survey of 1907, *West Ham*. If the work of Beveridge, Rowntree, and Hobson revealed the potentialities of the empirical tradition in its post-statistical mode, there were many studies which suggested an inclination to revert to type, a latent sterility springing from an overly administrative and "factual" orientation. *West Ham* was one such. If any single study could claim to represent British sociology in its first period it was this one. The survey was sponsored by a committee that included A. L. Bowley, W. H. Beveridge, Sir Edward Brabrook, James Bryce, L. T. Hobhouse, J. A. Hobson, E. J. Urwick, Beatrice Webb and J. Martin White. The organizing secretary, G. E. Arkell, had worked with Booth, and the chairman was Canon Barnett. The collection of data on rents, rates, and wages was meticulous and exhaustive. Yet the end-product is strangely emasculated. Apart from the enormous statistical tables the sense of evidence is weak. The central object of the study, to show that the system of casual labour was the mainspring of a spiral of economic dependence paralysing a whole neighborhood is simply not achieved—in part for want of any sort of comparative strategy or effort to control critical variables, but in part, too, for want of any clear conception of social structure. There is something desperately inconclusive, even mindless, about the whole work. Its intention is descriptive. Its perspective is administrative—again and again social behavior and experience are approached in terms of the question, Is such and such an Act of Parliament working as it

---

4   B. Webb and S. Webb, *Methods of Social Study*, p. 40.

should? What is most striking is the lack of any sense of sociological argument; in the end the study makes no claim to persuasiveness beyond the traditional one, "great pains have been taken to get exact facts." There would be many such studies in the next forty years.

What should we conclude? When a sociological profession did finally begin to take shape in Britain the whole social structure, including the university system, had been thoroughly shaken up. The profession grew up pooling resources culled from the tradition of social biology, from the poverty studies, from social anthropology, and from American work and American teachers. The links back to the sociology of the first generation are few and weak—the work of T. H. Marshall is an important exception. The discontinuities are great. And many valuable resources for sociology were lost as a result. The relevance of Hobhouse to a number of contemporary concerns has still to be perceived. Geddes' sense of the historical dimension of social organization might repay more careful formulation than he ever gave it. It is a pity that Spencer is remembered almost exclusively for what his contemporaries objected to. It is above all unfortunate that the effort of Hobhouse and Tylor to pull together the theory of social evolution, anthropological data, and statistical techniques in a systematic sociology of development was allowed to languish. At the end of *German Sociology* Raymond Aron observes that a comparative sociology of national development pursued in different countries is one of the more important tendencies in modern sociology displacing the old national schools. It is ironic that British sociologists should have pioneered this sort of work only to abandon it because of its historical involvement with a difficult moral philosophy. Marshall's *Citizenship and Social Class* apart, there is little British work since 1918 to be cited as contributing to this emerging theme of international sociology. We could do worse than rediscover Hobhouse and Tylor.

But though these and other discontinuities are unfortunate they were probably unavoidable. Sociology in its first manifestation in Britain failed to gain any control of the mainstream of national social thought. Partly, as Hobhouse saw, this was because there was too much to be done, and with only a few people in-volved, an impression of fragmentation was easily created. Partly it was because in the formative period of any science it is difficult to tell the central from the marginal concerns and equal emphasis tends to be given to both. But mainly it was because there were institutional resistances to sociology which sociologists alone could not break. In this essay I have tried to show how the history of ideas was contained and shaped by such institutional resistances and opportunities. What was needed for sociology to flourish in Britain was not a change of heart among Oxford professors but a social structure in which simple political responses to social problems were less easily available and less plausible than they had previously been in Britain, and in which, conversely, social problems were more *fundamentally* problematic than they had yet been in British experience. A double development of this kind would drastically increase the salience of hard social research. But it took the Second World War and five years of Labour government to produce such a change. Who but Marxists was interested in the theory of social class until manual workers began to earn as much or more than white collar workers? Political sociology was super-fluous until the Labour Party had lost control of the working-class vote. Only when the axioms of social organization as well as of social ideology had been shattered would a truly Spencerian sense of the depth and knotty complexity of social phenomena be widely diffused. And that was a necessary precondition for sociology.

II. From Statistics to Sociology

1
Robert Giffen

THE PROGRESS OF THE
WORKING CLASSES

IT SEEMS FAIRLY PROBABLE now that when we complete
our fiftieth year we shall have the round number of one thousand
members—a wonderful improvement upon the small number of
fifty years ago. On such an occasion I believe the subject on which
I propose to address you to-night will be not unsuitable—a review
of the official statistics bearing on the progress of the working
classes—the masses of the nation—in the last half century. If you
go back to the early records of the Society, you will find that one
of the leading objects of its founders was to obtain means by which
to study the very question I have selected. . . . I may remind you,
moreover, that one of the founders of the Society was Mr. Porter,
of the Board of Trade, whose special study for years was much the
same, as his well-known book, *The Progress of the Nation,* bears
witness; and that in one of the earliest publications of the Society,
a volume preceding the regular issue of the *Journal,* he has left a
most interesting account of what he hoped might be effected by
means of statistics in studying the subject I have put before you,
or the more general subject of the "Progress of the Nation." In
asking you, therefore, to look for a little at what statistics tell us of

Reprinted from "The President's Inaugural Address," *Journal of the Statistical Society,* 1883. This paper marks the apotheosis of the statistical
tradition conceived as the applied mode of political economy. As Giffen
makes clear, it was the product of intellectual crisis and its purpose was to
preserve tradition (in social organization as well as in ideology) in the
face of crisis. The reading that follows represents a more sociological, in-
novating way out of the crisis—a way Giffen was not willing to take.

the progress of the great masses of the nation, I feel that I am selecting a subject which is connected with the special history of the Society. That it happens for the moment to be attracting a considerable amount of popular attention in connection wtih sensational politics and sociology, with agitations for land nationalisation and collectivism among pretended representatives of the working classes, is an additional reason for our not neglecting this question; but it is a question to which the Society has a primary claim, and which the authors of the agitations I have referred to would have done well to study from the statistical point of view.

There are two or three ways in which statistics may throw light on such a question as I have put forward. The first and most direct is to see what records there are of the money earnings of the masses now and fifty years ago, ascertain whether they have increased or diminished, and then compare them with the rise or fall in the prices of the chief articles which the masses consume. Even such records would not give a complete answer. It is conceivable, for instance, that while earning more money, and being able to spend it to more advantage, the working classes might be no better off than formerly. There may be masses, as there are individuals, who do not know how to spend. The question of means, however, will carry us some distance on the road to our object. We shall know that the masses must be better off, unless they have deteriorated in the art of spending, a subject of separate inquiry.

In investigating such records, however, we have to recognise that the ideal mode of answering the question is not yet possible. That mode would be to draw up an account of the aggregate annual earnings of the working classes for a period about fifty years ago, and a similar account of the aggregate annual earnings of the same classes at the present time, and then compare the average per head and per family at the different dates. Having thus ascertained the increase or diminution in the amount per head at the different dates, it would be comparatively easy, though not in itself quite so easy a matter as it seems, to ascertain how much less or how much more the increased or diminished sum would buy of the chief articles of the workman's consumption. But no such account that I know of has been drawn up, except for a date about fifteen or sixteen years ago, when Mr. Dudley Baxter and Professor Leone Levi both drew up statements of enormous value as to aggregate earnings, statements which it would now be most desirable to compare with similar statements for the present time, if we could have them, and which will be simply invaluable to future generations. In the absence of such statements, all that can be done is to compare what appear to be the average wages of large groups of the working classes. If it is found that the changes in the money wages of such groups are in the same direction, or almost all in the same direction, then there would be sufficient reason for believing that similar changes had occurred throughout the entire mass. It would be in the highest degree improbable that precisely those changes which could not be traced were in the opposite direction. The difficulty in the way is that in a period of fifty years in a country like England the character of the work itself changes. The people who have the same names at different times are not necessarily doing the same work. Some forms of work pass wholly away and wholly new forms come into existence. Making all allowances, however, and selecting the best comparative cases possible, some useful conclusion seems obtainable.

What I propose to do first and mainly, as regards this point, is to make use of an independent official record which we have to thank Mr. Porter for commencing. I mean the record of wages, which has been maintained for many years in the Miscellaneous Statistics of the United Kingdom, and which was previously commenced and carried on in the volumes of Revenue and Population Tables which Mr. Porter introduced at the Board of Trade about fifty years ago. It is curious on looking back through these volumes to find how difficult it is to get a continuous record. The wages in one volume are for certain districts and trades; in a subsequent volume, for different districts and trades; the descriptive classifications of the workers are also constantly changing. Picking my way through the figures, however, I have to submit the following particulars of changes in money wages between a period forty to fifty years ago—it is not possible to get the same year in all cases to start from—and a period about two years ago, which may be taken as the present time. This comparison leaves out of account the length of hours of work, which is a material point I shall notice presently.

COMPARISON OF WAGES FIFTY YEARS AGO AND AT PRESENT TIME

[From *Miscellaneous Statistics of the United Kingdom*, and Porter's *Progress of the Nation*]

Occupation	Place	Wages Fifty Years ago, per Week	Wages Present Time, per Week	Increase or Decrease, Amount	per Cent
Carpenters	Manchester	24/–	34/–	10/– (+)	42
"	Glasgow	14/–	26/–	12/– (+)	85
Bricklayers	Manchester*	24/–	36/–	12/– (+)	50
"	Glasgow	15/–	27/–	12/– (+)	80
Masons	Manchester*	24/–	29/10	5/10 (+)	24
"	Glasgow	14/–	23/8	9/8 (+)	69
Miners	Staffordshire	2/8†	4/–†	1/4 (+)	50
Pattern weavers	Huddersfield	16/–	25/–	9/– (+)	55
Wool scourers	"	17/–	22/–	5/– (+)	30
Mule spinners	"	25/6	30/–	4/6 (+)	20
Weavers	"	12/–	26/–	14/– (+)	115
Warpers and beamers	"	17/–	27/–	10/– (+)	58
Winders and reelers	"	6/–	11/–	5/– (+)	83
Weavers (men)	Bradford	8/3	20/6	12/3 (+)	150
Reeling and warping	"	7/9	15/6	7/9 (+)	100
Spinning (children)	"	4/5	11/6	7/1 (+)	160

° 1825.   † Wages per day.

Thus in all cases where I have found it possible from the apparent similarity of the work to make a comparison there is an enormous apparent rise in money wages ranging from 20 and in most cases from 50 to 100 per cent, and in one or two instances more than 100 per cent. This understates, I believe, the real extent of the change. Thus, builders' wages are given at the earlier date as so much weekly, whereas in the later returns a distinction is made between summer and winter wages, the hours of labour being less in winter, and as the wages are so much per hour, the week's wages being also less, so that it has been possible to strike a mean for the later period, while it does not appear that anything more is meant at the early period than the usual weekly wage, which would be the summer wage. Without making this point, however, it is obvious that in all cases there is a very great rise.

The comparison is made between a period about fifty years ago and the present time only. It would have complicated the figures too much to introduce intermediate dates. I may state, however, that I have not been inattentive to this point, and that if we had commenced about twenty to twenty-five years ago, we should also have been able to show a very great improvement since that time, while at that date also, as compared with an earlier period, a great improvement would have been apparent. A careful and exhaustive investigation of the records of wages I have referred to, in comparison with the numbers employed in different occupations, as shown by the census reports, would in fact repay the student who has time to make it; and I trust the investigation will yet be made.

The records do not include anything relating to the agricultural labourer, but from independent sources—I would refer especially to the reports of the recent Royal Agricultural Commission—we may perceive how universal the rise in the wages of agricultural labourers has been, and how universal at any rate is the complaint that more money is paid for less work. Sir James Caird, in his *Landed Interest,* (p. 65), puts the rise at 60 per cent as compared with the period just before the repeal of the corn laws, and there is much other evidence to the same effect. The rise in the remuneration of labour in Ireland in the last forty years is also one of the facts which has been conspicuously brought before the public of late. In no other way is it possible to account for the stationariness of rents in Ireland for a long period, notwithstanding the great rise in the prices of the cattle and dairy products which Ireland produces, and which, it has been contended, would have justified a rise of rents. The farmer and the labourer together have in fact had all the benefit of the rise in agricultural prices.

The next point to which attention must be drawn is the shortening of the hours of labour which has taken place. While the money wages have increased as we have seen, the hours of labour have diminished. It is difficult to estimate what the extent of this diminution has been, but collecting one or two scattered notices I should be inclined to say very nearly 20 per cent. There has been at least this reduction in the textile, engineering, and house-building trades. The workman gets from 50 to 100 per cent more money, for 20 per cent less work; in round figures, he has gained from 70 to 120 per cent in fifty years in money return. It is just possible of course that the workman may do as much or nearly as much in the shorter period as he did in his longer hours. Still there is the positive gain in his being less time at his task, which many of the classes still tugging lengthily day by day at the oar would appreciate. The workman may have been wise or unwise in setting much store by shorter hours in bettering himself, but the shortening of the hours of labour is undoubtedly to be counted to the good as well as the larger money return he obtains.

We come then to the question of what the changes have been in the prices of the chief articles of the workman's consumption. It is important, to begin with, that as regards prices of commodities generally, there seems to be little doubt things are much the same as they were forty or fifty years ago. This is the general effect of the inquiries which have been made first as to the depreciation of gold consequent on the Australian and Californian gold discoveries, and next as to the appreciation of gold which has taken place within the last twenty years, consequent on the new demands for gold which have arisen, and the falling off in the supply as compared with the period between 1850 and 1860. It would burden us too much to go into these inquiries on an occasion like the present, and therefore I only take the broad result. This is that while there was a moderate rise of prices all round between the years 1847-50, just before the new gold came on the market, and the year 1862, when Mr. Jevons published his celebrated essay, a rise not exceeding about 20 per cent, yet within the last twenty years this rise has disappeared, and prices are back to the level, or nearly to the level, of 1847-50. The conclusion is that, taking things in the mass, the sovereign goes as far as it did forty or fifty years ago, while there are many new things in existence at a low price which could not then have been bought at all. If, in the interval, the average money earnings of the working classes have risen between 50 and 100 per cent, there must have been an enormous change for the better in the means of the working man, unless by some wonderful accident it has happened that his special articles have changed in a different way from the general run of prices.

But looking to special articles, we find that on balance prices are lower and not higher. Take wheat. It is notorious that wheat, the staff of life, has been lower on the average of late years than it was before the free trade era. The facts, however, deserve still more careful statement to enable us to realise the state of things fifty years ago and at the present time. Comparing the ten years before 1846 with the last ten years, what we find is that while the average price of wheat in 1837-46 was 58s. 7d., it was 48s. 9d. only in the last ten years—a reduction not of 5s. merely, but 10s. The truth is, the repeal of the Corn Laws was not followed by an *immediate* decline of wheat on the average. The failure of the potato crop, the Crimean War, and the depreciation of gold, all contributed to maintain the price, notwithstanding free trade, down to 1862. Since then steadily lower prices have ruled; and when we compare the present time with half a century ago, or any earlier part of the century, these facts should be remembered.

There is a still more important consideration. Averages are very good for certain purposes, but we all know in this place that a good deal sometimes turns upon the composition of the average, —upon whether it is made up of great extremes, or whether the individual elements depart very little from the average. This is specially an important matter in a question of the price of food. The average of a necessary of life over a long period of years may be moderate, but if in some years the actual price is double what it is in other years, the fact of the average will in no way save from starvation at certain periods the workman who may have a difficulty in making both ends meet in the best of times. What we find then is that fifty years ago the extremes were disastrous compared with what they are at the present time. In 1836 we find wheat touching 36s.; in 1838, 1839, 1840, and 1841, we find it touching 78s. 4d., 81s. 6d., 72s. 10d., and 76s. 1d.; in all cases double the price of the lowest year, and nearly double the "average" of the decade; and in 1847 the price of 102s. 5d., or three times the price of the lowest period, is touched. If we go back earlier we find still

more startling extremes. We have such figures as 106s. 5d. in
1810; 126s. 6d. in 1812; 109s. 9d. in 1813, and 96s. 11d. in 1817;
these figures being not merely the extremes touched, but the actual
averages for the whole year. No doubt in the early part of the
century the over-issue of inconvertible paper accounts for part of
the nominal prices, but it accounts for a very small part. What we
have to consider then is, that fifty years ago the working man with
wages, on the average, about half, or not much more than half,
what they are now, had at times to contend with a fluctuation in
the price of bread which implied sheer starvation. Periodic starvation was, in fact, the condition of the masses of working men
throughout the kingdom fifty years ago, and the references to the
subject in the economic literature of the time are most instructive.
M. Quetelet, in his well-known great book, points to the obvious
connection between the high price of bread following the bad
harvest of 1816, and the excessive rate of mortality which followed.
To this day you will find tables in the registrar-general's returns
which descend from a time when a distinct connection between
these high prices of bread and excessive rates of mortality was
traced. But within the last wenty years what do we find? Wheat
has not been, on the average, for a whole year so high as 70s., the
highest averages for any year being 64s. 5d. in 1867, and 63s. 9d.
in 1868; while the highest average of the last ten years alone is
58s. 8d. in 1873; that is only about 10s. above the average of the
whole period. In the twenty years, moreover, the highest price
touched at any period was just over 70s., viz., 70s. 5d., in 1867,
and 74s. 7d. in 1868; while in the last ten years the figure of 70s.
was not even touched, the nearest approach to it being 68s. 9d. in
1877. Thus of late years there has been a steadily low price, which
must have been an immense boon to the masses, and especially to
the poorest. The rise of money wages has been such, I believe, that
working men, for the most part, could have contended with extreme
fluctuations in the price of bread better than they did fifty years
ago. But they have not had the fluctuations to contend with.

It would be useless to go through other articles with the same
detail. Wheat had quite a special importance fifty years ago, and
the fact that it no longer has the same importance—that we have

ceased to think of it as people did fifty years ago—is itself significant. Still, taking one or two other articles, we find, on the whole, a decline:—

		1839–1840		*Present Time*	
		s.	*d.*	*s.*	*d.*
Sugar .... per cwt.		68	8	21	9
Cotton cloth exported .... per yard		–	5⅜	–	3¼
		(1840.)		(1882.)	
Inferior beasts .... per 8 lbs.		3	1	4	3¾
Second class .... ”		3	6	4	9¾
Third ” .... ”		3	11¾	5	7½
Inferior sheep .... ”		3	5	5	7
Second class .... ”		3	10¼	6	1¼
Large hogs .... ”		4	3½	4	6

I should have liked a longer list of articles, but the difficulty of comparison is very serious. It may be stated broadly, however, that while sugar and such articles have declined largely in price, and while clothing is also cheaper, the only article interesting the workman much which has increased in price is meat, the increase here being considerable. The "only" it may be supposed covers a great deal. The truth is, however, that meat fifty years ago was not an article of the workman's diet as it has since become. He had little more concern with its price than with the price of diamonds. The kind of meat which was mainly accessible to the workman fifty years ago, viz., bacon, has not, it will be seen, increased sensibly in price.

Only one question remains. Various commodities, it may be admitted, have fallen in price, but house rent, it is said, has gone up. We have heard a good deal lately of the high prices of rooms in the slums. When we take things in the mass, however, we find that however much some workmen may suffer, house rent in the aggregate cannot have gone up in a way to neutralise to any serious extent the great rise in the money wages of the workman. It appears that in 1834, when the house duty, which had existed up to that date, was abolished, the annual value of dwelling houses charged to duty was 12,603,000*l.*, the duty being levied on all

houses above 10*l*. rental in Great Britain. In 1881-82 the annual
value of dwelling houses charged to duty, the duty being levied on
houses above 20*l*. only, was 39,845,000*l*., while the value of the
houses between 10*l*. and 20*l*. was 17,040,000*l*., making a total of
56,885,000*l*., or between four and five times the total of fifty years
ago. Population, however, in Great Britain has increased from
about 16½ millions in 1831, to nearly 30 millions in 1881, or
nearly 100 per cent. Allowing for this, the increase in value would
be about 32 million pounds, on a total of about 25 million pounds,
which may be considered the increased rent which householders
above 10*l*. have to pay—the increase being about 130 per cent.
Assuming that houses under 10*l*. have increased in proportion, it
may be considered that house rents are now 1½ times more than
they were fifty years ago. In other words, a workman who paid 3*l*.
a year fifty years ago, would now pay 7*l*. 10*s*. Even, however, if
rent were a fourth part of the workman's earnings fifty years ago,
he would still be much better off at the present time than he was.
His whole wages have doubled, while the prices of no part of his
necessary consumption, except rent, as we have seen, have increased—on the contrary, they have rather diminished. Say then
that the rent, which was a fourth part of his expenditure, has increased 1½ times, while his whole wage has doubled, the account,
on a wage of 20*s*. fifty years ago, and 40*s*. now, would stand:—

	Fifty Years ago		Present Time	
	s.	*d.*	*s.*	*d.*
Wage	20	–	40	–
Deduct for rent	5	–	12	6
Balance for other purposes	15	–	27	6

—showing still an enormous improvement in the workman's
condition.

It may be pointed out, however, that houses are undoubtedly
of better value all round than they were fifty years ago. More rent
is paid because more capital is in the houses, and they are better
houses. It appears also that fifty years ago there were far more
exemptions than there are now, rural dwellings particularly being
favoured as regards exemption. The increase of rent for the same

accommodation, there is consequently reason to believe, has not been nearly so great as these figures would appear to show. It has further to be considered that the whole annual value of the dwelling houses under 10*l.* even now is 17,885,000*l.* only, the number of houses being 3,124,000. This must be a very small proportion of the aggregate earnings of those portions of the working classes who live in houses under 10*l.* rent, and even adding to it the value of all the houses up to 20*l.*, which would bring up the total to 34,925,000*l.*, the proportion would still be very small. On the five million families at least of the working classes in Great Britain, the sum would come to about 7*l.* per family, which is not the main portion of an average working man's expenditure.

We return then to the conclusion that the increase of the money wages of the working man in the last fifty years corresponds to a real gain. While his wages have advanced, most articles he consumes have rather diminished in price, the change in wheat being especially remarkable, and significant of a complete revolution in the condition of the masses. The increased price in the case of one or two articles—particularly meat and house rent—is insufficient to neutralize the general advantages which the workman has gained. Meat formerly was a very small part of his consumption, and allowing to house rent a much larger share of his expenditure than it actually bore, the increase in amount would still leave the workman out of his increased wage a larger margin than he had before for miscellaneous expenditure. There is reason to believe also that the houses are better, and that the increased house-rent is merely the higher price for a superior article which the workman can afford.

It has to be added to all this that while the cost of government has been greatly diminished to the working man, he gets more from the government expenditure than he formerly did. It would not do to count things twice over, and as the benefit to the working man of diminished taxes has already been allowed for in the lower prices of wheat and sugar, we need say nothing more on this head. But few people seem to be aware how, simultaneously with this reduction of the cost of government, there has been an increase of the expenditure of the government for miscellaneous civil purposes, of all of which the workman gets the benefit. It may be stated broadly that nearly 15 million pounds of the expenditure of the central government for education, for the post office, for inspection of factories, and for the miscellaneous purposes of civil government, is entirely new as compared with fifty years ago. So far as the expenditure is beneficial the masses get something they did not get before at all. It is the same even more markedly with local government. In Great Britain, the annual outlay is now about 60 million pounds, as compared with 20 million pounds fifty years ago. This 20 million pounds was mainly for poor relief and other old burdens. Now the poor relief and other old burdens are much the same, but the total is swollen by a vast expenditure for sanitary, educational, and similar purposes, of all of which the masses of the population get the benefit. To a great deal of this expenditure we may attach the highest value. It does not give bread or clothing to the working man, but it all helps to make life sweeter and better, and to open out careers even to the poorest. The value of the free library, for instance, in a large city, is simply incalculable. All this outlay the workman has now the benefit of as he had not fifty years ago. To repeat the words I have already used, he pays less taxes, and he gets more—much more—from the Government.

As already anticipated, however, the conclusion thus arrived at only carries us part of the way. Assuming it to have been shown that the masses have more money than they had fifty years ago, and that the prices of the chief articles they consume are cheaper rather than dearer, the question remains whether the condition of the masses has in fact been improved. This can only be shown indirectly by statistics of different kinds, which justify conclusions as to the condition of the people to whom they apply. To such statistics I propose now to draw your attention for a moment. I need hardly say that any evidence they contain as to the condition of the people having actually improved corroborates what has been already said as to their having had the means of improvement in their hands. The evidence is cumulative, a point of material importance in all such inquiries.

The first and the most important statistics on this head are those relating to the length of life among the masses of the nation.

Do the people live longer than they did? Here I need not detain you. A very effective answer was supplied last session by Mr. Humphreys, in his able paper on "The Recent Decline in the English Death-Rate." Mr. Humphreys there showed conclusively that the decline in the death-rate in the last five years, 1876–80, as compared with the rates of which Dr. Farr's *English Life Table* was based—rates obtained in the years 1838–54—amounted to from 28 to 32 per cent in males at each quinquenniad of the twenty years 5—25, and in females at each quinquenniad from 5—35 to between 24 and 35 per cent; and that the effect of this decline in the death-rate is to raise the mean duration of life among males from 39.9 to 41.9 years, a gain of 2 years in the average duration of life, and among females from 41.9 to 45.3 years, a gain of nearly 3½ years in the average duration of life. Mr. Haumphreys also showed that by far the larger proportion of the increased duration of human life in England is lived at useful ages, and not at the dependent ages of either childhood or old age. This little statement is absolutely conclusive on the subject; but we are apt to overlook how much the figures mean. No such change could take place without a great increase in the vitality of the people. Not only have fewer died, but the masses who have lived must have been healthier, and have suffered less from sickness than they did. Though no statistics are available on this point, we must assume that like causes produce like effects; and if the weaker, who would otherwise have died, have been able to survive, the strong must also have been better than they would otherwise have been. From the nature of the figures also the improvement must have been among the masses, and not among a select class whose figures throw up the average. The figures to be affected relate to such large masses of population, that so great a change in the average could not have occurred if only a small percentage of the population had improved in health.

I should like also to point out that the improvement in health actually recorded obviously relates to a transition stage. Many of the improvements in the condition of the working classes have only taken place quite recently. They have not, therefore, affected all through their existence any but the youngest lives. When the improvements have been in existence for a longer period, so that the lives of all who are living must have been affected from birth by the changed conditions, we may infer that even a greater gain in the mean duration of life will be shown. As it is, the gain is enormous. Whether it is due to better and more abundant food and clothing, to better sanitation, to better knowledge of medicine, or to these and other causes combined, the improvement has beyond all question taken place.

The next figures I shall refer to are those well known ones relating to the consumption of the articles which the masses consume. I copy merely the figures in the Statistical Abstract for the years 1840 and 1881:—

QUANTITIES OF THE PRINCIPAL IMPORTED AND EXCISEABLE ARTICLES RETAINED FOR HOME CONSUMPTION, PER HEAD OF THE TOTAL POPULATION OF THE UNITED KINGDOM

		1840	1881
Bacon and hams	lbs.	0.01	13.93
Butter	"	1.05	6.36
Cheese	"	0.92	5.77
Currants and raisins	"	1.45	4.34
Eggs	No.	3.63	21.65
Potatoes	lbs.	0.01	12.85
Rice	"	0.90	16.32
Cocoa	"	0.08	0.31
Coffee	"	1.08	0.89
Corn, wheat, and wheat flour	"	42.47	216.92
Raw sugar	"	15.20	58.92
Refined sugar	"	nil	8.44
Tea	"	1.22	4.58
Tobacco	"	0.86	1.41
Wine	galls.	0.25	0.45
Spirits	"	0.97	1.08
Malt	bshls.	1.59	1.91*

° Year 1878.

This wonderful table may speak for itself. It is an obvious criticism that many of the articles are also articles of home production, so that the increase does not show the real increase of the consumption of the whole population per head. Assuming a stationary production at home, the increased consumption per head cannot be so much as is here stated for the imported article only. There are other articles, however, such as rice, tea, sugar, coffee, tobacco, spirits, wine and malt, which are either wholly imported, or where we have the exciseable figures as well, and they all—with the one exception of coffee—tell a clear tale. The increase in tea and sugar appears especially significant, the consumption per head now being four times in round figures what it was forty years ago. There could be no better evidence of diffused material well-being among the masses. The articles are not such that the increased consumption by the rich could have made much difference. It is the consumption emphatically of the mass which is here in question.

As regards the articles imported, which are also articles of home production, it has, moreover, to be noted that in several of them, bacon and hams, cheese and butter, the increase is practically from nothing to a very respectable figure. The import of bacon and hams alone is itself nearly equal to the estimated consumption among the working classes fifty years ago, who consumed no other meat.

The only other figures I shall mention are those relating to education, pauperism, crime, and savings banks. But I need not detain you here. The figures are so well known that I must almost apologise for repeating them. I only insert them to round off the statement.

As to education, we have practically only figures going back thirty years. In 1851, in England, the children in average attendance at schools aided by parliamentary grants numbered 239,000, and in Scotland 32,000; in 1881 the figures were 2,863,000 and 410,000. If anything is to be allowed at all in favour of parliamentary grants as raising the character of education, such a change of numbers is most significant. The children of the masses are, in fact, now obtaining a good education all round, while fifty years ago the masses had either no education at all or a comparatively poor one. Dropping statistics for the moment, I should like to give my own testimony to an observed fact of social life—that there is nothing so striking or so satisfactory to those who can carry their memories back nearly forty years, as to observe the superiority of the education of the masses at the present time to what it was then. I suppose the most advanced common education forty or fifty years ago was in Scotland, but the superiority of the common school system there at the present day to what it was forty years ago is immense. If Scotland has gained so much, what must it have been in England where there was no national system fifty years ago at all? Thus at the present day not only do we get all children into schools, or nearly all, but the education for the increased numbers is better than that which the fortunate few alone obtained before.

Next as to crime, the facts to note are that rather more than forty years ago, with a population little more than half what it is now, the number of criminal offenders committed for trial (1839) was 54,000; in England alone 24,000. Now the corresponding figures are, United Kingdom 22,000, and England 15,000; fewer criminals by a great deal in a much larger population. Of course the figures are open to the observation that changes in legislation providing for the summary trial of offences that formerly went to the assizes may have had some effect. But the figures show so great and gradual a change, that there is ample margin for the results of legislative changes, without altering the inference that there is less serious crime now in the population than there was fifty years ago. Thus an improvement as regards crime corresponds to the better education and well-being of the masses.

Next as regards pauperism; here again the figures are so imperfect that we cannot go back quite fifty years. It is matter of history however that pauperism was nearly breaking down the country half-a-century ago. The expenditure on poor relief early in the century and down to 1830–31 was nearly as great at times as it is now. With half the population in the country that there now is, the burden of the poor was the same. Since 1849, however, we have continuous figures, and from these we know that, with a constantly increasing population, there is an absolute decline in the amount of pauperism. The earliest and latest figures are:—

PAUPERS IN RECEIPT OF RELIEF IN THE UNDERMENTIONED YEARS AT GIVEN DATES

	1849	1881
England	934,000	803,000
Scotland	122,000*	102,000
Ireland	620,000	109,000
United Kingdom ...	1,676,000	1,014,000

* 1859

Thus in each of the three divisions of the United Kingdom there is a material decline, and most of all in Ireland, the magnitude of the decline there being no doubt due to the fact that the figures are for a period just after the great famine. But how remote we seem to be from those days of famine.

Last of all we come to the figures of savings banks. A fifty years' comparison gives the following results for the whole kingdom:—

	1831	1881
Number of depositors	429,000	4,140,000
Amount of deposits	£13,719,000	£80,334,000
” per depositor	£32	£19

An increase of ten-fold in the number of depositors, and of five-fold and more in the amount of deposits! It seems obvious from these figures that the habit and means of saving have become widely diffused in these fifty years. The change is of course in part due to a mere change in the facilities offered for obtaining deposits; but allowing ample margin for the effect of increased facilities, we have still before us evidence of more saving among the masses.

To conclude this part of the evidence, we find undoubtedly that in longer life, in increased consumption of the chief commodities they use, in better education, in greater freedom from crime and pauperism, and in increased savings, the masses of the people are better, immensely better, than they were fifty years ago. This is quite consistent with the fact, which we all lament, that there is a residuum still unimproved, but apparently a smaller residuum, both in proportion to the population and absolutely, than was the case fifty years ago; and with the fact that the improvement, measured even by a low ideal, is far too small. No one can contemplate the condition of the masses of the people without desiring something like a revolution for the better. Still, the fact of progress in the last fifty years—progress which is really enormous when a comparison is made with the former state of things —must be recognised. Discontent with the present must not make us forget that things have been so much worse.

We may now conclude this long inquiry. It has been shown directly, I believe, that, while the individual incomes of the working classes have largely increased, the prices of the main articles of their consumption have rather declined; and the inference as to their being much better off which would be drawn from these facts is fully supported by statistics showing a decline in the rate of mortality, an increase of the consumption of articles in general use, an improvement in general education, a diminution of crime and pauperism, a vast increase of the number of depositors in savings banks, and other evidences of general well-being.

The facts are what we should have expected from the conditions of production in recent years. Inventions having been multiplied, and production having been increasingly efficient, while capital has been accumulated rapidly, it is the wages receivers who must have the benefit. The competition of capital keeps profits down to the lowest point, and workmen consequently get for themselves nearly the whole product of the aggregate industry of the country. It is interesting, nevertheless, to find that the facts correspond with what theory should lead us to anticipate.

The moral is a very obvious one. Whatever may be said as to the ideal perfection or imperfection of the present economic *régime,* the fact of so great an advance having been possible for the masses of the people in the last half-century is encouraging. It is something to know that whether a better *régime* is conceivable or not, human nature being what it is now (and I am one of those who think that the *régime* is the best, the general result of a vast community living as the British nation does, with all the means of healthy life and civilization at command, being little short of a marvel if we only consider for a moment what vices of anarchy and misrule in society have had to be rooted out to make this marvel); still, whether best or not, it is something to know that vast improvement has been possible with this *régime.* Surely the lesson is that the nation ought to go on improving on the same lines, relaxing none of the efforts which have been so successful. Steady progress in the direction maintained for the last fifty years must soon make the English people vastly superior to what they are now.

I should like to add just one or two remarks bearing on questions of the moment, and as to the desirability or possibility of a change of *régime* now so much discussed, which the figures I have brought before you suggest. One is, that apart from all objections of principle to schemes of confiscating capital,—land nationalisation, or collectivism, or whatever they may be called,—the masses could not hope to have much to divide by any such schemes. Taking the income from capital at 400 million pounds, we must not suppose that the whole of that would be divisible among the masses if capital were confiscated. What the capitalist classes spend is a very different thing from what they make. The annual savings of the country now exceed 200 million pounds, being made as a rule, though not exclusively, by the capitalist classes. If then the 400 million pounds were to be confiscated, one of two things would happen: either the savings would not be made, in which case the condition of the working classes would soon deteriorate, for everything depends upon the steady increase of capital; or the savings would be made, in which case the spending power of the masses would not be so very much increased. The difference would be that they would be owners of the capital, but the income would itself remain untouched. The system under which large capitals are in a few hands may, in fact, have its good side in this, that the Jay Goulds, Vanderbilts, and Rothschilds cannot spend their income. The consequent accumulation of capital is, in fact, one of the reasons why the reward for labour is so high, and the masses get nearly all the benefit of the great increase of production. The other remark I have to make is that if the object really aimed at by those who talk of land nationalisation and the like is carried out, the people who will suffer are those who receive large wages. To effect what they intend, the agitators must not merely seize on the property of a few, they must confiscate what are as much earnings as those of a mechanic or a labourer, and the wages of the most skilled mechanics and artizans themselves. The agitation is, in fact, to level down, to diminish the reward of labourers who receive a large wage because they can do the work the community requires, the proof being that in a market without favour they get the wage, and to increase the reward of other labourers beyond what in the same free market the community would freely give them. Whether the production would be continued at all if there were any success in these attempts, common sense will tell us. Those who have done some hard work in the world will, I am sure, agree with me that it is only done by virtue of the most powerful stimulants. Take away the rewards, and even the best would probably not give themselves up to doing what the community wants and now pays them for doing, but they would give themselves up either to idleness or to doing something else. The war of the land nationalizer and socialist is then not so much with the capitalist as with the workman, and the importance of this fact should not be lost sight of.

2

J. K. Ingram

THE NEED FOR SOCIOLOGY

THAT ECONOMIC PHENOMENA are capable of scientific treatment is a proposition which I do not intend to spend time in demonstrating. It is comprehended in the more general question of the possibility of a scientific Sociology; and any one who disputes it will have enough to do in combating the arguments by which Comte, and Mill, and Herbert Spencer have established that possibility. Nor do I intend to waste words in showing that if there be a science of society, no other branch of investigation can compete with it in importance or in dignity. It has the most momentous influence of all on human welfare. It presides, in fact, over the whole intellectual system—an office which some, mistaking the foundation for the crown of the edifice, have claimed for Mathematics. It receives contributions from all other departments of research—whether in the ascertainment of results, to be used for its purposes, or in the elaboration of methods to be applied in its inquiries. It is the most difficult of all the sciences, because it is that in which the phenomena dealt with are most complex and dependent on the greatest variety of conditions, and in which, accordingly, appearances are most deceitful, and error takes the most plausible forms. That the professors of the more

Reprinted from *Proceedings of the British Association for the Advancement of Science, 1878*, Section F, "Presidential Address." Giffen was of his time in making progress his central concern; but before 1883 many had felt the need for a subtler account of the structure of progress than the statistical method could yield. For public opinion at large Ingram's lecture was a critical step toward a new consciousness.

stably—because earlier—constituted branches of knowledge should ignore the claims of this great department of inquiry would be doubly disastrous—first, by tending to leave the scientific system without its necessary completion in a true theory of the highest and most important class of phenomena accessible to our researches; and secondly, by tending, so far as prejudice and misconception can temporarily produce such an effect, to hand over to minds of insufficient power, and destitute of the necessary preparation, studies which, more than any others, require a strong intelligence, disciplined in the methods and furnished with the results of the sciences of inorganic and organic nature. There is, in my judgment, no duty more incumbent in our day on the professors of these last, than that of recognising the claims om Sociology, whilst at the same time enforcing on its cultivators the necessity of conforming to the genuine scientific type. Yet it is now sought to expel from this Association, which ought to represent the harmonious union of all positive research, the very limited and inadequate portion of the science of society which has ever found recognition in its scheme.

I therefore hold by the truth, which has indeed now become a philosophic commonplace, that social phenomena generally, and amongst them the economic phenomena of society, do admit of scientific treatment. But I believe that the mode in which the study of these phenomena has been conceived and prosecuted in the hitherto reigning school, is open to serious objections; and the decline in the credit and influence of political economy, of which I have spoken, appears to me to be in a large measure due to the vicious methods followed by its teachers. The distrust of its doctrines manifested by the working classes is no doubt in a great degree owing to the not altogether unfounded belief, that it has tended to justify too absolutely existing social arrangements, and that its study is often recommended by the influential classes with the view of repressing popular aspirations after a better order of things. And it is doubtless true that some of the opposition which political economy encounters, is founded on the hostility of selfish interests, marshalled against the principles of free-trade, of which it is regarded as the representative.

But it is not with manifestations of this kind, which belong to politics rather than philosophy, that I am now chiefly concerned. It is more appropriate to this place to point to the growing coldness or distrust exhibited by the higher intellects towards political economy—a fact which lies on the surface of things, and shows itself everywhere in contemporary literature. The egoistic spirit in which it is steeped may explain the continued protest which Carlyle and Ruskin have, mainly as moral preachers, maintained against it—though that very spirit is, as I shall show, closely connected with vicious method. But what are we to say of Miss Martineau's final judgment? Speaking in her "Autobiography" of that part of her career in which, as Professor Jevons says, "she "successfully popularised the truths of political economy in her admirable tales," she tells us that what she then took to be the science of political economy as elaborated by the economists of our time, she had come to regard as being no science at all, strictly speaking. "So many of its parts," she adds, "must undergo essential change, that it may be a question whether future generations will owe much more to it than the benefit (incalculable to be sure) of establishing the grand truth, that social affairs proceed according to great general laws, no less than natural phenomena of every kind." Here is a conclusion resting essentially on intellectual, not moral, grounds; and I presume Professor Jevons will not explain it as a result of ignorant impatience.

But it is no longer necessary to consider scattered indications of the feeling of eminent individualities on this matter, for of late years the growing dissatisfaction has risen to the dimensions of a European revolt, whose organs have appeared not in the ranks of general literature, but within the sphere of economic investigation itself. It is a characteristic result of the narrowness and spirit of routine which have too much prevailed in the dominant English school of economists, that they are either unacquainted with, or have chosen to ignore, this remarkable movement.

The largest and most combined manifestation of the revolt has been in Germany, all whose ablest economic writers are in opposition to the methods and doctrines of the school of Ricardo. Roscher, Knies, Hildebrand, Nasse, Brentano, Held, Schmoller,

Schäffle, Schönberg, Samter, and others, have taken up this attitude. In Italy a group of distinguished writers, amongst whom are
named Luzzatti, Forti, and Lampertico, follow the same direction,
and have a special organ in which they advocate their views.

In France, the new direction is not so marked in the economic
world, strictly so called, though in that country it really first appeared. For the vices of the old school, which have led to the
development of the new, were powerfully stated more than forty
years ago by a French thinker, who is too little studied by the mass
of his countrymen, Auguste Comte, the greatest master who has
ever treated of sociological method. Considering the criticisms of
the great Frenchman to have been perfectly just when he wrote
them, and only requiring a certain correction now in view of the
healthier tendencies apparent in several quarters since his work
was published, I shall dwell at some length on the several grounds
of his censures, stating and illustrating them in my own way, which
will differ considerably from the mode of treatment which they
received in the controversy to which I have referred. Those
grounds, though nowhere by him formally enumerated, are essentially reducible to four, having relation—first, to the attempt
to isolate the study of the facts of wealth from that of the other
social phenomena; secondly, to the metaphysical or viciously
abstract character of many of the conceptions of the economists;
thirdly, to the abusive preponderance of deduction in their
processes of research; and fourthly, to the too absolute way in
which their conclusions are conceived and enunciated. It will be
found that these heads cannot be kept strictly apart, but run into
each other at several points. The separation of them will, however,
serve to give distinctness and order to the discussion.

The first objection is, as I have stated, to the pretension of the
economists to isolate the special phenomena they study, the economic phenomena of society, from all the rest—its material aspect
from its intellectual, moral, and political aspects, and to constitute
an independent science, dealing with the former alone, to the
exclusion of the latter. This question as to the relation of economic
studies to the general body of human knowledge, is really the most
radical and vital that can be raised respecting them, and on it more

than on any other depends, in my opinion, the future of these studies.

It is sometimes sought to get rid of this question in a very summary manner, and to represent those who raise it either as weakly sentimental persons, who shrink from studying the conditions of wealth apart, because there are better and higher things than wealth; or as persons of confused intellect, who wish to mix together things which are essentially different in their nature. On the former of these imputations it is unnecessary to dwell. I am far from undervaluing sentiment in its proper sphere; but I take up no sentimental ground on the present question. In denying the propriety of isolating economic investigation, I appeal to considerations derived from the philosophy of science. The second allegation is, therefore, the only one with which I am now concerned.

Of course we must do only one thing at a time. Only one out of several branches of a subject can be considered at a time: but they are yet branches of a single subject, and the relations of the branches may be precisely the most important thing to be kept in view respecting them. It might be said: "It is important, no doubt, that plant life and animal life should both be understood; but zoology and botany are different sciences; let them be studied apart; let a separate class of *savants* be appropriated to each, and every essential end is secured." But what says Professor Huxley, in unison with all the most competent opinion on the subject?— "The study of living bodies is really one discipline, which is divided into zoology and botany simply as a matter of convenience." They are, in fact, branches from the common stem of biology, and neither can be rightly conceived without bearing this in mind. Now I maintain that for still stronger reasons the several branches of social science must be kept in the closest relation.

Another biological analogy will place these reasons in the clearest light. When we pass from the study of the inorganic world to that of the organic, which presupposes and succeeds to the former, we come upon the new idea of a living whole, with definite structures appropriated to special actions, but all influencing one another, and co-operating to one result—the healthy life of the organism. Here, then, it is plain that we cannot isolate the study of one organ from that of the rest, or of the whole. We cannot break up the study of the human body into a number of different sciences, dealing respectively with the different organs and functions, and, instead of a human anatomy and physiology, construct a cardiology, a hepatology, an enterology. It is not of course meant that special studies of special organs and functions may not be undertaken—that they may not be temporarily and provisionally separated from each other; but the fact insisted on is, that it is essential to keep in view their relations and interactions, and that therefore they must be treated as forming part of the subject-matter of one and the same science. And what is thus true of theory is also true of practice—the physician who had studied only one organ and its function would be very untrustworthy even in the therapeutics of that organ. He who treats every disease as purely local, without regard to the general constitution, is a quack; and he who ignores the mutual action of the *physique* and the *moral* in disease, is not properly a physician, but a veterinary.

These considerations are just as applicable, *mutatis mutandis*, to the study of society, which is in so many respects kindred to biology. The most characteristic fact about what is well called the social system, is the consensus of its different functions; and the treatment of these functions as independent is sure to land us in theoretic and practical error. There is one great science of sociology; its several chapters study the several faces of social existence. One of these faces is that of the material well-being of society, its industrial constitution and development. The study of these phenomena is one chapter of sociology, a chapter which must be kept in close relation with the rest.

The justice of this view is clearly seen when we consider the two-fold aspect of sociology as statistical and dynamical—that is, as dealing on the one hand with laws of coexistence, and on the other with laws of succession. As in biology we have alongside of the theory of the constitution and actions of an organism, the further theory of its development in time: so in sociology we have, beside the doctrine of the constitution and actions of society, the doctrine of its evolution from a primitive to a higher condition.

Now nothing is plainer than that in the course of the human evolution the several social elements did not follow separate and independent processes of growth. The present economic condition, for example, of the nations of western Europe, as a group, or of any individual one amongst them, is the result of a great variety of conditions, many of them not in their own nature economical at all. Scientific, moral, religious, political ideas and institutions have all concurred in determining it. But if they worked in this manner in the past, it follows that they are working so in the present. It is therefore impossible rationally to conceive or explain the industrial economy of society without taking into account the other coexisting social factors.

In nothing is the eminent superiority of Adam Smith more clearly seen than in his tendency to comprehend and combine in his investigations all the different aspects of social phenomena. Before the term "social science" had been spoken or written, it could not be expected that he should have conceived adequately the nature and conditions of that branch of inquiry—much less founded it on definite bases—a task which was to be achieved more than fifty years later by the genius of Comte. But he proceeded as far in this direction as it was possible to do under the intellectual conditions of his time.

In striking contrast with this spirit of the master is the affectation, habitual in his followers, of ignoring all considerations except the strictly economic—though in doing so they often pass over agencies which have important effects on material well-being. This is the very pedantry of purism; and the purism is not merely exaggerated, it is really altogether out of place. Mill, though, as I believe, he did not occupy firm ground in relation to the constitution of social science, is free from any such narrowness as this:— "For practical purposes," he says, "political economy is inseparably intertwined with many other branches of social philosophy. Except on matters of mere detail, there are perhaps no practical questions, even among those which approach nearest to the character of purely economic questions, which admit of being decided on economic premises alone." This is true; but it is only part of the truth. For purposes of theory as well as of practice, the several branches of social inquiry are inseparably intertwined; and this larger proposition Mill in another place has stated with all the desirable fulness of enunciation, declaring that "we can never understand in theory or command in practice the condition of a society in any one respect, without taking into consideration its condition in all other respects."

The second common error of the political economists since the time of Adam Smith, consists in this, that, mainly by the influence of Ricardo, they have been led to conceive and present, in a viciously abstract way, the conceptions with which they deal.

Abstraction is, indeed, necessary to all science, being implied in the search after unity amidst variety. The criterion of true or false science lies precisely in the right or wrong institution of the relation between the abstract and the concrete. Now, in matters of human life especially, we have only to carry abstraction far enough in order to lose all hold on realities, and present things quite other than they in fact are; and, if we use these abstractions in the premises of our reasonings, we shall arrive at conclusions, either positively false, or useless for any practical purpose. As Comte remarked, the most fundamental economic notions have been sub- tilised in the ordinary treatises, till the discussions about them often wander away from any relation to fact, and lose themselves in a region of nebulous metaphysics; so that exact thinkers have felt themselves obliged to abandon the use of some of the most necessary terms, such as *value, utility, production,* and to express the ideas they attach to them by circuitous phrases. I am far from condemning the effort after accuracy of language and well-defined terms; but the endless fluctuations of economists in the use of words certainly indicate a very general failure to apprehend and keep steadily in view the corresponding realities.

There is a common economic abstraction, which by the un- sympathetic colour it has given to political economy, has tended— perhaps more than anything else—to repel the working classes from its study. By habitually regarding labour from the abstract point of view, and overlooking the personality of the labourer, economists are led to leave out of account some of the considera- tions which most seriously affect the condition of the working man.

He comes to be regarded exclusively as an agent—I might almost say, an instrument of production. It is too often forgotten that he is before all things a man and a member of society—that he is usually the head of a household, and that the conditions of his life should be such as to admit of his maintaining the due relations with his family—that he is also a citizen, and requires for the intelligent appreciation of the social and political system to which he belongs a certain amount of leisure and opportunity for mental culture. Even when a higher education is now sought for him, it is often conceived as exclusively designed to adapt him for the effective exercise of his functions as a producer, and so is reduced to technical instruction; whereas moral and social ideas are for him, as for all of us, by far the most important, because most directly related to conduct. Labour, again, is viewed as a commodity for sale, like any other commodity; though it is plain that, even if it could be properly so called at all, yet in some particulars, as in the difficulty of local transfer (a family having to be considered), and in the frequent impossibility of waiting for a market, it is quite exceptional amongst commodities. By a further abstraction, the difference of the social vocations of the sexes is made to disappear, in economic as in political reasoning, by means of the simple expedient of substituting for man in every proposition *person* or *human being;* and so by little else than a trick of phraseology, self-support is made as much an obligation of the woman as of the man. It is true that ungenerous sentiment has much to do with the prevalence of these modes of thought; but what it is most suitable to insist on here, is that the science on which they rest, or in which they find justification, is false science. By merely keeping close to facts and not hiding realities under lax generalisations, we shall be led to more humane, as well as truer, conceptions of the proper conditions of industrial life.

The third prevailing error of the economists—and, with the exception of the isolation of their study, this is the most serious of all—is that of exaggerating immensely the office of deduction in their investigations. Deduction has indisputably a real and not inconsiderable place in sociology. We can sometimes follow the method which Mill calls the *à priori* deductive, that is, we can, from

what we know of the nature of man and the laws of the external
world, see beforehand what social phenomena will result from
their joint action; but though the economists of the so-called
orthodox school recognise no other method, we cannot really proceed far in this way, which is available only in simple cases. Social
phenomena are in general too complex, and depend on too manifold conditions, to be capable of such *à priori* determination. In
so far as the method can be used, the vital condition of its legitimate employment is the ascertainment of the consilience of the
results of deduction with those of observation; and yet such
verification from fact of the conclusions of theory, though essential
to the admissibility of this process of inquiry, is too often entirely
overlooked. Much more commonly the function of deduction is
different from what has just been described, and its relation to
observation is inverted. The laws of the economic constitution and
movement of society are ascertained by observation, whether
directed to contemporary life or the history of the past. The office
of deduction is then to verify and control the inductions which
have been arrived at, using for this purpose considerations founded
on the qualities of human nature and the external conditions to
which society is subjected. Results which could not have been
elicited by *à priori* reasoning from the latter data, may, when
inductively obtained, be in this way checked and rationalised. The
pretension of the economists to deduce all the phenomena of the
industrial life of communities from four propositions, is one that
cannot be sustained. But conclusions derived from observation
may be placed in relation with the laws of the world and of human
nature, so far at least as to show that they contradict nothing we
know respecting those laws. This method, in which inductive research preponderates, and deduction takes a secondary place as
means of verification, is the really normal and fruitful method of
sociological inquiry. Finding its principal resources in human
history, it may be best called the historical method.

It must not, however, be supposed that by this expression we
mean nothing more than the ascertainment of fact by historical
investigation. This is the indispensable basis, but by itself it would
be matter rather of erudition than of science. We mean further,

the comparison of the successive states of society in order to discover the laws of social filiation—a process similar in principle to the biological comparison of organisms of different degrees of development. If we followed exclusively the *à priori* deductive method, in (for example) economic research, and sought to infer the economic facts of life from the nature of the world and man, we could arrive only at one determinate order of things, whilst we know that in reality the economic organisation and functions of society vary in time according to definite laws of succession. Mr. Lowe, indeed, will have it "political economy is founded on the attributes of the human mind, and nothing can change it;" which means, I suppose, that its formulas must always correspond with the phenomena. But how can this view be reconciled with the now ascertained fact, that society has passed through states in which the modern economic constitution was so far from existing, that property did not belong to the individual, but to the community? The *à priori* method, in fact overlooks what is the main agency in the social movement—namely, the accumulated influence of anterior on subsequent generations of mankind; an influence too complex to be estimated deductively. Every department of social life, and amongst the rest the industrial system, undergoes transformation—not arbitrarily indeed, but in accordance with law; and if we wish to understand any of those departments, we must study its transformations, considering each successive form in relation to all the preceding and contemporary conditions.

There is, indeed, no more important philosophical theorem than this: that the nature of a social fact of any degree of complexity cannot be understood apart from its history. "Only when its genesis has been traced," says Mr. Herbert Spencer, "only when its antecedents of all orders have been observed in their cooperation, generation after generation, through past social states—is there reached that interpretation of a fact which makes it a part of sociological science." To understand, for example, the true meaning of the trade societies of modern times, so important an object of economic study, "we must," he says, "go back to the older periods when analogous causes produced analogous results. And facts of this order," he adds, "must be studied not merely in their own successive forms, but in relation to the other phenomena of their time—the political institutions, the class distinctions, the family arrangements, the modes of distribution and degree of intercourse between localities, the amounts of knowledge, the religious beliefs, the morals, the sentiments, the customs." These considerations all point to the historical method, and, I may add, they all confirm what I have already urged, that the economic phenomena of society cannot be isolated from its other aspects. When our object is not the explanation of any past or present fact, but the prevision (within possible limits) of the future, and the adoption of a policy in relation to that future, our guide must still be the historic method, conceived as indicating, from the comparison of successive states, the general tendency of society with respect to the phenomenon considered, and the agencies which are in course of modifying existing systems. "Legislative action of no kind," again says Mr. Spencer, "can be taken that is not either in agreement with or at variance with the processes of national growth and development as naturally going on." We can by judicious action modify in their special mode of accomplishment or in the rate of their development, but cannot alter in their fundamental nature, the changes which result from the spontaneous tendencies of humanity. An attempt to introduce any social factor which is not essentially conformable to the contemporary civilisation, will result, if not in serious disturbance, at least in a mere waste of effort. Any proposal of social action, therefore, should repose on a previous analysis of those spontaneous tendencies, and this is possible only by the historic method. Let me give an example from an economic subject which happens just at present to offer a special interest. Attention has been called by Sir Henry Maine, to the general law that property in land originally belongs, not to individuals, nor even to families in the modern sense, but to larger societies, and that in the progress of mankind there is a natural movement from common to separate ownership. This historical result has been elaborated by a number of independent inquirers; and M. de Laveleye in a work of great research has brought together a vast mass of evidence, both establishing the main fact, and exhibiting the varied features which the common evolution has assumed in different countries. From the general appearance of this collective ownership in an early stage of society, it is sometimes argued that it is a *natural* system; but the historic method shows that it is just as natural that it should disappear at a more advanced stage. Serving useful ends in the former period, it becomes in the latter an obstruction to progress by stereotyping agricultural art, and impeding that individual initiative which is an indispensable condition of social improvement.

I observed before that Mill betrayed some uncertainty of view as to the precise relation of economic inquiries to general sociology. As to the proper method of the social science also, he appears to me not strictly consistent with himself. That method he declares, in so many words, to be the direct (or *à priori*) deductive. Yet elsewhere he as plainly agrees with Comte, that in the general science of society, as distinguished from its separate departments, nothing of a scientific character is possible except by the inverse deductive—as he chooses to call the historical— method. In one place he seems to assert that the general course of economic evolution could be predicted from the single consideration of the desire of wealth. Yet again he admits that no one could determine *à priori* from the principles of human nature and the general circumstances of the race the order in which human development takes place. Now this involves the conclusion, that the laws of economic progress—like all dynamic laws of sociology— must be ascertained by observation on the large scale, and only verified by appeal to the laws of the external world and human nature: in other words, that the right method for their study is the historical.

Lastly has to be noticed the too absolute character of the theoretic and practical conclusions of the political economists. It follows (as I have already indicated) from their *à priori* and unhistoric method that they arrive at results which purport to apply equally to all states of society. Neglecting the study of the social development, they tend too much to conceive the economic structure of society as fixed in type, instead of as undergoing a regular modification in process of time, in relation to the other changing elements of human condition. Similar consequences arose in other branches of sociological inquiry from the prevalence of unhistoric methods. But reforms have been largely carried into effect from the increasing recognition of the principle, that the treatment of any particular aspect of society must be dominated by the consideration of the general contemporary state of civilisation. Thus, in jurisprudence there is a marked tendency to substitute for the *à priori* method of the Benthamites a historical method, the leading idea of which is to connect the whole juristic system of any epoch with the corresponding state of society; and this new method has already borne admirable fruits, especially in the hands of Sir Henry Maine. Again, the old search after the best government, which used to be the main element of political inquiry, is now seen to have been radically irrational, because the form of government must be essentially related to the stage of social development, to historic antecedents, and the question, what is best? admits of no absolute answer.

Mill admits that there can be no separate science of government; in other words, that the study of the political phenomena of society cannot be conducted apart, but must, in his own words, stand part of the general science of society, not of any separate branch of it. And why? Because these phenomena are so closely mixed up, both as cause and effect, with the qualities of the particular people, or of the particular age. Particular age must here mean the state of general social development. But are not economic phenomena very closely bound up with the particular state of development of the society which is under consideration? Mr. Bagehot, indeed, takes up the ground that political economy is "restricted to a single kind of society, a society of competitive commerce, such as we have in England." And Mill himself, whilst stating that only through the principle of competition, as the exclusive regulator of economic phenomena, has political economy any claim to the character of a science, admits that competition has, only at a comparatively modern period, become in any considerable degree the governing principle of contracts; that in early periods transactions and engagements were regulated by custom, and that to this day in several countries of Europe, in large departments of human transactions, custom, not competition, is the arbiter.

The truth is, that in most enunciations of economic theorems by the English school, the practice is tacitly to presuppose the state of social development, and the general history of social conditions, to be similar to that of modern England; and whenever this supposition is not realised, those theorems will be found to fail.

Let me now recapitulate the philosophical conclusions which I have been endeavouring to enforce. They are the following:—

(1) That the study of the economic phenomena of society ought to be systematically combined with that of the other aspects of social existence; (2) That the excessive tendency to abstraction and to unreal simplifications should be checked; (3) That the *à priori* deductive method should be changed for the historical; and (4) That economic laws and the practical prescriptions founded on those laws should be conceived and expressed in a less absolute form. These are, in my opinion, the great reforms which are required both in the conduct of economic research, and in the exposition of its conclusions.

I am far from thinking that the results arrived at by the hitherto dominant economic school ought to be thrown away as valueless. They have shed important partial lights on human affairs, and afforded salutary partial guidance in public action. The task incumbent on sociologists in general, or such of them as specially devote themselves to economic inquiries, is to incorporate the truths already elicited into a more satisfactory body of doctrine, in which they will be brought into relation with the general theory of social existence, to recast the first draughts of theory, which, however incomplete, in most cases indicate real elements of the question considered, and to utilise the valuable materials of all kinds which their predecessors have accumulated. Viewed as provisional and preparatory, the current political economy deserves an approbation and an acceptance to which I think it is not entitled, if regarded as a final systemisation of the industrial laws of society.

Returning now from our examination of the condition and

prospects of economic study in the general field of human knowledge to the consideration of its position in this association, what
seems to follow from all I have been saying? I do not take into
account at all the suggestion that that study should be removed
from what professes to be a confederation of the sciences. As has
been well said, the omission from the objects of this body of the
whole subject of the life of man in communities, although there is
a scientific order traceable in that life, would be a degradation of
the association. If the proper study of mankind is man, the work
of the association, after the extrusion of our section, would be like
the play with the part of the protagonist left out. What appears
to be the reasonable suggestion, is that the field of the section
should be enlarged, so as to comprehend the whole of sociology.
The economic facts of society, as I have endeavoured to show, cannot be scientifically considered apart; and there is no reason why
the researches of Sir Henry Maine, or those of Mr. Spencer, should
not be as much at home here as those of Mr. Fawcett or Professor
Price. Many of the subjects, too, at present included in the artificial assemblage of heterogeneous inquiries known by the name
of anthropology, really connect themselves with the laws of social
development; and if our section bore the title of the sociological,
studies like those of Mr. Tylor and Sir John Lubbock concerning
the early history of civilisation would find in it their most appropriate place. I prefer the name sociology to that of social science,
which has been at once rendered indefinite and vulgarised in common use, and has come to be regarded as denoting a congeries of
incoherent details respecting every practical matter bearing directly or remotely on public interests, which happens for the
moment to engage attention. There are other societies in which an
opportunity is afforded for discussing such current questions in a
comparatively popular arena. But if we are to be associated here
with the students of the other sciences, it is our duty, as well as
our interest, to aim at a genuine scientific character in our work.
Our main object should be to assist in fixing theoretic ideas on the
structure, functions, and development of society. Some may regard
this view of the subject with impatience, as proposing to us investigations not bearing on the great and real needs of contempo-

rary social life. But that would be a very mistaken view. Luciferous research, in the words of Bacon, must come before fructiferous. "Effectual practice," says Mr. Herbert Spencer, "depends on superiority of ideas; methods that answer are preceded by thoughts that are true." And in human affairs, it is in general impossible to solve special questions correctly without just conceptions of *ensemble*—all particular problems of government, of education, of social action of whatever kind, connect themselves with the largest ideas concerning the fundamental constitution of society, its spontaneous tendencies, and its moral ideal.

I have as yet said nothing of statistics, with which the name of this section at first exclusively connected it, and which are still recognised as forming one of its objects. But it is plain that though statistics may be combined with sociology in the title of the section, the two cannot occupy a co-ordinate position. For it is impossible to vindicate for statistics the character of a science; they constitute only one of the aids or adminicula of science. The ascertainment and systematic arrangement of numerical facts is useful in many branches of research, but, till law emerges, there is no science; and the law, when it does emerge, takes its place in the science whose function it is to deal with the particular class of phenomena to which the facts belong. We may ascertain and arrange meteorological facts of this kind as well as sociological; and if they help us to the discovery of a law, the law belongs to meteorology, as in the other case, to sociology. More frequently social statistics are used, not to assist us towards scientific generalisations, but as subservient to the direct practical action of the statesman by indicating the condition of the body politic. From this point of view, they may be compared with a description of the condition, pathological or otherwise, of a particular living organism for hygienic or diagnostic purposes. The questions to be asked by the observer are dictated, and the interpretation to be put upon the answers is supplied, in the latter case by physiology, in the former by sociology. But as the facts observed and recorded are not general but individual, we are here in the domain of practical theapeutics or practical politics—not in that of science properly so called.

But though the character of a science cannot be claimed for

statistics, it is obvious that if the views I have advocated as to the true nature and conditions of economic study should prevail, the importance of statistical inquiries will rise as the abstract and deductive method declines in estimation. Senior objected to the saying that political economy was *avide de faits*, because, according to him and the school of Ricardo in general, its work was mainly one of inference from a few primary assumptions. But if the latter notion is given up, every form of careful and conscientious search after the realities of the material life of society, in the present as in the past, will regain its normal importance. This search must, of course, be regulated by definite principles, and must not degenerate into a purposeless and fortuitous accumulation of facts; for here, as in every branch of inquiry, it is true that *"Prudens interrogatio est dimidium scientiæ."*

I do not expect that the views I have put forward as to the necessity of a reform of economic studies will be immediately adopted either in this section or elsewhere. They may, I am aware, whilst probably in some quarters meeting with at least partial sympathy, in others encounter determined hostility. And it is possible that I may be accused of presumption in venturing to criticise methods used in practice, and justified in principle, by many distinguished men. I should scarcely have undertaken such an office, however profoundly convinced of the urgency of a reform, had I not been supported by what seemed to me the unanswered arguments of an illustrious thinker, and by the knowledge that the growing movement of philosophic Europe is in the direction he recommended as the right one. No one can feel more strongly than myself the inadequacy of my treatment of the subject. But my object has not been so much to produce conviction as to awaken attention. Our economists have undeniably been slow in observing the currents of European thought. Whilst such foreign writers as echo the doctrines of the so-called orthodox school are read and quoted in England, the names of those who assume a different and more independent attitude are seldom heard, and their works appear to be almost entirely unknown. But the fence of self-satisfied routine within which in these countries we formerly too often entrenched ourselves is being broken down at every point; and no really vital body of opinion can now exist abroad without speedily disturbing our insular tranquillity. The controversy, therefore, as to the methods of economic research and its relations to sociology as a whole, cannot long be postponed amongst us. It has, in fact, been already opened from different sides by Mr. Leslie and Mr. Harrison, and it is desirable that it should arrive as promptly as possible at a definite issue. If I have done anything to-day to assist in launching this great question on the field of general English discussion, the purpose I have set before me will have been abundantly fulfilled.

III. The Nature of Sociology

1
Herbert Spencer

GROWTH, DEVELOPMENT, STRUCTURE, AND FUNCTION

SETTING OUT with this general principle, that the properties of the units determine the properties of the aggregate, we conclude that there must be a Social Science expressing the relations between the two, with as much definiteness as the natures of the phenomena permit. Beginning with types of men who form but small and incoherent social aggregates, such a science has to show in what ways the individual qualities, intellectual and emotional, negative further aggregation. It has to explain how slight modifications of individual nature, arising under modified conditions of life, make somewhat larger aggregates possible. It has to trace out, in aggregates of some size, the genesis of the social relations, regulative and operative, into which the members fall. It has to exhibit the stronger and more prolonged social influences which, by further modifying the characters of the units, facilitate further aggregation with consequent further complexity of social structure. Among societies of all orders and sizes, from the smallest and rudest up to the largest and most civilized, it has to ascertain what traits there are in common, determined by the common traits of human beings; what less-general traits, distinguishing certain groups of societies, result from traits distinguishing certain races of men; and what peculiarities in each society are traceable to the peculiarities of its members. In every case it has for its subject-

Reprinted from *The Study of Sociology*, 1873, chapter 3.

matter the growth, development, structure, and functions of the social aggregate, as brought about by the mutual actions of individuals whose natures are partly like those of all men, partly like those of kindred races, partly distinctive.

These phenomena of social evolution have, of course, to be explained with due reference to the conditions each society is exposed to—the conditions furnished by its locality and by its relations to neighbouring societies. Noting this merely to prevent possible misapprehensions, the fact which here concerns us, is, not that the Social Science exhibits these or those special truths, but that, given men having certain properties, and an aggregate of such men must have certain derivative properties which form the subject-matter of a science.

What Biography is to Anthropology, History is to Sociology— History, I mean, as commonly conceived. The kind of relation which the sayings and doings that make up the ordinary account of a man's life, bear to an account of his bodily and mental evolution, structural and functional, is like the kind of relation borne by that narrative of a nation's actions and fortunes its historian gives us, to a description of its institutions, regulative and operative, and the ways in which their structures and functions have gradually established themselves. And if it is an error to say that there is no Science of Man, because the events of a man's life cannot be foreseen, it is equally an error to say that there is no Science of Society, because there can be no prevision of the occurrences which make up ordinary history.

Of course, I do not say that the parallel between an individual organism and a social organism is so close, that the distinction to be clearly drawn in the one case may be drawn with like clearness in the other. The structures and functions of the social organism are obviously far less specific, far more modifiable, far more dependent on conditions that are variable and never twice alike. All I mean is that, as in the one case so in the other, there lie underneath the phenomena of conduct, not forming subject-matter for science, certain vital phenomena, which do form subject-matter for science. Just as in the man there are structures and functions which make possible the doings his biographer tells of, so in the nation there are structures and functions which make possible the doings its historian tells of; and in both cases it is with these structures and functions, in their origin, development, and decline, that science is concerned.

To make better the parallel, and further to explain the nature of the Social Science, we must say that the morphology and physiology of Society, instead of corresponding to the morphology and physiology of Man, correspond rather to morphology and physiology in general. Social organisms, like individual organisms, are to be arranged into classes and sub-classes—not, indeed, into classes and sub-classes having anything like the same definiteness or the same constancy, but nevertheless having likenesses and differences which justify the putting of them into major groups most-markedly contrasted, and, within these, arranging them in minor groups less-markedly contrasted. And just as Biology discovers certain general traits of development, structure, and function, holding throughout all organisms, others holding throughout certain great groups, others throughout certain sub-groups these contain; so Sociology has to recognize truths of social development, structure, and function, that are some of them universal, some of them general, some of them special.

So that whether we look at the matter in the abstract or in the concrete, we reach the same conclusion. We need but to glance, on the one hand, at the varieties of uncivilized men and the structures of their tribes, and, on the other hand, at the varieties of civilized men and the structures of their nations, to see inference verified by fact. And thus recognizing, both *à priori* and *à posteriori*, these relations between the phenomena of individual human nature and the phenomena of incorporated human nature, we cannot fail to see that the phenomena of incorporated human nature form the subject-matter of a science.

And now to make more definite the conception of a Social Science thus shadowed forth in a general way, let me set down a few truths of the kind indicated. Some that I propose to name are very familiar; and others I add, not because of their interest or importance, but because they are easy of exposition. The aim is simply to convey a clear idea of the nature of sociological truths.

Take, first, the general fact that along with social aggregation there always goes some kind of organization. In the very lowest stages, where the assemblages are very small and very incoherent, there is no established subordination—no centre of control. Chieftainships of settled kinds come only along with larger and more coherent aggregates. The evolution of a governmental structure having some strength and permanence, is the condition under which alone any considerable growth of a society can take place. A differentiation of the originally-homogeneous mass of units into a co-ordinating part and a co-ordinated part, is the indispensable initial step.

Along with evolution of societies in size there goes evolution of their co-ordinating centres; which, having become permanent, presently become more or less complex. In small tribes, chieftainship, generally wanting in stability, is quite simple; but as tribes become larger by growth, or by reduction of other tribes to subjection, the co-ordinating apparatus begins to develop by the addition of subordinate governing agencies.

Simple and familiar as are these facts, we are not, therefore, to overlook their significance. That men rise into the state of social aggregation only on condition that they lapse into relations of inequality in respect of power, and are made to cooperate as a whole only by the agency of a structure securing obedience, is none the less a fact in science because it is a trite fact. This is a primary common trait in social aggregates derived from a common trait in their units. It is a truth in Sociology, comparable to the biological truth that the first step in the production of any living organism, high or low, is a certain differentiation whereby a peripheral portion becomes distinguished from a central portion. And such exceptions to this biological truth as we find in those minute non-nucleated portions of protoplasm that are the very lowest living things, are paralleled by those exceptions to the sociological truth, seen in the small incoherent assemblages formed by the very lowest types of men.

The differentiation of the regulating part and the regulated part, is, in small primitive societies, not only imperfectly established but vague. The chief does not at first become unlike his fellow-savages in his functions, otherwise than by exercising greater sway. He hunts, makes his weapons, works, and manages his private affairs, in just the same ways as the rest; while in war he differs from other warriors only by his predominant influence, not by ceasing to be a private soldier. And along with this slight separation from the rest of the tribe in military functions and industrial functions, there is only a slight separation politically: judicial action is but very feebly represented by exercise of his personal authority in keeping order.

At a higher stage, the power of the chief being well established, he no longer supports himself. Still he remains undistinguished industrially from other members of the dominant class, which has grown up while chieftainship has been getting settled; for he simply gets productive work done by deputy, as they do. Nor is a further extension of his power accompanied by complete separation of the political from the industrial functions; for he habitually remains a regulator of production, and in many cases a regulator of trade, presiding over acts of exchange. Of his several controlling activities, this last is, however, the one which he first ceases personally to carry on. Industry early shows a tendency towards self-control, apart from the control which the chief exercises more and more as political and military head. The primary social differentiation which we have noted between the regulative part and the operative part, is presently followed by a distinction, which eventually becomes very marked, between the internal arrangements of the two parts: the operative part slowly developing within itself agencies by which processes of production, distribution, and exchange are co-ordinated, while co-ordination of the non-operative part continues on its original footing.

Along with a development which renders conspicuous the separation of the operative and regulative structures, there goes a development within the regulative structures themselves. The chief, at first uniting the characters of king, judge, captain, and often priest, has his functions more and more specialized as the evolution of the society in size and complexity advances. Though remaining supreme judge, he does most of his judging by deputy; though remaining nominally head of his army, the actual leading of it falls more and more into the hands of subordinate officers; though still retaining ecclesiastical supremacy, his priestly functions practically almost cease; though in theory the maker and administrator of the law, the actual making and administration lapse more and more into other hands. So that, stating the facts broadly, out of the original co-ordinating agent having undivided functions, there eventually develop several co-ordinating agencies which divide these functions among them.

Each of these agencies, too, follows the same law. Originally simple, it step by step subdivides into many parts, and becomes an organization, administrative, judicial, ecclesiastical, or military, having graduated classes within itself, and a more or less distinct form of government within itself.

I will not complicate this statement by doing more than recognizing the variations that occur in cases where supreme power does not lapse into the hands of one man (which, however, in early stages of social evolution is an unstable modification). And I must explain that the above general statements are to be taken with the qualification that differences of detail are passed over to gain brevity and clearness. Add to which that it is beside the purpose of the argument to carry the description beyond these first stages. But duly bearing in mind that without here elaborating a Science of Sociology, nothing more than a rude outline of cardinal facts can be given, enough has been said to show that in the development of social structures, there may be recognized certain most-general facts, certain less-general facts, and certain facts successively more special; just as there may be recognized general and special facts of evolution in individual organisms.

To extend, as well as to make clearer, this conception of the Social Science, let me here set down a question which comes within its sphere. What is the relation in a society between structure and growth? Up to what point is structure necessary to growth? after what point does it retard growth? at what point does it arrest growth?

There exists in the individual organism a duplex relation between growth and structure which it is difficult adequately to express. Excluding the cases of a few low organisms living under special conditions, we may properly say that great growth is not possible without high structure. The whole animal kingdom, throughout its invertebrate and vertebrate types, may be cited in evidence. On the other hand, among the superior organisms, and especially among those leading active lives, there is a marked tendency for completion of structure to go along with arrest of growth. While an animal of elevated type is growing rapidly, its organs continue imperfectly developed—the bones remain partially cartilaginous, the muscles are soft, the brain lacks definiteness; and the details of structure throughout all parts are finished only after growth has ceased. Why these relations are as we find them, it is not difficult to see. That a young animal may grow, it must digest, circulate blood, breathe, excrete waste products, and so forth; to do which it must have tolerably-complete viscera, vascular system, &c. That it may eventually become able to get its own food, it has to develop gradually the needful appliances and aptitudes; to which end it must begin with limbs, and senses, and nervous system, that have considerable degrees of efficiency. But along with every increment of growth achieved by the help of these partially-developed structures, there has to go an alteration of the structures themselves. If they were rightly adjusted to the preceding smaller size, they are wrongly adjusted to the succeeding greater size. Hence they must be re-moulded—unbuilt and re-built. Manifestly, therefore, in proportion as the previous building has been complete, there arises a great obstacle in the shape of un-building and re-building. The bones show us how this difficulty is met. In the thigh-bone of a boy, for instance, there exists between the head and the cylindrical part of the bone, a place where the original cartilaginous state continues; and where, by the addition of new cartilage in which new osseous matter is deposited, the shaft of the bone is lengthened: the like going on in an answering place at the other end of the shaft. Complete ossification at these two places occurs only when the bone has ceased to increase in length; and, on considering what would have happened had the bone been ossified from end to end before its lengthening was complete, it will be seen how great an obstacle to growth is thus escaped. What holds here, holds throughout the organism: though structure up to a certain point is requisite for growth, structure beyond that point impedes growth. How necessary is this relation we shall equally perceive in a more complex case—say, the growth of an entire limb. There is a certain size and proportion of parts, which a limb ordinarily has in relation to the rest of the body. Throw upon that limb extra function, and within moderate limits it will increase in strength and bulk. If the extra function begins early in life, the limb may be raised considerably above its usual size; but if the extra function begins after maturity, the deviation is less: in neither case, however, being great. If we consider how increase of the limb is effected, we shall see why this is so. More active function brings a greater local supply of blood; and, for a time, new tissue is formed in excess of waste. But the local supply of blood is limited by the sizes of the arteries which bring it; and, though, up to a certain point, increase of flow is gained by temporary dilatation of them, yet beyond that point increase can be gained only by un-building and re-building the arteries. Such alterations of arteries slowly take place—less slowly with the smaller peripheral ones, more slowly with the larger ones out of which these branch; since these have to be altered all the way back to their points of divergence from the great central blood vessels. In like manner, the channels for carrying off waste products must be re-modelled, both locally and centrally. The nerve-trunks, too, and also the centres from which they come, must be adjusted to the greater demands upon them. Nay, more; with a given visceral system, a large extra quantity of blood cannot be permanently given to one part of the body, without decreasing the quantities given to other parts; and, therefore, structural changes have to be made by which the drafting-off of blood to these other parts is diminished. Hence the great resistance to increase in the size of a limb beyond a certain moderate limit. Such increase cannot be effected without un-building and re-building not only the parts that directly minister to the limb, but, eventually, all the remoter parts. So that the bringing of structures into perfect fitness for certain requirements, immensely hinders the adaptation of them to other requirements—re-adjustments become difficult in proportion as adjustments are made complete.

How far does this law hold in the social organism? To what extent does it happen here, too, that the multiplying and elaborating of institutions, and the perfecting of arrangements for gaining immediate ends, raise impediments to the development of better institutions and to the future gaining of higher ends? Socially, as well as individually, organization is indispensable to growth: beyond a certain point there cannot be further growth without further organization. Yet there is not a little reason for suspecting that beyond this point organization is indirectly repressive—increases the obstacles to those re-adjustments required for larger growth and more perfect structure. Doubtless the aggregate we call a society is much more plastic than an individual living aggregate to which it is here compared—its type is far less fixed. Nevertheless, there is evidence that its type tends continually to become fixed, and that each addition to its structures is a step towards the fixation. A few instances will show how this is true alike of the material structures a society develops and of its institutions, political or other.

Cases, insignificant, perhaps, but quite to the point, are furnished by our appliances for locomotion. Not to dwell on the minor ones within cities, which, however, show us that existing arrangements are impediments to better arrangements, let us pass to railways. Observe how the inconveniently-narrow gauge (which, taken from that of stage-coach wheels, was itself inherited from an antecedent system of locomotion), has become an insuperable obstacle to a better gauge. Observe, also, how the type of carriage, which was derived from the body of a stage-coach (some of the early first-class carriages bearing the words *"tria juncta in uno"*), having become established, it is immensely difficult now to introduce the more convenient type later established in America; where they profited by our experience, but were not hampered by our adopted plans. The enormous capital invested in our stock of carriages cannot be sacrificed. Gradually to introduce carriages of the American type, by running them along with those of our own type, would be very difficult, because of our many partings and joinings of trains. And thus we are obliged to go on with a type that is inferior.

Take, again, our system of drainage. Urged on as it was some thirty years ago as a panacea for sundry sanitary evils, and spread as it has been by force of law through all our great towns, this system cannot now be replaced by a better system without extreme difficulty. Though, by necessitating decomposition where oxygen cannot get, and so generating chemical compounds that are unstable and poisonous, it has in many cases produced the very diseases it was to have prevented; though, by delivering the morbid products from fever-patients, &c., into a branching tube which, communicating with all houses, effectually conveys to them infecting gases that are kept out only so long as stink-traps are in good order; yet it has become almost out of the question now to adopt those methods by which the *excreta* of towns may be got rid of at once innocuously and usefully. Nay, worse—one part of our sanitary administration having insisted on a sewage-system by which Oxford, Reading, Maidenhead, Windsor, &c., pollute the water London has to drink, another part of our sanitary administration makes loud protests against the impurity of the water, which it charges with causing disease (not remarking, however, that law-enforced arrangements have produced the impurity). And now there must be a re-organization that will be immensely impeded by the existing premature organization, before we can have either pure air or pure water.

Our mercantile arrangements, again, furnish abundant illustrations teaching the same lesson. In each trade there is an established course of business; and however obvious may be some better course, the difficulties of altering the settled routine are, if not insurmountable, still very considerable. Take, for instance, the commerce of literature. In days when a letter cost a shilling and no book-post existed, there grew up an organization of wholesalers and retailers to convey books from publishers to readers: a profit being reached by each distributing agent, primary and secondary. Now that a book may be ordered for a half-penny and sent for a few pence, the old system of distribution might be replaced by one that would diminish the cost of transfer, and lower the prices of books. But the interests of distributors practically negative the change. An advertised proposal to supply a book direct by post at a reduced rate, offends the trade; and by ignoring the book they check its sale more than its sale is otherwise furthered. And so an old organization, once very serviceable, now stands in the way of a better organization. The commerce of literature furnishes another illustration. At a time when the reading public was small and books were dear, there grew up circulating libraries, enabling people to read books without buying them. At first few, local, and unorganized, these circulating libraries have greatly multiplied, and have become organized throughout the kingdom: the result being that the demand for library-circulation is in many cases the chief demand. This arrangement being one which makes few copies supply many readers, the price per copy must be high, to obtain an adequate return on the edition. And now reading people in general, having been brought up to the habit of getting books through libraries, usually do not think of buying the books themselves—would still get most of them through libraries even were they considerably cheapened. We are, therefore, except with works of very popular authors, prevented by the existing system of book-distribution in England from adopting the American system—a system which, not adjusting itself to few libraries but to many private purchasers, issues large editions at low prices.

Instances of another class are supplied by our educational institutions. Richly endowed, strengthened by their *prestige,* and by the bias given to those they have brought up, our colleges, public schools, and other kindred schools early founded, useful as they once were, have long been enormous impediments to a higher education. By subsidizing the old, they have starved the new. Even now they are retarding a culture better in matter and manner; both by occupying the field, and by partially incapacitating those who pass through them for seeing what a better culture is. Evidence of a kindred kind is offered by the educational organization developed for dealing with the masses. The struggle going on between Secularism and Denominationalism in teaching, might alone show to any one who looks for the wider meanings of facts, that a structure which has ramified throughout a society, acquired an army of salaried officials looking for personal welfare and promotion, backed by classes, ecclesiastical and political, whose ideas and interests they further, is a structure which, if not unalterable, is difficult to alter in proportion as it is highly developed.

These few examples, which might be supported by others from the military organization, the ecclesiastical organization, the legal organization, will make comprehensible the analogy I have indicated; while they make clearer the nature of the Social Science, by bringing into view one of its questions. That with social organisms, as with individual organisms, structure up to a certain point is needful for growth is obvious. That in the one case, as in the other, continued growth implies un-building and re-building of structure, which therefore becomes in so far an impediment, seems also obvious. Whether it is true in the one case, as in the other, that completion of structure involves arrest of growth, and fixes the society to the type it has then reached, is a question to be considered. Without saying anything more by way of answer, it is, I think, manifest enough that this is one belonging to an order of questions entirely overlooked by those who contemplate societies from the ordinary historical point of view; and one pertaining to that Social Science which they say does not exist.

2

B. Seebohm Rowntree

THE CAUSES OF POVERTY

IT IS NO PART of the object of this chapter to discuss the ultimate causes of poverty. To attempt this would be to raise the whole social question. The object is rather to indicate the immediate causes of (a) "primary" poverty, and (b) "secondary" poverty in York.

a) Immediate Causes of "Primary" Poverty
These appear to fall under the following headings:—
1) Death of chief wage-earner.
2) Incapacity of chief wage-earner through accident, illness, or old age.
3) Chief wage-earner out of work.
4) Chronic irregularity of work (sometimes due to incapacity or unwillingness of worker to undertake regular employment).
5) Largeness of family, *i.e.* cases in which the family is in poverty because there are more than four children, though it would not have been in poverty had the number of children not exceeded four.
6) Lowness of wage, *i.e.* where the chief wage-earner is in regular work, but at wages which are insufficient to maintain a

Reprinted from *Poverty: A Study of Town Life*, 1901, chapter 5, "The Immediate Causes of Poverty." By 1900 the new consciousness generated by Spencer, Booth, and the debates of the previous generation was beginning to take shape in empirical sociology. Of a large number of studies Rowntree's is unquestionably the one that comes nearest to satisfying all the professional criteria of modern social science—if only because it uses an empirical method for clearly specified analytical purposes.

moderate family (*i.e.* not more than four children) in a state of physical efficiency.

On analysing the cases of "primary" poverty in York, we find that they are immediately due to one or other of the above causes in the following proportions:—

Sec-tion	No. of House-holds affected	Immediate Cause of "Primary" Poverty	No. of Chil-dren af-fected	No. of Adults af-fected	Total Num-ber af-fected	Percentage of Total Population living under "Primary" Poverty Line
1.	403*	Death of chief wage-earner .	460	670	1130	15.63
2.	146	Illness or old age of chief wage-earner	81	289	370	5.11
3.	38	Chief wage-earner out of work	78	89	167	2.31
4.	51	Irregularity of work	94	111	205	2.83
5.	187	Largeness of family, *i.e.* more than four children	1122	480	1602	22.16
6.	640	In regular work, but at low wages	2380	1376	3756	51.96
	1465		4215	3015	7230	100.00

° In this section are also included fourteen cases of women deserted by, or separated from, their husbands.

Let us now examine in greater detail the above sections of the population living in "primary" poverty. Sections 1 and 2 may be suitably considered together, the immediate cause of poverty being either the death or the incapacity of the chief wage-earner.

SECTIONS 1 AND 2

Comprising together 20.74 per cent of the population living in "primary" poverty.

	Section 1 (Death of Chief Wage-Earner)	Section 2 (Ill-ness or Old Age of Chief Wage-Earner)
Total number of persons	1130	370
Number of families	403	146
Average size of family	2.85	2.53
Average family earnings	8s. 7d.	5s. 7¼d.
Average rent	2s. 11½d.	2s. 8¾d.

The families in these two sections are, with few exceptions, included in Class "A," described on pp. 58 *et seq.* A brief summary of their economic condition will therefore suffice here.

Only 367 of the 549 families are earning money, their aggregate weekly earnings amounting to £200:11s., which is equal to 10s. 11d. per family. This sum is contributed by householders and supplementary workers in the following proportion:—

	Total Sum			Per Family	
	£	s.	d.	s.	d.
Contributed by householders	136	8	0	7	5¼
Contributed by supplementary earners	64	3	0	3	5¾
	£200	11	0	10	11

The occupations of the 367 householders who are earning money are as under:—

> 165 are charwomen.
> 78 are washerwomen.
> 28 take lodgers.
> 18 are dressmakers, etc.
> 16 are labourers (old men).
> 12 are field labourers (women).
> 10 are nurses.
> 10 are North Eastern Railway Company's employees (women).
>   8 work in confectionery factories.
>   7 are small shopkeepers.
>   4 are employed in glass works (women).
>   4 are pensioners.
>   3 are shoemakers.
>   2 are hawkers.
>   1 is a tinner (old).
>   1 is a joiner (old).
> ———
> 367

As far as could be ascertained, the remaining 182 householders are earning no money, but are dependent upon public and private charity for their support.

Considering the two sections as a whole we find that the total rent paid weekly amounts to £73:12:3, equal to an average of 2s. 10¾d. per family.

The economic condition of these two sections may be gathered from the following statement:—

Income	£	s.	d.	Expenditure	£	s.	d.
Weekly estimated income of 367 families	200	11	0	Weekly rent	73	12	3
182 families without income	0	0	0	Weekly minimum cost of food and sundries, necessary to maintain 959			
Weekly poor relief	64	3	6*	adults and 541 children			
Weekly balance—				in a state of physical			
Deficiency	111	13	5	efficiency	302	15	8
(= 4s. 10¾d. per family)							
	£376	7	11		£376	7	11

* These figures, and others on subsequent pages, regarding poor relief were obtained by examination of the official records.

A consideration of this statement of income and expenditure, and of the number of persons who are living under the conditions which it indicates, reminds us how precarious are the lives of the poor, who are at all times liable to be plunged into poverty by the death or illness of the chief wage-earner. It must be borne in mind that Sections 1 and 2 comprise not only adults, but 541 children.

SECTION 3

Comprising 2.31 per cent of the total population living in "primary" poverty.

IMMEDIATE CAUSE OF POVERTY: CHIEF WAGE-EARNER
OUT OF WORK

Total number of persons	167
Number of families	38
Average size of family	4.34
Average family income	5s. 3d.
Average rent	3s. 1½d.

The occupations ordinarily followed by the men returned as out of work are as follows:—

25 labourers	3 comb makers
1 gardener	1 butcher
1 waiter	1 sawyer
1 gilder	1 grocer's assistant
1 wheelwright	1 bricklayer
1 carter	38
1 gasfitter	

This list does not include all the men out of work in York, but only those whose lack of work causes them to come below the "primary" poverty line. It must also be remembered that, as pointed out on p. 74, the inquiry was made at a time when there was an almost unexampled demand for labour (summer 1899).

The total weekly earnings of this section amount to £10, equal to 5s. 3d. per family. This is all earned by supplementary earners.

The following statement shows the weekly income and necessary expenditure of Section 3:—

Income				*Expenditure*			
	£	s.	d.		£	s.	d.
Weekly income of 38 families	10	0	0	Weekly rent	5	18	8
Weekly poor relief	1	0	0	Weekly minimum cost of food			
Weekly balance—Deficiency	25	15	8	and sundries necessary to			
(= 13s. 6¾d. per family)				maintain 89 adults and			
	£36	15	8	78 children in a state of			
				physical efficiency	30	17	0
					£36	15	8

The heavy deficiency, amounting to 13s. 6¾d. per family, is met mainly by foregoing the necessaries of physical efficiency, and by running into debt, especially with the pawnbroker, the landlord, and with small shopkeepers. If the lack of work continues for a considerable period, the burden of debt upon the family becomes very heavy, and may take years to clear off. A part of the above deficiency may be precariously relieved by private charity and by picking up "odd jobs."

Section 5

Comprising 22.16 per cent of the total population living in "primary" poverty.

Immediate Cause of Poverty: Largeness of Family°

Total number of persons	1602
Number of families	187
Average size of family	8.56
Average family earnings	29s. 6½d.
Average rent	4s. 4½d.

° The average size of families in York, according to the 1901 census returns, was 4.71; the figure for England and Wales was 4.61.

A large family is, of course, only a cause for poverty so long as the children are dependent upon the wages of the householder. As soon as the children begin to earn money they become a source of income. But the poverty period, with its accompaniments of underfeeding, scanty clothing, and overcrowding, lasts during the first ten or more years of their lives, a circumstance which cannot fail to arrest their mental and physical development.

This section comprises almost a quarter of those who are living in "primary" poverty. The number of children per family varies from five to ten, the average being six.

There are 66 households with 5 children

    "   76   "   6   "

    "   29   "   7   "

    "   12   "   8   "

    "   3   "   9   "

    "   1   "   10   "

       187

The total weekly income of this section is £276:6:6, which is contributed by householders and supplementary earners in the following proportions:—

	Total Sum			Per Family	
	£	s.	d.	s.	d.
Contributed by householders	243	13	0	26	0¾
	32	13	6	3	5¾
Contributed by supplementary workers	£276	6	6	29	6½

The occupations of the heads of households are as follows:—

27 blacksmiths, strikers, etc.	4 butchers
15 painters	3 glassblowers
16 joiners, etc.	3 plumbers
6 bricklayers	3 bootmakers
14 railway employees	2 confectioners
6 furnishing trades	2 police constables
6 tailors	1 corkcutter
1 electrician	1 schoolmaster
1 maltster	1 asylum attendant
1 sweep	7 clerks
1 commercial traveller	47 labourers
1 waiter	4 carters
1 general shopkeeper	3 dairymen
1 compositor	4 cabdrivers
1 postman	3 watermen
1 druggist	

    187

The following statement shows the income and estimated necessary expenditure of Section 5:—

Income	£	s.	d.	Expenditure	£	s.	d.
Weekly income of 187 families	276	6	6	Weekly rent	40	18	7
Weekly parish relief	2	5	0	Weekly minimum cost of food and sundries necessary to maintain 480 adults and 94 children in a state of physical efficiency	264	1	10
Weekly balance— Deficiency .... (= 2s. 9¾d. per family)	26	8	11				
	£305	0	5		£305	0	5

SECTION 6

Comprising 51.96 per cent of the total population living in "primary" poverty.

IMMEDIATE CAUSE OF POVERTY: LOWNESS OF WAGE

Total number of persons	3756
Number of families	640
Average size of family	5.86
Average family earnings	18s. 9d.
Average rent	3s. 6½d.

This section comprises more than half of the persons who are living in "primary" poverty.

The total weekly earnings of this section amount to £600, which is contributed by householders and supplementary workers in the following proportions:—

	Total Sum			Per Family	
	£	s.	d.	s.	d.
Contributed by householders	586	14	0	18	4
Contributed by supplementary workers	13	6	0	0	5*
	£600	0	0	18	9

* It will be noticed that the average sum earned by the supplementary earners is much smaller than in the other sections. The explanation of this is to be found in the fact, that in this section the chief wage-earner is in every case in receipt of a regular income, and as soon as the earnings of the children become considerable the family rises above the "primary" poverty line. The families below it are therefore chiefly those with young children who are not earning wages.

The occupations of the heads of households in this section are as follows:—

469 general labourers*
47 carters, cabmen, grooms, etc.
21 painters' labourers
19 railway employees
12 small shopkeepers
12 cobblers
9 clerks
8 chimney sweeps
7 gardeners
5 butchers
5 tailoring trade

8 postal service, etc.
3 watermen
3 furniture removers
2 porters
2 packers
8 —one each tanner, milkman, waiter, lamplighter, teacher of music, barman, hairdresser, and bookbinder

_____
640

* Many of these are engaged in factories or on the railway.

The following statement shows the income and estimated necessary expenditure of Section 6:—

Income	£	s.	d.	*Expenditure*	£	s.	d.
Weekly income of 640 families	600	0	0	Weekly rent	112	15	5
Weekly balance—				Weekly minimum cost of food and sundries necessary to maintain 1376 adults and 2380 children in a state of physical efficiency	648	2	0
Deficiency	160	17	5				
(= 5s. 0¼d. per family)							
	£760	17	5		£760	17	5

It will have been noticed that Section 6 consists of unskilled workers of various grades, 73 per cent being general labourers; whilst the others holding the lower posts in their respective occupations are employed upon work which is scarcely more difficult or responsible than that of the general labourer, and whose wages are consequently only slightly, if at all, in excess of those paid to the latter. That so many wage-earners should be in a state of primary poverty will not be surprising to those who have read the preceding pages. Allowing for broken time, the average wage for a labourer in York is from 18s. to 21s.; whereas, according to the figures given earlier in this chapter, the minimum expenditure necessary to maintain in a state of physical efficiency a family of two adults and three children is 21s. 8d,[1] or, if there are four children, the sum required would be 26s.

It is thus seen that *the wages paid for unskilled labour in York are insufficient to provide food, shelter, and clothing adequate to maintain a family of moderate size in a state of bare physical efficiency.* It will be remembered that the above estimates of necessary minimum expenditure are based upon the assumption that the diet is even less generous than that allowed to able-bodied paupers in the York Workhouse, and that *no allowance is made for any expenditure other than that absolutely required for the maintenance of merely physical efficiency.*

And let us clearly understand what "merely physical efficiency" means. A family living upon the scale allowed for in this estimate must never spend a penny on railway fare or omnibus. They must never go into the country unless they walk. They must never purchase a halfpenny newspaper or spend a penny to buy a ticket for a popular concert. They must write no letters to absent children, for they cannot afford to pay the postage. They must never contribute anything to their church or chapel, or give any help to a neighbour which costs them money. They cannot save, nor can they join sick club or Trade Union, because they cannot pay the necessary subscriptions. The children must have no pocket money for dolls, marbles, or sweets. The father must smoke no tobacco, and must drink no beer. The mother must never buy any pretty clothes for herself or for her children, the character of the family wardrobe as for the family diet being governed by the regulation, "Nothing must be bought but that which is absolutely necessary for the maintenance of physical health, and what is bought must be of the plainest and most economical description." Should a child

		s.	d.
1	This estimate is arrived at thus:		
	Food—two adults at 3s.	6	0
	three children at 2s. 3d.	6	9
	Rent—say	4	0
	Clothes—two adults at 6d.	1	0
	three children at 5d.	1	3
	Fuel	1	10
	All else—five persons at 2d.	0	10
	Total	21	8

fall ill, it must be attended by the parish doctor; should it die, it must be buried by the parish. Finally, the wage-earner must never be absent from his work for a single day.

If any of these conditions are broken, the extra expenditure involved is met, *and can only be met,* by limiting the diet; or, in other words, by sacrificing physical efficiency.

That few York labourers receiving 20s. or 21s. per week submit to these iron conditions in order to maintain physical efficiency is obvious. And even were they to submit, physical efficiency would be unattainable for those who had three or more children dependent upon them. It cannot therefore be too clearly understood, nor too emphatically repeated, *that whenever a worker having three children dependent on him, and receiving not more than 21s. 8d. per week, indulges in any expenditure beyond that required for the barest physical needs, he can do so only at the cost of his own physical efficiency, or of that of some members of his family.*

If a labourer has but two children, these conditions will be better to the extent of 2s. 10d.; and if he has but one, they will be better to the extent of 5s. 8d. And, again, as soon as his children begin to work, their earnings will raise the family above the poverty line. But the fact remains that every labourer who has as many as three children must pass through a time, probably lasting for about ten years, when he will be in a state of "primary" poverty; in other words, when he and his family will be *underfed.*[2]

[2]   Some readers may be inclined to say, upon reading the above, "This surely is an over-statement. Look at the thousands of families with incomes of 18s. to 21s., or even less, where the men *do* smoke and *do* spend money upon drink, and the women *do* spend money on dress and recreation, and yet, in spite of it all, they seem happy and contented, and the men make good workmen!" Such arguments against the actual pressure and the consequences of poverty will, however, upon closer investigation be found to be illusory. They come amongst a class of arguments against which Bastiat, the French economist, warned his readers in a series of articles entitled, "That which is seen, and that which is not seen." In these articles the writer pointed out the danger of forming judgments upon social and economic questions without thoroughly investigating them.

In the argument referred to above, the money spent by the poor upon

The life of a labourer is marked by five alternating periods of want and comparative plenty. During early childhood, unless his father is a skilled worker, he probably will be in poverty; this will last until he, or some of his brothers or sisters, begin to earn money and thus augment their father's wage sufficiently to raise the family above the poverty line. Then follows the period during which he is earning money and living under his parents' roof; for some portion of this period he will be earning more money than is required for lodging, food, and clothes. This is his chance to save money. If he has saved enough to pay for furnishing a cottage, this period of comparative prosperity may continue after marriage until he has two or three children, when poverty will again overtake him. This period of poverty will last perhaps for ten years, *i.e.* until the first child is fourteen years old and begins to earn wages; but if there are more than three children it may last longer.[3] While the children are earning, and before they leave the home to marry, the man enjoys another period of prosperity—possibly, however, only to sink back again into poverty when his children have married and left him, and he himself is too old to work, for

---

drink, dress, or recreation is one of the *"things that are seen."* There are, however, consequences of poverty which are *"not seen."*

We *see* that many a labourer, who has a wife and three or four children, is healthy and a good worker, although he only earns a pound a week. What we do *not see* is that in order to give him enough food, mother and children habitually go short, for the mother knows that all depends upon the wages of her husband.

We *see* the man go to the public-house and spend money on drink; we do *not see* the children going supperless to bed in consequence.

These unseen consequences of poverty have, however, to be reckoned with—the high death-rate among the poor, the terribly high infant mortality, the stunted stature and dulled intelligence,—all these and others are not seen unless we look beneath the surface; and yet all are having their effect upon the poor, and consequently upon the whole country.

I would therefore ask any readers who think I have over-stated my case in the preceding pages to defer judgment until they read Chapter VII., where the question of "Poverty and the Health Standard" is dealt with.

3   It is to be noted that the family are in poverty, and consequently are underfed, during the first ten or more years of the children's lives.

his income has never permitted his saving enough for him and his wife to live upon for more than a very short time.

A labourer is thus in poverty, and therefore underfed—

a In childhood—when his constitution is being built up.

b In early middle life—when he should be in his prime.

c In old age.

It should be noted that the women are in poverty during the greater part of the period that they are bearing children.

We thus see that the 7230 persons shown by this inquiry to be in a state of "primary" poverty, *represent merely that section who happened to be in one of these poverty periods at the time the inquiry was made.* Many of these will, in course of time, pass on into a period of comparative prosperity; this will take place as soon as the children, now dependent, begin to earn. But their places below the poverty line will be taken by others who are at present living in that prosperous period previous to, or shortly after, marriage. Again, many now classed as above the poverty line were below it until the children began to earn. The proportion of the community who at one period or other of their lives suffer from poverty to the point of physical privation is therefore much greater, and the injurious effects of such a condition are much more widespread than would appear from a consideration of the number who can be shown to be below the poverty line at any given moment.

How widespread the effects of "primary" poverty are cannot be exactly stated, but when (in Chap. VII.) we consider the connection existing between poverty and a low physical condition, figures will be put forward which will throw some light upon the matter.[4]

The above remarks regarding the poverty periods in a labourer's life emphasise the fact that the great opportunity for a

---

[4]   There is no doubt that poor people are often very good to each other, and that those who are in the poverty period not infrequently receive gifts of clothes and food from friends and relatives who are in the stages of less pressure. Whilst such assistance mitigates the full pressure of want in certain cases, it is neither general enough nor sufficient in amount to interfere with the argument set forth above.

labourer to save money is after he has reached manhood, and before marriage. In view of this consideration, it was felt that it would be of interest to ascertain whether the age at which labourers marry is early in comparison with that of other sections of the community.

With this object the writer has obtained particulars regarding the marriages which took place in York during 1898 and 1899, the age and occupation of the bridegroom and the age of the bride being ascertained in each case. In most cases the street in which the bridegroom lived was ascertained, but the name of bride or bridegroom was not ascertained in any case. Information was obtained regarding 1123 marriages of persons belonging to the working class. In the case of 626 of these the bridegrooms were skilled workers, while 497 were unskilled labourers.

An examination of the ages at which these 1123 persons married shows that while nearly one-third of the labourers married under twenty-three years of age, less than one-fifth of the skilled workers did so, and that 58 per cent of the labourers married under twenty-six years as compared with 49 per cent of the skilled workers.

The following table shows the number of each class who married at various ages (1898–99) :

Age at Marriage	Skilled Workers		Labourers	
	Number	Per Cent	Number	Per Cent
Under 20	3	.5	21	4.2
20–22	114	18.2	138	27.2
23–25	188	30.0	132	26.5
26–30	174	27.8	117	23.5
31–35	61	9.8	40	8.1
36–40	19	3.0	22	4.5
41–45	29	4.6	7	1.4
46–50	15	2.4	7	1.4
Over 50	23	3.7	13	2.7
	626	100.0	497	100.0

In view of the above figures, it is clear that a considerably larger proportion of labourers than of skilled workers marry young. This fact no doubt indicates how the exercise of prudence and of forethought increases as you advance in the social scale, but two other important causes of early marriages amongst the labouring class must not be overlooked, viz.—

1. The overcrowded condition of the homes from which the labourers chiefly come makes them anxious to have a home of their own, in which, at any rate, so long as there are no children, they will be free from the many inconveniences inseparable from overcrowded surroundings.

2. Generally speaking, the labourers have fewer intellectual interests and pleasures than skilled workers, and doubtless some of them enter upon marriage partly with a view to relieving the monotony of their lives.

Immediate Causes of "Secondary" Poverty

Number of persons living in "secondary"
    poverty in York 13,072
Percentage of total population 18.51
Percentage of working-class population 28

It will be remembered that the amount of "secondary" poverty was arrived at by estimating the total poverty in York, and then subtracting the "primary" poverty, which had been previously ascertained.

The amount of "primary" poverty was based upon a low estimate of the minimum expenditure necessary for the maintenance of physical efficiency. Had a higher estimate been adopted, the effect would have been to increase the proportion of "primary" poverty and to decrease the proportion of "secondary" poverty.

On p. 144 it was pointed out that in addition to those returned as being in "primary" poverty, there are no fewer than 2312 persons belonging to families with incomes only 2s. above the standard adopted in fixing the "primary" poverty line. In other words, these families are living practically *on* the "primary" poverty line. Had they been included amongst those returned as being in "primary" poverty, the proportion of "primary" to total poverty would have been raised from 35.6 per cent to 47 per cent, and the proportion of "secondary" to total poverty would have fallen correspondingly from 64.4 per cent to 53 per cent. It is thus seen that the point at which "primary" passes into "secondary" poverty is largely a matter of opinion, depending upon the standard of well-being which is considered necessary. But even if a higher standard were chosen than that adopted in the preceding chapter when fixing the "primary" poverty line, there would still remain a considerable amount of poverty indisputably "secondary" which would appear to be mainly due to the following immediate causes, namely— Drink, betting, and gambling. Ignorant or careless housekeeping, and other improvident expenditure, the latter often induced by irregularity of income. It is not possible to ascertain the proportion of "secondary" poverty assignable to each of the above causes; probably all are factors in the poverty of many households, and they act and react powerfully upon each other. There can be but little doubt, however, that the predominant factor is drink. I have been unable to form any close estimate of the average sum spent weekly upon drink by working-class families in York, but a careful estimate has been made by others of the average sum expended weekly by working-class families throughout the United Kingdom. This average is arrived at, in the first instance, by dividing that portion of the yearly national drink-bill which competent authorities assign to the working classes by the number of working-class families in England. This results in a figure of 6s. 10d. as the average weekly sum spent upon drink by each such family. This estimate has been examined in great detail by Messrs. Rowntree and Sherwell, who have tested the figure in a great number of ways. The result of their investigation is summed up as follows:—"That a large proportion of the working classes spend very much less than the amount suggested is certain, but it is equally certain that a considerable number spend very much more, and when all possible deductions have been made, it is doubtful if the average family expenditure of the working classes upon intoxicants can be reckoned at less than 6s. per week."

There is no reason to suppose that the average sum spent upon drink by working-class families in York is lower than the average for the United Kingdom. An expenditure of 6s. per family upon drink would absorb more than one-sixth of the average total family income of the working classes of York.

With regard to betting and gambling, it is obviously not possible to obtain even approximate statistics regarding the extent to which the habit prevails amongst the working classes, or to measure the amount of poverty which it causes. There is, however, ample evidence that it is very largely indulged in not only by working men, but also by women, and, to a lesser extent, even by children. Some evidence regarding the magnitude of the evil is afforded by the following extract from *The Bulletin*, November 1896: "A York bookmaker was shown to have had 3500 transactions in one month, in sums varying from 6d. to 4s. This did not include York races." A good deal of general evidence in support of the view that the habit of betting and gambling is not only a great but a growing evil amongst the working classes was gathered during the course of the present inquiry, but it is difficult to reduce it to any definite statement.

Though we speak of the above causes as those mainly accounting for most of the "secondary" poverty, it must not be forgotten that they are themselves often the outcome of the adverse conditions under which too many of the working classes live. Housed for the most part in sordid streets, frequently under overcrowded and unhealthy conditions, compelled very often to earn their bread by monotonous and laborious work, and unable, partly through limited education and partly through overtime and other causes of physical exhaustion, to enjoy intellectual recreation, what wonder that many of these people fall a ready prey to the publican and the bookmaker? The limited horizon of the mother has a serious effect upon her children; their home interests are narrow and unattractive, and too often they grow up prepared to seek relief from the monotony of their work and environment in the public-house, or in the excitement of betting.

The writer is not forgetful of the larger questions bearing upon the welfare of human society which lie at the back of the considerations just advanced. It would, however, lead into fields of thought beyond the scope of this volume adequately to state these problems. Probably it will be admitted that they include questions dealing with land tenure, with the relative duties and powers of the State and of the individual, and with legislation affecting the aggregation or the distribution of wealth. While the immediate causes of "secondary" poverty call for well-considered and resolute action, its ultimate elimination will only be possible when these causes are dealt with as a part of, and in relation to, the wider social problem.

3

J. A. Hobson

SOCIOLOGICAL INTERPRE-
TATION OF A GENERAL
ELECTION

IF, AS HAS BEEN SAID, prophecy is the most gratuitous
form of human error, interpretation of current politics may be
conceded the second place. For the ideal interpreter is himself a
contradiction in terms. Interpretation is impossible without a
sympathetic understanding, and a sympathy directed with entire
impartiality and, what is more, capable of convincing others of
that impartiality, is not attainable. For what sort of a citizen would
he be, who in the present current of public affairs, could guarantee
to himself or to others this complete impartiality? An intelligent
foreigner might indeed set forth the measurable facts of the subject without bias, but he could hardly give them the meaning and
the valuation essential to the process of interpretation.

I shall not pretend the impossible. Though my treatment will
be as 'sociological' as I can make it, the fact that I entertain certain
political opinions implies, even in selection and ordering of material, still more in valuation and interpretation, a measure of bias
for which each member of my audience must make his own allowance. I shall be content if I can keep this bias within bounds

Reprinted from "The General Election: A Sociological Interpretation,"
The Sociological Review, 1910. So far as I know this was a new departure
in British social analysis. Since Hobson used no survey procedures his work
hardly bears comparison with electoral sociology since *The People's
Choice.* Nevertheless his attempt to interpret gross turn-out and party-
preference data in terms of class and regional variations clearly places Hobson in the modern rather than the classical tradition of political science.

and fairly constant in direction and intensity. For then I shall afford to those who see events with different eyes the best conditions for making an intelligible adjustment for themselves.

In laying before you what appear to me to be the chief measurable facts disclosed by the result of the general election, I must ask your further to remember that time compels a very rigorous economy of selection. Much relevant and interesting matter must be omitted from our survey.

The election results must be considered in the first place as disclosing two facts: first, the present judgment of the electorate upon a set of issues forming the substance of two, or in some cases three, policies, and recommended by the prestige of party names and leaders; second, the change that has taken place in the electoral preference since the election of four years ago qualified by some eighty bye-elections. For our purpose it is best to pay most attention to analysis and interpretation of the present judgment; for, if we hold the electoral choice to be directed at least as much by consideration of policy as of party allegiance, we shall recognise that the shift of important issues since 1906 has been so considerable as to invalidate to an unknown extent an attempt to interpret the swing of the pendulum in any close relation to particular issues.

For obvious convenience I shall in most of my account omit Ireland, confining myself to the election in Great Britain. Some of the few figures I present will be merely approximate, partly because exact figures are not always attainable, partly because round figures are more easily comprehended and do no harm where no argument depends on their exactness.

Taking first the General Election as a Plebiscite, and counting Liberal and Labour votes together, as we are justified in doing from their close agreement on the dominant issues, we reach the following result for Great Britain:—

Liberal and Labour	Unionist	Majority
3,185,250	2,904,001	281,249

a majority amounting to about 4¾ per cent. This plebiscite is of course very differently proportioned in relation to the different groups of constituencies. In London the Unionist majority amounted to about 6¾ per cent.: in the English boroughs the Liberal majority was about 4 per cent., in the English counties about ⅞ per cent. In Wales the Liberal vote was considerably more than double the Unionist vote (206,288 to 97,126) : in Scotland the majority was nearly 20 per cent.

It will be evident from consideration of this result that, as usual, the numbers of members of the parties elected bear no just relation to the aggregate party vote.

If an equal value were secured for every vote, the majority for the Liberal and Labour parties in Great Britain would be, not 63, the actual number, but 27. The operation of our electoral machinery, as is well recognised, tends to favour the stronger party, giving it a majority in excess of its proportionate majority of votes. This excess, though considerable, is, however, far smaller than in most recent elections, as the following figures show:—

Vote Majorities

	1895	1900	1906	1910
Great Britain	U. 310,632	322,974	L. 636,418	L. 281,249
Maj. in Seats	U. 213	U. 195	L. 289	L. 63

In regarding the election as a measure of public opinion, it would, however, be necessary to exclude plural voting. This introduces a considerable element of conjecture into our arithmetic. The number of out-voters is not known. It is often roughly estimated, upon what evidence I know not, at half a million, or about 1 in 13 of the votes cast. If this is even approximately true, it evidently makes a considerable readjustment necessary in estimating the election as a plebiscite. For no one will contend that these outvotes are equally apportioned between the two parties. In the recent election it is not unreasonable to believe that four out of five were cast for the Unionist party. This estimate is defended by urging that plural voting is virtually confined to men of property, the overwhelming majority of whom, especially in the South of England where outvoters chiefly dwell, vote conservative. If half a million of such votes were actually cast and four out of five went to a Unionist, this would be equivalent to a weighting of the Unionist poll by an additional 10 per cent. of votes. Or, putting the matter in another way, the abolition of the plural voting at this election would have doubled the actual majority of Liberal votes in Great Britain, raising the majority of Liberal and Labour members, under a system of one vote one value, to a figure a little below the 63 which is their actual majority.

It is now time to consider the geographical and economic distribution of political opinion as indicated by party victories in the election. First, we are confronted by that remarkable contrast of North and South which first strikes the eye on glancing at the electoral map. A line drawn across Great Britain along the Mersey and the Trent shows an overwhelming majority of Liberal and Labour seats in the northern section, an almost equally overwhelming majority of Unionist seats in the southern section, if Wales be left out of the account. This geographical generalisation, however, requires important qualifications. The uniformity of the Unionist South is broken by substantial patches of Liberalism in the industrial part of the Metropolis, in Cornwall and Devon, and in Norfolk and Lincolnshire. Upon the other hand Unionism makes two considerable encroachments upon the Liberal North, one along the sea-coast constituencies East and West, another in a slanting wedge working through Staffordshire and Cheshire towards a point in North Lancashire. The predominance of Unionism throughout the coast constituencies is very marked, amounting in the south to an almost complete possession. The general contrast of North and South is sharpened by the fact that the further North you go the greater the compactness and the uniformity of Liberalism, while Conservatism becomes correspondingly more intense the further South you go.

The list of party gains which marks most forcibly the change of political opinion since 1906 gives striking testimony to the same general truth, showing that the Liberalism of the North is virtually unmoved, during a period when the South has undergone a profound change. For, of the 117 seats gained by Unionists in England, 13 only stand above the line of Trent and Mersey, while 9 Liberal and Labour gains above that line reduce the net Unionist gain in the Northern Counties to 4. In Scotland the net Unionist gain was none, five seats being won by them and five lost.

A truer electoral map, which indicated by a deepening of the representative colours the size or proportion of the majority by which each seat was held, would upon the whole enforce still further the contrast of North and South, showing proportionate Liberal majorities which grew larger as you went further North, Unionist majorities largest in the most Southern Counties. The special case of the Birmingham sphere of influence would, however, qualify the operation of this general rule.

Before turning to the interpretation of these broad results I ought to remind you that the proportion of the distribution of seats in North and South respectively gives of necessity a very exaggerated notion of the distribution of political opinion. So long as there is no provision for the proportionate representation of minorities this is inevitable. The effect is to induce a belief that the North is more Liberal, the South more Conservative than is actually the case. Even in Lancashire where the Liberals claim a signal victory it is asserted by the *National Review* that nearly 45 per cent. of the votes recorded were cast for Tariff Reform.

Now, taking this geographical distribution of parties as indicated by the electoral results, we can easily apply some general principles of economic criticism. North and South correspond with certain economic distinctions. The great productive industries of manufacture and of mining are almost entirely Northern, while the South is more agricultural, its manufactures are small and less highly organised, and it contains a large number of pleasure resorts and residential towns and villages.

The statement that industrial Britain is Liberal, rural and residential Britain Conservative, is substantially accurate. It may be tested variously. London itself may be cited as a witness. Indeed the geographical distribution of electoral results in the Metropolis is the most striking corroboration of the economic interpretation of the larger contrast between North and South. For in London, East and West correspond economically with the division of North and South in the country taken as a whole, and, as a glance at the map will show, the East is entirely Liberal, the West entirely

Unionist, in each case with the one exception which saves the appearance of unnatural exactitude. But when we turn from London, whose industrial conditions are unique, to the great manufacturing towns of the Midlands and the North, we find an overwhelming preponderance of Liberal seats. Even the exceptions form the rule, for Birmingham, Liverpool, Wolverhampton, Nottingham, Preston, Sunderland, are all susceptible of easy explanations based upon the special conditions of employment or of unemployment, or upon the chance of a three-cornered contest. Every other great industrial city in the country has returned a majority of Liberal members, or of Liberal votes, while the dominance of Liberalism north of the Tweed carried even the great residential capital of Scotland.

Where industrialism is most highly organised and most concentrated, upon the great coalfields of Lancashire and Yorkshire, Derbyshire, Northumberland and Durham, not to mention South Wales, the greatest intensity of Liberalism and Labourism prevails. The textile, machine-making and mining constituencies yielded almost universally the largest Liberal majorities, infecting with their views even most of the semi-agricultural constituencies in their near neighbourhood. The Liberal predominance in the North may be thus summarised. Scotland and North England, including Lancashire, Yorkshire, Durham, Northumberland, Cumberland, Westmorland, Derbyshire and Cheshire, send to Parliament 175 Liberal and Labour men and 54 Unionists. Hardly less concentrated is the Unionist power in the home and Southern counties. Kent, Surrey, Sussex, Hertfordshire and Huntingdon are held entire, while Middlesex and Warwickshire show only one Liberal seat. Almost every old cathedral city, with the exception of one or two important industrial centres such as Durham, York, and Norwich, nearly all the dockyard and service towns, the watering places and pleasure resorts, the county towns throughout the South, the old market towns, which return a member of bulk largely in some county constituency, cast substantial majorities for the Unionists.

Most instructive is the test of Unionist gains. With the exception of a few seats in Lancashire and Staffordshire and half a dozen of the London seats, the 117 Unionist gains in England were almost wholly composed of non-industrial towns and purely agricultural or residential county constituencies.

This tabulation will suffice to enable us to understand why the political issues set before the electorate produced such different results in North and South Britain. The three positive issues of prime importance were the Lords' Veto, the Land policy contained in or associated with the Budget, and Tariff Reform. Two other issues, though of inferior formal importance, namely, the liquor taxation and the German scare must, however, be accorded a prominent part in influencing votes, particularly in London and in the smaller older boroughs. To Home Rule, the Education Question and other older issues I do not assign wide influence in determining votes or the results of elections, except in a few special cases.

To attempt any assessment of the relative value of these issues as influencing the result of elections is of course a very hazardous proceeding. The view stated here is only to be taken as a register of the impressions gathered from conversation with active politicians, some personal observation and copious reading of the press of both parties.

The solidarity of Liberalism in the North and generally in the great industrial centres may, I think, be regarded as an endorsement of an Anti-Veto policy, Land Reform and Free Trade, with a fairly equal valuation of the three issues. The Lords and the Land probably bulked more largely as the really live issues in Scotland and the Northern English counties, where Tariff Reform propaganda has made less progress. Though Liberal candidates and leading platform speakers all over the country placed the issue of the Lords in the front of their appeal, it did not play so considerable a part off the platform, and in the Midlands and South it was certainly a subordinate influence in determining elections. The Unionist victories in the South must be attributed chiefly to a successful propaganda of Tariff Reform, mainly directed to the issue of unemployment, assisted by the unpopularity of the liquor taxes and a half-military, half-industrial fear of Germany. There are, I am aware, many other factors which deserve attention. One deserves, I think, especial mention: the failure of the Government to secure the effective administration of the Small Holdings Act was an important contributory cause to the loss of Liberal seats in the rural South.

Assuming that this general assessment of electoral issues is substantially correct, it is worth while briefly to consider the methods by which they were made effective for influencing votes. Here of course we enter the shadowy, or shady, region of the arts of electioneering. How far, and in what sense, can the verdict of the electorate be regarded as a reasoned judgment, how far was it procured by strong subconscious or irrational suggestion, how far by the mere mechanics of electioneering, how far by intimidation of sheer bribery? No man can answer such questions with confidence or any safe precision. I will, however, venture the following opinions. The abnormal fierceness of a contest in which pocket-interests bulked more largely and more clearly than at any previous election, probably evoked a certain recrudescence of those practices of bribery, treating and intimidation, which, once general, have never died out of our electioneering. In certain constituencies where traditions of corruption and servility survive, and where the conditions of work enable pressure to be brought to bear upon numbers of poor electors in precarious employment, such malpractices may have affected the result. But, making due allowance for the tendency of the defeated party to exaggerate the amount of unfair play, where some unfairness exists, I am not disposed to set down very much to the score of bribery or direct intimidation. No doubt 'moral influence,' to use a dubious phrase, which comprises respect for the known opinion of 'our betters' and a general desire to stand well with the gentry and those who can influence business or employment, counted more heavily than usual. But even then the line between such personal influence and the impersonal appeal of political issues is hard to draw. Personal or business interests everywhere help to drive home arguments or to give efficacy to emotional suggestions.

No student of electioneering is likely to underrate the part played by emotional suggestion. But it may easily be exaggerated. Even the familiar appeals to party allegiance are not merely emotional, still less merely subconscious; they contain some element of rational appeal. The figure of a Duke who asks you to 'get off his earth,' of a foreigner who has 'got your job,' or of a dissipated London corner-man who 'wants work,' are no doubt intended to impose rather than to educate opinion. But none the less they do serve to evoke reflection. Everywhere knots of men, gathering round these placards, were stimulated or provoked to reasoned controversy. I would venture to assert that there has never been an election in which reasoned discussion has been so widespread and played so large a part in determining results. Nor would I apply this only to the North, where by general consent the level of intelligence and intellectual interest among the working classes is higher than in the South.

The Tariff Reform victory in the South was obtained upon the whole by convincing the understanding of the active minds of the electorate. Although many of the facts adduced were false and most of the reasoning faulty, it was a serious attempt to present a reasoned fiscal policy, directed chiefly to prove that Protection could increase employment. Indeed the failure of Free Trade to find effective platform arguments to meet the contention entitles Protectionists fairly to claim an argumentative victory upon this head. Though political education of a formal sort has made little advance in any class, the magnitude and even the dramatic character of the new issues do much more than influence the passions; everywhere in various degrees they awaken reflection and stimulate the reasoning faculties. The result is that elections are coming gradually to depend less, not more, upon mere skill of electioneering: sound facts and right reasoning are gradually coming to possess an increased advantage over unsound facts and false reasoning. It is easier to impose true than false suggestions, for they are less likely to be 'found out' when every electorate comes to contain a leaven of intelligent and informed minds.

One other point connected with electioneering deserves mention. It is probably the case that in the South, where men of property are more numerous and are more predominantly Conservative, the mere mechanics of electioneering was used with more effect than any sort of bribery or intimidation to secure Conservative majorities. The machinery of registration, the co-operation of 'the trade' and of other outside agencies, and, in particular, the services of the motor car, probably account to a considerable extent for the increase in the Unionist poll.

Having now disposed, however imperfectly, of the main external features of the general election, let us turn once more to investigate more closely the significance of the contrast between political opinion in the North and South, in industrial and non-industrial Britain. What is the difference in character or disposition of electors which induces the cathedral and residential cities of the well-to-do, the watering places, service towns and feudal ruralism to vote for Tariff Reform and the Lords, while the manufacturing and mining centres with the more independent agricultural population of the North declare for the Budget, Land Reform and the legislative liberty of the representative House? Before suggesting an answer to this question, it is, however, right to call attention to one interesting result of the election which appears to conflict with the economic generalisation presented here. I allude of course to what is known as the Birmingham area. In this part of the Midlands a large group of definitely industrial constituencies has severed itself from the rest of industrial Britain. This severance would itself form a valuable subject of sociological enquiry. How much weight should be assigned to the extraordinary personal prestige of Mr. Chamberlain, how much to efficient operation of the political machine first made in Birmingham, how much to the fact that a large number of the trades upon which this district is dependent, are carried on in small factories or workshops which do not favour effective Trade Unionism, and are engaged in making goods which are exposed to close foreign competition, to an unusual extent? I do not possess knowledge enabling me to answer these questions: it is, however, probable that each of the considerations I suggest contributes to the result, and perhaps further allowance should be made for obscure but strong influences of local pride in adhering to a policy which has evoked so much interest and so much criticism.

But the importance of this exceptional area is not such as to destroy the validity of the general distinction between industrial North and non-industrial South.

The two Englands, to which the electoral map gives substantially accurate expression, may be described as a Producer's England and a Consumer's England, one England in which the well-to-do classes, from their numbers, wealth, leisure and influence, mould the external character of the civilisation and determine the habits, feelings and opinions of the people, the other England in which the structure and activities of large organised industries, carried on by great associated masses of artisans, factory hands and miners, are the dominating facts and forces. The Home Counties, the numerous seaside and other residential towns, the cathedral and university towns, and in general terms, the South, are full of well-to-do and leisured families, whose incomes, dissociated from any present exertion of their recipients, are derived from industries conducted in the North or in some over-sea country. A very large share, probably the major part, of the income spent by these well-to-do residential classes in the South, is drawn from possessions or investments of this nature. The expenditure of these incomes calls into existence and maintains large classes of professional men, producers and purveyors of luxuries, tradesmen, servants and retainers, who are more or less conscious of their dependence on the goodwill and patronage of persons 'living on their means.' This class of 'ostentatious leisure' and 'conspicuous waste' is subordinated in the North to earnest industry: in the South it directs a large proportion of the occupations, sets the social tone, imposes valuations and opinions. This England is primarily regarded by the dominant class as a place of residence and a playground, in which the socially reputable sports and functions (among which church-going, the theatre, art, and certain mild forms of literary culture are included), may be conducted with dignity and comfort. Most persons living in the South certainly have to work for a living, but much of this work is closely and even consciously directed by the will and the demands of the moneyed class, and the prestige of the latter imposes habits, ideas and feelings antagonistic alike to useful industry and to democracy. Moreover (a feature related closely to the character of the expenditure) the occupations of the people in the South are principally those of retail traders, small tenant farmers with ill-paid labourers, and numbers of small local businesses supplying the needs of local groups of consumers. The only great widespread industry, building, is in structure and working widely sundered from the great manufacturing and mining industries, and its instability affects gravely the character of its employees. In the South there is a great gulf fixed between the gentry and the working classes, a class of peculiarly servile shopkeepers furnishing no proper bridge. In the North a large proportion of the well-to-do are actively engaged in organising and directing industry, and, more important still, the industries support large classes of regular, well-paid, intelligent artisans and other skilled workers. Here we reach the chief clue to the difference of political opinion in North and South. The Liberalism and Labourism of the North is mainly dependent on the feelings and opinions of this upper grade of the wage-earners, the large, new middle-class. The strength of Liberalism, as attested by the election, varies directly with the relative size and compactness of this artisan element. Almost everywhere is set against it the opinion and the vote of the great majority of the employing, the professional, the shopkeeping, the leisured classes upon the one hand, and a large proportion, usually a majority, of the casual or semi-employed manual labour, and of clerks and shop-assistants, upon the other.

Never has the cleavage been so evident before. It is organised labour against the possessing and educated classes, on the one hand, against the public house and unorganised labour, on the other. So general a statement, of course, requires qualification. With the solid mass of organised workers stands a minority of well-to-do progressives and a large various scattering of lower-grade workers. But it is substantially true that organised labour furnishes the body of the liberal electorate. It is this body that has declared most solidly and definitely for the Budget, against the Lords and against Protection. This solidarity and definiteness are so marked as to constitute a new position in our politics. Taken in conjunction with our analysis of Southern England, with its unassociated servile and ill-paid labour, it serves to bring into relief the deeper interpretation of the election. Never before have the main issues of an election been charged with so much definitely economic import. This growing pressure of economic issues is of course not now confined to this country. But recent events have accelerated the pace and imparted clearer consciousness to the movement. Imperialism, Militarism, Protection, Oligarchy, are suddenly exhibited as a dramatic company on the stage of practical politics. The party which still retains the title Conservative has delivered itself over to the powers of reaction, embodied in explicit demands for Protection and Conscription and an assertion by the hereditary House of a control over finance.

The foreign and domestic policy involved in the new front of Conservatism, aggressively reactionary in form, is best interpreted as belonging to the traditional defences to which the ruling and possessing classes instinctively resort to meet a popular attack upon their economic and social privileges. The policy of land, industrial and social reform, with its accompanying fiscal policy, to which Liberalism and Labourism are now committed, is naturally regarded by them and their intellectual and economic dependents as an attack upon property. Its advocates prefer to describe it as a readjustment of the rights of property upon a basis of greater equality of individual opportunity, with a fuller recognition of state rights in socially-erected property. However described, it involves considerable interference with, and some curtailment of, existing rights of property in land values, liquor licenses and in other sources of unearned or superfluous wealth. The organised artisans, who are the strength of the attacking or reforming forces, are not socialists or conscious idealists of any order. Though there is some logic in their aims and purposes, it is made applicable to the redress of particular concrete grievances rather than to the realisation of large general aspirations. Some patches of consciousness, dim or clear, show here and there in the general will, but for the most part the movement is instinctive. Definite problems of poverty and injustice have been stirring the minds of the working and poorer classes, and in the group-mind of the associated workmen a number of separate demands have grown into a more or less coherent policy. Freer access to land and a curbing of landlordism in town and country, public assistance against the risks and injuries of proletarian life, and a definite constructive public policy for the prevention and redress of destitution, are the strongest strains in the policy. No doubt other larger, vaguer aspirations are present, making for a fuller life, more pleasure, more knowledge, and a larger share of the wealth and leisure and other opportunities which they see provided for the few by the heavy unremitting toil of the many. Though some active minds among them form general conceptions of a socialistic state, or ride some narrower theory of a panacea, the general mind of this Liberalism is groping after near and tangible results. But the reforms they seek indisputably imply disturbances in the present private system of property and industry, and the public finance which they demand, as an adjunct, involves direct encroachments upon the possessions and incomes of the well-to-do. The power of associated labour is growing, and it is setting itself with more persistency and skill to use the machinery of politics and party. How shall the threatened interests now defend themselves? They can seek to recover some of the positions, constitutional and economic, they had lost. Here is the first meaning of Tariff Reform and of the new legislative claim of the Lords. But Tariff Reform has two purposes. No government in modern times can prevent a constant growth of public expenditure, and modern Conservatism, whether instructive or enlightened, accepts a large and expensive policy of doles to distressed interests, and such 'social reforms' as eleemosynary and police considerations dictate. More money must be found. By direct taxation the body of the people can best be made to pay their share, and an indirect taxation, which at the same time serves those business interests that are bulwarks of Conservatism, will of necessity be preferred.

It is only when we thus conceive the situation as one which is fundamentally an attack upon and a defence of the present distribution of rights of property, that we can resolve some of the paradoxes that appear upon the surface. Why for instance should the great consuming South uphold Protection, the first effect of which is to raise the prices of consumables, against the producing

North? Why, again, should the 'educated' classes hold so lightly the teaching of history that they should be prepared to fling an obsolete constitutional barrier across the flowing stream of popular liberties?

This election presents more plainly than ever before the instinctive rally of the classes and interests, whose possessions, prestige, privileges and superiority of opportunity, are menaced by the new forces of constructive democracy. Landowners are put to the defence of unearned increments and land assessments; licence-owners fear the loss of their monopoly; great manufacturers and employers fear increased taxation of wealth and the legal strengthening of labour organisations; the Church, conscious of the indifference of the working classes to its spiritual authority and fearing disestablishment and disendowment, defends its hold upon the schools; the services are natural allies of force and economic privilege; the Universities fear lest a too utilitarian populace should repudiate their academic values and explode the solemn futilities of a too decorative culture.

In setting this array of Conservative forces against the pressure of the organised workers for economic security and opportunity, as the central fact of present politics, I am no doubt giving a too exclusively materialistic interpretation. The spirit of both parties is also nourished on finer sentiments and less selfish convictions. Everywhere in town and country sturdy Nonconformity has given a moral glow and a crusading enthusiasm to the radical cause, and has infused a religious passion into the demand for the land.

On the other hand the ranks of Conservatism are sustained by a corresponding glow of patriotism, in the feeling that they are defending the very pillars of the social order threatened by disintegrating forces of socialism within and the menace of a foreign enemy without. This genuine sentimentalism half supplements and half conceals the play of the driving and directing forces which animate politics.

One point, in conclusion, deserves particular attention, for it contains the chief justification of democracy. Though I have found a larger play of rationalism and of conscious individual judgment in this election than in any former one, I cannot attribute to this individual rationalism the chief place as determinant. Organisation and intelligent association for common human purposes constitute the strength of civilised society. Where masses of men are thus associated for work and life, there exist the best conditions for the emergence and the operation of that sane collective will and judgment which, in the sphere of politics, constitutes the spirit and the policy of progressive democracy. It is not mere individual self-interest, or more intimate acquaintance with the facts of trade and industry, which leads the Lancashire or Yorkshire mill-operative or the Northumbrian miner to reject the Tariff that seems so alluring to the London clubman or the country vicar or the half-pay officer at Brighton or Bournemouth. There is, I feel sure, a half-instinctive, half-conscious drive of collective wisdom, set up by the associated working class life which the needs of modern capitalistic production have established, a genuine spirit of the people, however incomplete in its expression, which makes for political righteousness.

The intelligence of associated labour is less likely to be led astray by sophistry or sentimentalism than the more cultivated but more individualised intelligence of the scholar, the professional man, or the member of that swell-mob commonly termed 'Society.' Nor is its superiority shown merely in the avoidance of error, an instinct of wholesome Conservatism. From the will of such a people proceeds a constructive political energy, moving somewhat blindly and unevenly, and not with firm persistent direction, towards rather shapeless ideals. It is the creative instinct of the collective mind seeking to express itself in politics, very uncertain in its crude handling of material, groping after ill-conceived effects, wasting much, spoiling some, but learning the art called democracy.

I do not mean to claim that the artisans of the North are 'the people.' In some respects they are very limited in aims and outlook. There may even be a certain danger of a new though wider class government, if their superior organisation enabled them to wield for a while the same measure of dominance in politics as that possessed formerly by the landed aristocracy, or latterly by the mercantile and middle trading classes. I can conceive that collective mechanic mind and will impressing themselves too hardly upon our social institutions, and with too little tenderness towards those above and those below, too rigorous in the regimentation of the weaker grades of workers, shirkers and defectives. But all the same it is to this associated labour power that we must look for the rudiments of any coming art of democracy, and to my mind the most significant lesson of the election is the geographical and social testimony to the emergence of this popular power.

IV. Lines Forward

1

L. T. Hobhouse

SOCIOLOGY, GENERAL, SPECIAL, AND SCIENTIFIC

THE *Sociological Review* takes the place of the annual volume of collected "Papers" in which proceedings of the Sociological Society have been published hitherto. By quarterly publication it is possible to secure greater continuity of treatment and more scope for the scientific handling of the subject; and the publishing of a Review is felt to be the best method of putting the work of the Society on a permanent footing and rendering it accessible to the world. The work of the Society, has, among other things, done something towards clearing up misconceptions of the nature and problems of Sociology, and defining the scope of any sociological journal. But it would be ill to pretend that we have arrived at general agreement on this initial question. We cannot yet assume that Sociology means the same thing to all people or that there would be universal agreement as to the appropriate contents of a sociological journal. Not only are there still many who deny the bare existence of Sociology, but, what is more serious, among Sociologists there are still many deep divergences of view as to the nature and province of the enquiries which they professedly pursue in common. This divergence is, however, not a sign of disease but rather of the raw vigour and

---

Reprinted from *The Sociological Review*, 1908. This was the editorial article Hobhouse wrote for the first issue of the Sociological Society's journal. It is as near to an agreed manifesto as any group of British sociologists has ever produced.

exuberance of youth. An enemy is doubtless entitled to make the most of the fact that the enthusiasts for a science have not hitherto been able to decide among themselves what their science is about. But if disagreement as to its fundamental definitions is used as a proof that a science does not exist and cannot be brought into existence, it is to be feared that other sciences will follow Sociology to annihilation. Political Economy is generally admitted to be a science, but economists would not seek to prove it by pointing to the general agreement in their definitions of Wealth, of Capital, of Production and other fundamental conceptions. Biology is a science, but how many Biologists can satisfy themselves—to say nothing of satisfying one another—with any definition of Life. What in the light of recent researches is the limit between Chemistry and Physics? Is it certain that the present demarcation between the sciences of Life and those which deal with inanimate matter is of any permanent validity? Indeed if a science sets out to deal with the properties of matter, must we demand that it should first define satisfactorily what matter is and what it means by a property, and if so, should we find that any physical science can yet be reckoned among the number of human achievements? In reality it is precisely the most elementary conceptions that remain longest in the dark. The physicist can far more readily teach us what matter does than what matter is. The dialectician may prove that this is absurd, but the fact is so. The biologist finds it a great deal easier to tell us about life than to tell us what that life is which he is talking about. We are able to follow him (if we are not dialecticians) because we already have some rough notion of what life means. We are not prepared with a definition but "if you do not ask we understand." So it is with the biologist himself. He has a rough, broad conception which serves as a starting point for his investigations. He finds it difficult to put this conception into a rigid formula, and if he succeeds in doing so the very progress of his enquiry will probably confute him. As he learns more and more about his subject matter so does his original conception of that matter grow and change and remodel itself under his hands. The more he knows about living things the more adequate his definition of Life. But if this is so it is clear that the definition which is to satisfy everybody must come not at the beginning but at the end of discovery. We must know what we are investigating only in the sense that we must have a rough and provisional outline of the field of work. If this imperfect and broken knowledge be ruled out, it remains that we can only know what we are looking for when we have found it.

What may be fairly demanded of Sociologists then is not that they should have a nicely rounded definition of the object of sociological investigation which should command universal agreement, but rather that they should have sufficient common understanding of the nature and aims of a science of Society to render discussion fruitful and co-operation possible. They must have a rough and professional conception of "Society" just as in Biology students must have a rough and provisional conception of Life. That is, the term must be at once generic and distinctive. It must serve to group certain matters together and to distinguish them from others, as possible objects of scientific investigation. Does the phrase science of sociology serve this purpose? If it allows room for cavil among sociologists it is probably in the use of the term "science" rather than of the term "society." Some would doubtless prefer to speak of Social Philosophy and deny that Society can be an object of a science comparable to Physics or Biology. This objection, however, can only be grounded on the more restricted use of the term science in which it is opposed to philosophy. If by science we mean merely unprejudiced investigation, accurately measured statement and the systematic prosecution of a subject through all the windings of interrelated facts —then philosophy itself aims at being a science. It is only if certain presuppositions as to the subject matter of science be allowed, if for example there is a separation between "nature" and that which is not of nature, or between the sphere of law and that of "freedom," and if science be restricted to one side of the partition, that any question can arise as to the use of the term in connection with society. As long as no such presuppositions are covertly introduced by the use of the term probably all Sociologists will agree that their object is the Science of Society. They hold that is to say that the Social Life constitutes a distinct field for investigation, and that it should be investigated in a scientific spirit—that is to say in the spirit which makes the ascertainment of the truth the immediate object, which aims at accurately measured statement, and at the systematic interconnection of the facts which it ascertains. I do not know whether all who profess and call themselves Sociologists would accept this account of their views, but on the other hand I do not know of any serious work on sociology which does not on its own lines seek to fulfill this purpose.

Within the limits of such a conception, however, very great variety of treatment is of course possible and the reader who wishes to know something of the scope and plan of a new journal may be expected to ask for something more definite. It is not, fortunately, among the recognised duties of an Editorial Committee to produce definitions, but in view of the admitted divergencies in the handling of sociological investigations, it is perhaps well for those responsible for a sociological journal to give some indication of the ground which they hope to cover. This ground, I think, can only be marked off at the present stage by reference to the actual work done or in the doing by sociologists, that is, by all who treat problems of social life in the scientific spirit. As already pointed out this would by no means exclude many of those who would maintain that their own method was not scientific but philosophical. The fundamental questions of social life were for long studied mainly under the aegis of political philosophy and one of the first points which a modern sociologist, seeking to define his subject, has to consider is the relation of his method to this older discipline. He finds to begin with that systematic political thinking developed in close connection with the general movement of metaphysics and moral philosophy. For this there is a double reason. On the one hand political philosophy whether in Hobbes or Locke, in Rousseau or Bentham, in John Mill or T. H. Green, closely resembles general philosophy in its method. Like metaphysics or ethics, it takes as its starting point common current conceptions, conceptions of law and government, of liberty and obligation, of the individual and society, conceptions which we all use and all suppose ourselves to understand until someone asks us what we mean by them. This someone is the philosopher and in the use of such conceptions as have been instanced, it is the political philosopher. That is to say, the political philosopher has sought for light by scrutinising those principles of human association which are so fundamental that everybody else takes them for granted. In other words he is dealing according to his lights with the most general conditions of social life, the intimate nature of the social bond, the problems arising out of the bare fact that distinct personalities form a social whole. On this side then he is in line with contemporary enquirers into those broad sociological principles which are independent of time and place. He has been and is laying down the lines of a general sociology. On the other side political thought has been closely associated with moral philosophy. For political thinkers have not merely sought to determine what society is, but have pretty uniformly conceived their analysis as having at least an important bearing on the question, what it ought to be. On the face of the facts these are two very distinct questions, and if there is any ultimate sense in which they are one that sense is only reached by a long philosophical analysis which not all will follow. But without such analysis many people confuse them or at least pass from the one to the other without sufficiently clear consciousness of the step that they are taking. It may be that some schools of political philosophy have fused, if they have not confused, these two questions. Be that as it may, sociological thinking must start with a clear cut distinction between the "is" and the "ought," between the facts of social life and the conditions on which society actually rests and the ideal to which society should conform. If indeed it finds that any element of the ideal enters into the facts or the conditions, that is matter of fact, capable of proof or disproof. But it must hold in full clearness from the outset that the question of fact is one thing and the question of right and wrong another. An ideal is not proved to be an actual condition of social life because it is an ideal nor is a factor in the actual life of society to be identified with a moral law merely because it is proved to be a factor. The "laws" of Political Economy are not as the old jest has it laws to be "obeyed," but statements of certain relations of cause and effect to be taken into account by anyone who wishes to achieve certain economic results; and so with any other "laws" of Sociology.

Political Philosophy, if this view is correct, has concerned itself with two questions which in thought are quite distinct. The first of these questions concerns the general conditions of social life; the second is the problem of Moral Philosophy. It may be asked whether this latter problem is properly the concern of Sociology at all. Sociology, it may be said, is a science, and science is to be understood in a more limited sense than that given above. A science deals with facts and the interconnection of facts. It discovers laws and makes predictions. Hence it tells us what has been, what is, and what will be, but it has no concern with what ought to be. Not that social science leaves ethics out of account. There is the science of Comparative Ethics which tells what men have thought and think about right and wrong. It may even help us to forecast what they are likely to think about right and wrong, but it does not profess to say what they ought to think about right and wrong. If this is a question which can be determined at all it belongs to Philosophy and not to science. Sociology as a science then, it may be said, has no concern with the right and wrong of human conduct, or with the good and bad of social life, but only with the nature and conditions of the social structure and the observable laws of its growth and decay.

But the very terms of the protest show how impossible it is to keep Sociology—especially the broader investigations of general Sociology—in permanent separation from all ethical considerations. On the one side if right conduct is truly social conduct the results of sociology cannot be indifferent to the moral philosopher. We said above, that to discover one of the conditions of human association is not all one with discovering an element in the ethical ideal. But there are circumstances in which the two come very nearly to the same thing. For if the condition is a vital and unalterable condition of social life, if science proves that the social life cannot subsist without it, and if moral philosophy regards the maintenance of the social life as a necessary part of its ideal then the scientific truth is at once translateable into a moral command. The deliverance of science and the deliverance of moral philosophy on the subject are still distinct. The one states a fact and the other lays down an injunction. But the fact and the injunction issue from two sides, if the phrase be allowed, of the same human consciousness in relation to the same human data. More generally, those who take seriously the social side of Ethics look forward to the gradual formation of an Applied Ethics which will stand in much closer relation to life than the disputations of the schools, that is in effect to an Art which, resting on Moral Philosophy as its theoretical foundation, would use the results of the social sciences as Medicine uses those of Physiology. The widest conception of Sociology then—and however individual thinkers may differ, it is the widest conception that should shape the policy of a review—takes the subject as embracing not only a Science, but a Philosophy and an Art, as dealing not only with the facts and conditions of social life, but with its ideals, and the means of their realisation.

Indeed, if Sociology as a science of facts and conditions is important to Ethics, it may equally be argued that Ethics cannot be indifferent to a student of Sociology. For what after all is the material of Sociology? It is the kind of common life achieved by human beings, beings that is to say moved by impulses and purposes. The interplay of purpose we may say, is to Sociology what mass and motion are to physics or the metabolism of cellular tissue to Biology. Doubtless there are conditions, physical conditions, biology conditions, for example, which come cramping in, hedging round the play of purpose, sometimes determining its direction, sometimes twisting its result. But the distinctive feature of our subject matter, the feature that makes Sociology a distinct science is the web of purpose wherein men act on one another and react on the conditions that make them. But purpose and the relations of purpose also constitute the subject of the ethical judgment. Ethics and social science have, generically, the same subject matter and though they regard it from different points of view yet as every sociologist is also a man he cannot, so to say, wholly divest himself of the one kind of consciousness in putting on the other. Nor is it desirable that he should do so. The Ethical judgment is scientifically by far the most important judgment which has to be passed on human purposes. For we cannot ask any more vital questions about purposes than how far they attain their ends, whence our fundamental question about the interaction of distinct purposes and the purposes of separate personalities is how far they tend to frustrate or to further one another, how they conflict or harmonise. But to raise this question is at once to revert to the old ethical problem of the individual and the common good. And any answer that we give to this question, that is as much as to say any deep-reaching definitions, classifications, any conception of growth, development or decay in human society will consciously or unconsciously be framed in terms of our conception of the common good. It is better for the sake of clearness that it be done consciously, and accordingly our most purely "scientific" work in Sociology is likely to be done best, if we have in mind an articulate system of clear cut ethical conceptions.

Even were it otherwise, were the scientific, the philosophic, and the practical sides of sociological work separate in essence rather than distinct in thought, a Review which seeks to offer common ground for sociological workers to meet upon could hardly neglect the speculative or the practical approach to the subject. Its conductors would have to realise that a subject which is treated by some as a science in the more limited sense of that term, is, and has been, approached by others from the speculative and by still more from the human and practical point of view. They would have to take these points of view into account and to bear in mind, among other things, that the "practical" interest in Sociology has often taken, and seems more and more likely to take shape in the form of experiments in verification of hypotheses, experiments which the most precisely limited science cannot ignore. So what a Review has to ask is that the sociological interest, whether practical or theoretical, should be "scientific" in the broad sense here given to that term, that to find expression in these pages it should be prompted by an unprejudiced desire for truth, rendered in measured accuracy of expression, and be such as to assist in the systematic following up of interconnected facts.

So far we have spoken of General Sociology and have seen

reasons for giving the term for our purposes a wide interpretation. But the advance of Sociology in recent years has been more marked in the growth of special sciences than in the fresh development of fundamental ideas. Indeed sociology as a general discipline has been sometimes threatened with destruction at the hands of its own offspring. It tends to be dispersed and disappear into a number of specialisms. In place of sociology we have social sciences and the question of urgency for sociology is whether they are to develop independently each on its own lines or are to be kept in touch with one another and with the fertilising principle of social unity by means of a general study of Sociology.

The division of Sociology into special sciences is in itself only in accordance with the normal conditions of scientific growth. So vastly complex a whole as Social Life cannot be studied for long without a division of labour, and as soon as certain elements can be distinguished, certain fields of work marked out in *prima facie* distinctness from the remainder, economy suggests a concentration of different minds on each of these in turn. The selection is justified and the economy is real on two conditions. (1) There must be real cohesion of certain social phenomena which brings them closer to one another than they are to other sides of social life, and (2) since society is after all one, and no portion of its life can be really divorced from the remainder, the specialist should be ready at every stage to take into account the influence in his own sphere of forces emanating from some other part of the field. It is on this side that the natural limitations of specialism are often the cause of confusion of voices, stagnation in discovery, and positive errors in the practical guidance of affairs—and this not in Sociology alone. It is here that the function of General Sociology becomes all important. Properly considered General Sociology is neither a separate science complete in itself before specialism begins, nor is it a mere synthesis of the social sciences consisting in a mechanical juxtaposition of their results. It is rather a vitalising principle that runs through all social investigation nourshing and nourished by it in turn, stimulating inquiry, correlating results, exhibiting the life of the whole in the parts and returning from the study of the parts to a fuller comprehension of the whole. We cannot indeed attempt any reasoned distribution of social functions among separate sciences without being struck by the unsubstantial nature of our divisions. We may think of Society first as a Structure and consider its constitution, the main groups of which it is composed, the mode of government by which it is held together, the nature of its relation to other societies. We see here foundations for the study of the Family, the Class, the Tribe, the Nation; for the Science of Government; or for the study of International Law. We may turn to the Directive Conceptions and Institutions which condition the life of society, and distinguish law, ethics, religion; industrial organisation; science and philosophy; literature and art. The systematic treatment of any of these is on one side a sociological investigation, and each in turn may be subdivided into further specialisms. We may enquire into the concrete facts of society, the actual life of a people as affecting and affected by the constitution and the directive institutions of the social structure, and then we obtain demographical investigations of the life conditions of the social classes, and of the distribution of personal qualities among groups. In any or all of these departments a science may be "Descriptive," limited to a straightforward account of the facts of a given time and place; it may be Analytical, resolving complex effects into elementary principles, causes, or conditions; and it may be Comparative bringing phenomena of different societies into relation with one another and seeking through comparison and classification to discover lines of growth. But we can no sooner make these or any similar divisions of the possible field of sociology than we become aware of forces that pass over all our boundaries. What can we know of the nature, say, of the family and of the various forms which it has assumed without taking some account of general ethics, of religion, law, and even of industrial and governmental organisation? How far could we carry a treatise on government without law, or on law without reference to religion and ethics, and what mountains of specialism we must raise between our eyes and the facts before we could fail to see the interaction of any one of these with the contemporary state of science and philosophy, of literature and art. We may carry specialism further in one field than in another according as the facts are more or less closely knit but whenever we take one side of social life, be it the economic, the religious, or any other, and treat it as though it stood alone we are on the road to fallacy.

It is not the function of a sociological journal to produce a ready made scheme of Sociology. But it is its function to assist in the work which General Sociology has to do, in bringing the work of specialists together and in affording facilities for the discussion of the broad sociological bearing of each specialistic investigation. It should aid in familiarising the Economist with the conclusions of Comparative Jurisprudence or with the philosophic analysis of society; the historian of thought with the facts of industrial and political development; the investigators of contemporary social conditions with the earlier phases of social life; and all students of society with the best that is known or thought of the bearings of Biology and Psychology on their own investigations. At the same time it will afford them collectively the opportunity of defending the study of society from aggressions which would destroy its character as a distinct science or from usurpations which would merge it in the work of one of its own departments. It must give a fair field and no favour to the practical interest in Sociology. Needless to say it will approach questions of living interest without party bias, but it will be among its prime objects to show that even questions of the day, like questions of 3,000 years ago, can be approached in a scientific spirit with a distinterested desire to find out the truth about them.[1]

It may be objected that the Review would on these lines become an organ of all the specialisms, an attempt which considerations of print and paper forbid. But this is once again to mis-

---

[1]   By restricting the term science to its narrower sense of an inquiry into facts as opposed to ideals we may make the result of the discussion clear by a systematic arrangement. Thus:

Sociology

Sociology as Science		Moral Philosophy
General	Special	

Applied Social Ethics.

apprehend the position of Sociology. It does not lie within our province to cater for the detailed investigations of the recognised specialist. We invite him rather to discuss his principles and broad results with representatives of other specialisms and in the presence of those interested in Sociology at large.

We seek to touch each specialism at the point where it comes in contact with General Sociology. In each department there are matters of little interest except to those far advanced in that branch —matters of controversy on which the specialist alone can decide, investigations of detail of which he alone can see the bearing. The natural home for discussion of such points is the journal of the specialism. But there are also in each branch matters of general interest, results of importance to other investigators, controversies in which a material part of the evidence falls within the competence of another department, and of these the natural home is the journal for sociologists in general. Thus, Economics is logically a branch of Sociology and every economic truth is a sociological truth. But there are economic investigations which would be best suited to the Economic Journal, and others—such as touch most nearly the general life of the people—that would find an appropriate place in the Sociological Review.

We shall, therefore, welcome contributions alike from the philosopher and the specialist, from the comparative sciences which search the whole human record for their data, and from the detailed study of contemporary tendencies. We shall hope to show that in the study of social evolution the organisation of a mediæval city, or the genesis of an Oriental religion have their place alongside of the analysis of contemporary institutions. We hope to show at the same time that the problems of the day are just as much objects of science as any period of past history or any phase of primitive life. To the sociologist "nothing that is human is foreign." Not that such scattered fragments of Sociology are of real value for the science till they are brought or rather till they grow together. On the contrary it is one of the functions of Sociological criticism to prevent the crude use of fragments of history and of empirical generalisation from isolated cases. But the main problem of Sociology at the present day is to build up the great Comparative

Science which alone can put the theory of social evolution on a firm basis. To form by a philosophic analysis a just conception of human progress, and trace this progress in its manifold complexity in the course of history, to test its reality by careful classification and searching comparisons, to ascertain its conditions, and if possible to forecast its future—this is the comprehensive problem towards which all sociological science converges and on the solution of which reasoned sociological effort must finally depend. In the light of this conception everything that concerns human development acquires value and all sociological work achieves unity. The comparative study of law, of government and the social fabric; the history of science and philosophy, of art and literature; the study of the ethical and religious consciousness in their manifold phases; the story of the industrial arts and the gradual conquest of nature, all these have their sociological side. All contribute to the general enquiry into the nature, conditions, and possibilities of human progress and to understand their contributions is the work of sociology.

2

Francis Galton

SOCIOLOGY AS EUGENICS

THE AIM OF THIS LECTURE is to give a scientific basis to the problem of race improvement under the existing conditions of civilisation and sentiment. It leads to many subsidiary problems, each interesting to anthropologists on its own account.

Men differ as much as dogs in inborn dispositions and faculties. Some dogs are savage, others gentle; some endure fatigue, others are soon exhausted; some are loyal, others are self-regarding. They differ no less widely in specialities, as in herding sheep, retrieving, pointing at game, and following trails by scent. So it is with men in respect to the qualities that go towards forming civic worth, which it is not necessary at this moment to define particularly, especially as it may be a blend of many alternative qualities. High civic worth includes a high level of character, intellect, energy, and physique, and this would disqualify the vast majority of per-

Reprinted from "The Possible Improvement of the Human Breed under the Existing Conditions of Law and Sentiment," *Man*, 1901. Eugenicists made numerous indirect contributions to sociology; among other things they took up the study of cultural constraints on political action as they became increasingly aware of the resistance of law and sentiment to eugenic proposals. And their insistence on a relatively strict mathematical method eventually had an influence, in only by reaction, on those who refused to see social problems as primarily problems of heredity. Note that by 1900 it was de rigueur to use or pay lip service to Booth's data in all social investigations. Galton was no exception. This was not one of the papers Galton read to the Sociological Society in its early days. But it indicates better than those programmatic statements do the sort of work he wanted the Society to take up.

sons from that distinction. We may conceive that a committee might be entrusted to select the worthiest of the remaining candidates, much as they select for fellowships, honours, or official posts.

Distribution in a Population—It is a fair assumption that the different grades of civic worth are distributed in accord with the familiar normal law of frequency. This means nothing more than that the causes why civic worth varies in amount in different persons are numerous and act independently, some pulling this way, some that, the results being due to the ordinary laws of combination. As it is found that such very different variables conform fairly to this law, as Stature, Bullet holes around the bull's eye, Error of judgment of astronomers, and Marks gained by candidates at examinations, whether in simple or in grouped subjects, there is much reason to bèlieve that civic worth will do so also. The figures will then come out as follows: Let the average civic worth of all the male adults of the nation be determined and its value be called M, one-half of them having less and the other more than M. Let those who have more than M be similarly subdivided, the lower half will then have M *plus* something that does not exceed a sharply-defined amount, which will be called 1°, and is taken as the unit of distribution. It signifies the height of each step or grade between the limits of the successive classes about to be described. We therefore obtain by familiar methods the result that 25 per cent. lie between M and M $+ 1°$ (call it for brevity $+ 1°$); 16 per cent. between $+1°$ and $+ 2°$; 7 between $+ 2°$ and $+3°$, and 2 for all beyond $+ 3°$. There is no outer limit; the classification might proceed indefinitely, but this will do at present. Similarly for the negative grades below M. It is convenient to distinguish the classes included between these divisions by letters, so they will be called R, S, T, U, &c., in succession upwards, and *r, s, t, u,* &c., in succession downwards, *r* being the counterpart of R; *s* of S, and so on.

These normal classes were compared with those of Mr. Charles Booth in his great work, *Labour and Life of the People of London.* His lower classes, including the criminals and semi-criminals, correspond in numbers with "*t* and below"; those higher than small shopkeepers and subordinate professional men correspond with "T and above," and the large body of artisans who earn from 22s. to 30s. a week exactly occupy the place of mediocrity; they include the upper four fifths of r and the lower four fifths of R. So far as these may represent civic worth they confirm as far as they go its fairly normal distribution.

The differences between the classes are exemplified by the figures relating to the stature of many thousand adult males, measured at the Health Exhibition. Their average height was nearly 5 ft. 8 in., the unit of distribution was nearly 1¾ in., so the class U exceeded 6 ft. 1 in.; consequently even U overlooks a mob, while V, who exceed 6 ft. 2¾ in., and much more the higher grades, tower above it in an increasingly eminent degree.

Worth of a Child—Dr. Farr calculated the value at its birth of a baby born of the wife of an Essex labourer, supposing it to be an average specimen of its class in length of life, in cost of maintenance while a child and in old age, and in earnings during youth and manhood. He capitalised with actuarial skill the prospective values at the time of birth, of the outgoings and the incomings, and on balancing the items found the newly-born infant to be worth 5l. A similar process would conceivably bring out the money value at birth of children destined when they grew up to fall into each of the several classes, and by a different method of appraisement to discover their moral and social worth. As regards the money value of men of the highest class, many found great industries, establish vast undertakings, increase the wealth of multitudes and amass large fortunes for themselves. Others, whether rich or poor, are the guides and light of the nation, raising its tone, enlightening its difficulties and imposing its ideals. The more gifted of these men, members of our yet undefined X class, would be each worth thousands of pounds to the nation at the moment of their birth.

Augmentation of Favoured Stock—Enthusiasm to improve our race might express itself by granting diplomas to a select class X of young men and women, by encouraging their intermarriages and by promoting the early marriage of girls of that high class. The means that are available consist in dowries, where a moderate sum is important, help in emergencies, healthy homes, pressure of public opinion, honours, and the introduction of religious motives, which are very effective as in causing Hindoo girls and most Jewesses to marry young. The span of a generation would be thereby shortened, which is equivalent to increasing the fertility of one that was unshortened. It would also save the early years of the child-bearing period from barrenness. Healthy homes would diminish mortality among children, and in that way increase the output of adult offspring. There is a tendency among girls to shrink from marriage on prudential grounds. This feeling might be directed in the opposite way, by making it an imprudence in an X girl not to gain the advantages that would reward the indulgence of a natural instinct. It was concluded that the effect of a widely-felt enthusiasm for improving the race might be expected to add an average increment of one adult son and one adult daughter to the prospective offspring of each X girl. These would be distributed among the X, W, and V classes much as the offspring of V parentages are distributed among the V, U, and T classes, but not in quite such high proportions.

Economical Problem—The problem to be solved now appears in a clear shape. An X child is worth so and so at birth and one of each of the inferior grades respectively is worth so and so; 100 X-favoured parentages will each produce a gain of so many; the total value of their produce can therefore be estimated by an actuary, consequently it is a legitimate expenditure to spend up to such and such an amount on each X parentage. The distinct statement of a problem is often more than half way towards its solution. There seems no reason why this one should not be solved between limiting values that are not too wide apart to be useful.

Existing Agencies—Leaving aside profitable expenditure from a money point of view the existence of large and voluntary activities should be borne in mind that have nobler aims. It appears that the annual voluntary contributions to public charities in the British Isles amount on the lowest computation to 14,000,000*l.*, and that, as Sir H. Burdett asserts on good grounds, is by no means the maximum attainable (*Hospitals and Charities*, 1898, p. 85).

A custom has existed in all ages of wealthy persons befriending poor and promising youths which might be extended to young and promising couples. It is a conspicuous feature in the biographies of those who have risen from the ranks, that they were indebted for their first start in life to this cause. Again, it is usual among large landowners to proceed not on the rackrent principle, but to select the worthiest all round for tenants and others in their employ, and to give them good cottages at low rents and other facilities. The advantage of being employed on one of those liberally-conducted properties being thoroughly appreciated, there are usually many applicants to each vacancy, so selection can be exercised. The result is that the tenants and servants of all kinds to be found about them are a finer stamp of men to those in similar positions elsewhere. It might easily become an avowed object of noble families to gather fine specimens of humanity around them, as it is to produce fine breeds of cattle and so forth, which are costly but repay in satisfaction.

Finally, there are building societies that have higher ends than mere investments and which have been endowed with princely generosity. A settlement of selected persons might conceivably be maintained that should bear some analogy to colleges with their fellowships, and include a grant of rooms for a term of years at low cost. A select class would create through their own merits an attractive settlement, distinguished by energy, intelligence, and civic worth, just as a first-rate club attracts desirable candidates by its own social advantages.

Prospects—It is easy to indulge in Utopias, including a vast system of statistical registration, but the pressing need is to establish a firm basis of fact for the roads that lead towards race improvement. The magnitude of the inquiry is great, but its object is one of the highest that man can hope to accomplish, and there seems no reason to doubt its practicability to a greater or less degree. The question of how much may be reasonably anticipated must be delayed until the problems that have been indicated are more or less satisfactorily solved.

3

Patrick Geddes

SOCIOLOGY AS CIVICS

THE SOCIOLOGIST has not merely to repeat criticisms of the inadequacy of pecuniary-mechanistic culture, and to insist, with Comte and Spencer alike, upon the full recapitulation and application of biological and psychological as well as physical science. He has further to insist upon fully executed geographical, naturalistic and social surveys; and these carried into detail, regional, and civic, that meet those of Humboldt, Ritter and Reclus. So, too, he has to consider the work of Montesquieu, Buckle, Taine, &c., upon the important bearing of environment on organism, of place on people. But if we go so far, there is no escaping the further steps made by Frédéric Le Play: and these not merely as regards his family budgets, at length accepted in current schools of economics. We need to follow up his substantial initiative towards the study of the nature-occupations, as fundamental and initiative for those of our whole complex modern world. Important for human biology and anthropology as is Darwin's *Descent of Man* and all that has followed it, fascinating also as is his rediscovery of relations like those of worms and soil fertility, of flowers and insects, and of other webs of natural evolution, the Le Play line of social evolution is most productive and fascinating of all. Hence it must before long be recognised, even by the most up-to-date "fundamentalists" in economics, that the whole modern complex of occupations and

Reprinted from *Cities in Evolution*, 1915, chapter 17, and *The Coal Crisis and the Future*, 1926, chapter 1.

division of labour, in any great city has thus to be re-interpreted upon evolutionary lines: since all traceably arising from the simple occupations still manifest in every region, as we survey it from hill-tops to sea. Economists have of course had some inkling of this: indeed, their Physiocratic beginnings were substantially in terms of the peasant civilisation of rural France; while their later discussions of "hunting, pastoral and agricultural phases" were attempts towards extending this basal realism, albeit too hypothetically, and apart from the contemporary progress of geography and anthropology.

It is assumed in Universities, and still too much throughout research and education alike, and hence by the public, that Geography, Economics and Anthropology are distinct subjects, to be prosecuted independently, each in its own academic department or learned society. But life cannot be found in "environment" apart from "organism," nor yet in "organism" apart from "environment": it exists in (and during) their interaction: an interaction in which, though the environment conditions the organism, the organism reacts upon the environment. This is obvious for man as organism, and from his life-breath throughout all other organic functioning: but his social life remains unintelligible, or misinterpreted, so long as we fail to see also the strict parallelism of his whole social life to his organic functioning. For each given place cannot but so far condition its inhabitants, its people: but every living people must so far also recondition their place. The greater their difficulties, the higher may thus rise their economic efficiency, indeed, hence their advancing civilisation. Switzerland, and yet more Holland, each a region of peculiar difficulties, yet of corresponding mastery of them, are thus obvious examples in point. In short, then, Place, Work, People, have not merely to be separately analysed, as into the geo-morphology, the market economics, and the cranial anthropology which still go on, in necessary detachment from each other, in separate academic departments, in museums, and in learned societies. They have also, and above all, to be seen in living unity. These three, and long apparently distinct studies, are now-a-days increasingly uniting.

Within the single chord of social life all three combine; yet with definite inter-relations, by help of which all the fields, sub-divisions and details of their past studies may be more fully and freshly re-investigated, related and harmonised. In a word, these three studies of place, work and people thus revive, from so many separate and analytic enquiries, each like a post-mortem examination, into a vivid presentment of the living unity of society. In fact, Geography, Economics and Anthropology are so intimately related (as every open-minded traveller has seen from of old), that it can hardly be much longer before all their separate cultivators realise their co-operation and union within the field of Sociology, thus fertilised anew by their associated labours.

Further developments of this approach to Sociology—first by Le Play's French disciples, in their books and reviews (*La Science Sociale* especially), and next in our own Society and its *Review* —are thus easily referred to. Moreover, current archæology and anthropology have long been tracing the evolution of occupations; as from the simple gathering, hunting and fishing of Palæolithic man up to his neotechnic agriculture. But between these simple societies and our present age the sociologist has observantly and interpretatively to work out the steps and phases of development. Hence his increasing insistence upon regional survey, as preliminary to urban studies, to civic survey, and city improvement.

"We learn by living"; the student of medicine must go to the bedside as well as to dissecting-room and study before he really understands the working of the human frame; and likewise with the student of cities; he must work in and for his city, were it but to investigate it more clearly. Still, in medicine and public health, it is found best to let diagnosis precede treatment, and not, as with the would-be "practical man" so much hitherto, to adopt the best advertised panacea of treatment, before any diagnosis worth the name. So it is with cities; the rival panaceas of their party politicians have too long been delaying the surveys and diagnoses of the civic sociologist.

The "Survey of Cities," which we thus reach must take in all aspects, contemporary as well as historic. It must be geographic and economic, anthropological and historical, demographic and eugenic, and so on: above all, it aims towards the reunion of all these studies, in terms of social science, as "Civics." This youngest branch of science, as yet but a little-noticed bud upon the ever-spreading tree of knowledge, may before long be recognised as one of the most fruitful of all. Its legitimacy and its interest are still often unrecognised by the sociologist, himself too abstract, or merely anthropological or racial, for lack of civics.

This too general thinker upon human affairs has for some time been seeing that between his long favourite extremes of Individual and State, there lies the Family; but here the City is shown to mould the individual (it may be even more strongly), and—not merely as governing metropolis—to dominate the State. So far we see to-day; hence our civic observations, speculations, and controversies, our emerging theories—in a word, the rebirth of sociology, as above all the Science of Cities.

We visualise and depict our city from its smallest beginnings, and its immediate and wider setting, as of valley, river, and routes; we spread it upon its plain, tower it upon its hills, or throne it more spaciously by the sea. Our synoptic vision of the city, for each and all of its growth-phases, thus ranges through region to homes, and back again, and with pictured completeness as well as plans; first a rough jewel on the breast of Nature, then the wrought clasp upon her rich-embroidered garments of forest, vineyard, or orchard, of green pastures or golden fields.

As with geography, so with history: we design or renew the city's pageant, scene by scene. No minuteness of local archaeologist and antiquarian can be spared, no contact with the outer world of which the general historian tells; yet the main task is too commonly missed between these—the problem of presentment of its characteristic life at each period. We have to see it as it lived in pre-Roman, Roman, and barbarian times, in early and later mediæval days, and at the Renaissance, as well as in its modern industrial growth since the steam-engine and the railway.

The too purely spectacular pageant of a city—with its loosely strung succession of incidents, themselves too often of external contacts—despite its splendour, has failed to satisfy the public. But here we come in sight of its next development—that of the more interpretative masque of the city's life; the seven ages, as it were, of its being—though happily not too closely corresponding to Shakespeare's individual ones, themselves sadly degenerate from a nobler tradition. And though at many points our masque must still be eked out with pageant, at others it may well rise towards epic. Here, in fact, a new form of epic begins to appear; that of each and every city and region throughout the ages.

We are thus reaching the very portal of literature; yet, thanks to our outdoor survey and its exhibition, we can look back from it upon life, which everywhere creates it. We realise for ourselves how this dull town has had beauty and youth. We see how it has lived through ages of faith and had its great days of fellowship; how it has thrilled to victory, wept in defeat, renewed its sacrifices and strifes, and so toiled on, through generation after generation, with ever-changing fortunes, and in mind and spirit more change-ful still. But since in the mass of prosperous English and American cities we too readily forget our historic past, and think only of our town in its recent industrial and railway developments, we have come to think of this present type of town as in principle final, instead of it itself in change and flux.

It is a blind view of history, as something done elsewhere and recorded in books—instead of being, as it is, the very life-process of our city, its heredity and its momentum alike—which delays the perception of civic change among the intelligent, and still retards comprehension of it among even the progressive. Where even the theologian has too much failed to awaken to the current judgment-day, with its inexorable punishments, its marvellous re-wards, we cannot wonder that the economist should have been slow to realise the limitations of his Paleotechnic age; to analyse, yet correlate its complex of evils, its poverty—and luxury—dis-eases, its vices and crimes, its ignorances and follies, its apathy and indolence; or conversely, to appreciate and to support its Neotechnic initiatives and quests.

From past romancers to modern realists—Sir Walter to Zola, Reade to Bennett—the stuff of literature is life; above all, then, city-life and region-life. Ideas, as Bergson rightly teaches, are but sections of life: movement is of its essence. This life-movement proceeds in changing rhythm initiated by the genius of the place, continued by the spirit of the times, and accompanied by their good and evil influences. How else should we hear in our survey as we go, at one moment the muses' song, at another the shriek of furies!

Our survey, then, is a means towards the realisation of our community's life-history. This life-history is not past and done with; it is incorporated with its present activities and character. All these again, plus such fresh influences as may arise or intervene, are determining its opening future. From our survey of facts we have to prepare no mere material record, economic or structural, but to evoke the social personality, changing indeed so far with every generation, yet ever expressing itself in and through these.

Here, in fact, is the higher problem of our surveys, and to these the everyday purposes of our previous chapters will all be found to converge. He is no true town planner, but at best a too simple engineer, who sees only the similarity of cities, their common network of roads and communications. He who would be even a sound engineer, doing work to endure, let alone an artist in his work, must know his city indeed, and have entered into its soul— as Scott and Stevenson knew and loved their Edinburgh; as Pepys and Johnson and Lamb, as Besant and Gomme their London. Oxford, Cambridge, St. Andrews, Harvard, have peculiarly inspired their studious sons; but Birmingham and Glasgow, New York or Chicago, have each no small appeal to observant and active minds. In every city there is much of beauty and more of possibility; and thus for the town planner as an artist, the very worst of cities may be the best.

Hence we are but at the beginning of the study of cities in evolution. We should now pass through a representative selection of cities. We need to search out sociological interpretations of all these unique developments; indeed, it is for lack of such concrete inquiries that sociology has been so long marking time, between anthropology and metaphysics, and with no sufficient foothold in social life as it is lived to-day in cities. We need to search into the life of city and citizen, and the interrelation of these, and this as intensively as the biologist inquires into the interaction of individual and race in evolution. Only thus can we adequately handle the problems of social pathology; and hence again rise to the hope of cities, and with clearer beginnings of civic therapeutics, of social hygiene.

In such ways, and through such studies, the incipient civic renaiscence is proven to be no mere utopia; and its needed policy may be more clearly discerned, even devised. Thus we return, upon a new spiral, to town planning as City Design. City by city our civic ideals emerge and become definite; and in the revivance of our city we see how to work towards its extrication from its Paleotechnic evils, its fuller entrance upon the better incipient order. Education and industry admit of reorganisation together, towards sound mind and vigorous body once more. This unification of idealistic feeling and of constructive thought with practical endeavour, of civic ethics and group-psychology with art, yet with economics, is indeed the planning of Eutopia—of practical and practicable Eutopias, city by city.

Such then, is the vital purpose of all our surveys: and though their completion must be left to others, fresh chapters for city after city—indeed sometimes a volume for each—might here be added, with their Surveys, of things as they are and as they change, passing into Reports, towards things as they may be.

Every town planner is indeed moving in this direction more or less; no one will now admit himself a mere procrustean engineer of parallelograms, or mere draughtsman of perspectives; but long and arduous toil and quest are still before us ere we can really express, as did the builders of old, the spirit of our cities. Spiritually, artistically, we are but in the day of small things, however big be our material responsibilities. Hence the justification of the inner rooms of our Outlook Tower, and of the Cities and Town Planning Exhibition, with their drafts, sketches, and sometimes beginnings towards the realisable Eutopia of cities, as of Edinburgh and Dunfermline, of Chelsea or Dundee, of Dublin or Madras.

Without such increasing, deepening, and generally diffusing realisation of the character and spirit of our city, our town planning and improvement schemes are at best but repeating (though no doubt in better form and upon a further spiral) those "bye-law streets" with which the past generation was too easily content, but with which we are now becoming so thoroughly disenchanted, as but slums after all, and in some ways the worse for being standardised.

Take next a fuller line of historico-sociological treatment. What is the characteristic field, and essential concept, of sociology? The mathematician's mind deals with concepts of movement in space and time, the physicists with the phenomena of matter and energy, and the biologist's with those of life. What are these last? And how related, to the social, how distinguished also?

Obviously for every living being, from humblest to highest, there must be nutritive and reproductive functionings; and these in relation to their environment. Moreover, despite the long traditional error of political economists in insisting essentially on egoism, the primary self-regarding functions of life become increasingly subservient to the species-regarding (and so far altruistic) ones. In fact, this is a main process, and test, of evolutionary advance, and more important than any others, however earlier applied.

But sociology, while utilising all the preceding biological concepts, has its own distinctive field beyond them. Its essential and distinctive concept is not merely of "Society," for animals have their societies, and with their "Consciousness of Kind," their "Herd-instinct," &c., Human societies show a course of changes far beyond those of animal societies; since these are largely cumulative, (in ways transcending those of biological heredity) throughout the filiation of human generations (and in the "*durée*" of individual life also.) Sociology is thus distinguished by its study of this manifold heritage of civilisation: and alas, also by its corresponding recognition of correspondingly transmissible burdens, with increasing enquiry into these.

The clear distinctiveness of this social heritage from organic heredity (and correspondingly of social burdens from organic ones) is of course here essential; since too often "Heritage" and "Heredity" have been confused, and still sometimes are.

This main problem of sociology thus becomes seen as of the fullest evolutionary range; and its treatment has thus to be more comprehensive and thoroughgoing than have been as yet those of contemporary economics; or even of politics, great though its activities have been, both as regards heritages and burdens. The still customary discussions and treatments of all these, too independently of their historic filiations and their mutual interactions, &c., are thus necessarily inadequate; indeed too often futile or misleading, when not positively disastrous.

4

A. L. Bowley

THE PROBLEM OF

SOCIAL CLASSES

WE NOW COME to the very troublesome problem of defining or describing social classes. We may consider either families or households or individuals; we may place them by birth, by rank, by occupation, by income, or by habits.

Birth will not give a classification, because it can only throw the problem back a generation. Rank will take us a very little way, though perhaps for some purposes, even in modern times, it may be worth while to enumerate the hereditary titles whose possession is a patent of nobility, and rank in the Army and Navy, and the learned professions; but official rank makes so little social difference except on ceremonial occasions, and affects so small a proportion of the population that it is not sociologically important.

We may suggest as a definition of a social class that it consists of a group of persons and their dependants (in the sense discussed above) who have intercourse on equal terms so far as sex and age allow. The determinants will then be occupation, income, and habits. It is at once clear that there can be no hard and fast line separating one class from another, and perhaps the most hopeful

Reprinted from *The Nature and Purpose of the Measurement of Social Phenomena*, 1915. The problem of social class was curiously ignored in British sociology between 1880 and 1910—perhaps because Liberal ideology was so resistant to the idea that class was a significant element of social structure. Thus Bowley virtually pioneered the methodology of research on social class—which was to become such a major theme of sociological work in Britain in the following forty years.

way of identifying classes will be to try to find a few distinct types and suppose people grouped in classes about those types which they most resemble. This is a task for a critic of life and manners rather than for a statistician, and I do not propose to attempt it at length.

As typical of the *upper class* we should take people of large and so-called independent means, in other words, owners of property on a considerable scale, who have acquired the habits appropriate to dignified leisure, to public service, or to the management of land or of persons on a large scale; with them we must group other persons whom they are pleased to admit into their ranks.

A glance at the census of occupations will show how sadly mixed the *professional class* is. Essentially it contains those who, having passed through a definite course of intellectual and technical training, have been admitted to the rank of clergyman, barrister, physician, etc., by competent authority. But teachers satisfy the definition very nearly, and there is an unbroken grading from a university professor to an uncertificated teacher in a village school, or a nursery governess. Musicians, artists, authors and actors have also an intellectual training and frequently a degree or diploma; but a street-musician,[1] a pavement-artist, a lithographer, a shorthand writer, and a pantomime child are at the other end of continuous scales of which the top is occupied by developed genius. An arbitrary separation must be made by the tests of intercourse and income, and at least three sections will be found.

Somewhere we must find room for people who will not have intercourse with a class they consider below them, and whom the class to which they aspire will not admit—a very numerous body in all grades of society.

In industry and commerce we may distinguish an employing class, with numerous subdivisions based mainly on income, and an employed class, containing clerks and manual workers, as al-

[1]   In the English census a street-singer is a musician, an organ-grinder is a worker in Sundry Industries, and a pavement-artist is without specified occupation.

ready discussed. Clerks (of similar ages) can only be graded arbitrarily by the test of income and intercourse.

It is evident that such classification is not definite, for the same family may contain members of each class so far named except manual workers, and intercourse may be complete. On the other hand, family intercourse may become nominal or non-existent, while men as they grow older tend more and more to associate with others of similar habits, income and occupation. But the intercourse test will give lines cutting across the occupation test, since persons engaged in professions meet on equal terms those of similar incomes engaged in commerce. If we merge all in one great middle-class, we can imagine a grading by income which would nearly correspond to the test of intercourse.

To get any clear division between the middle and the manual-working class, we must deal only with adults in their final position. For the middle class is continually recruited from the working class: the children of artisans become clerks and teachers with increasing frequency; very often the girls become shop-assistants, milliners, dressmakers, and so on; more rarely they enter professions, or become employers.

A classification by social position can only be complete if we allow a place for the young, no longer dependent, who are passing out of their parents' class. Many cases were found in the town inquiries, which are summarized in the table on the opposite page.

We can only make the observation in the relatively small number of households where there are children at work and still living with their parents.

Further details are given in the Appendix.

Mr. Booth gave a very interesting empirical classification in his *Life and Labour in London* (Final Volume, 1902, pp. 6 *seq.*), based for the richer classes on the number of persons per servant, and for the poorer on the number of persons per room. This is, of course, arbitrary, for well-to-do families of similar occupations and incomes vary greatly in their expenditure on rent and arrangements for service, while working-class families tend to take the best houses they can afford and then accommodate themselves to the house.

STATUS OF CHILDREN COMPARED WITH THAT OF
THEIR FATHER

Status of occupier	Status of children living with parents	No. of Households			
		North-ampton	Warring-ton	Read-ing	To-gether
Unskilled:					
	No children placed	60	154	146	360
	Children in same grade as father ..	13	66	75	154
	One or more children skilled or apprenticed	29	21	18	68
	One or more children employed as clerks	—	6	8	14
Skilled:					
	None	288	205	180	673
	Fallen	13	21	23	57
	Same	173	77	64	314
	Risen	22	11	12	45
Clerk:					
	None	11	14	18	43
	Fallen	2	4	2	8
	Same	—	4	—	4
	Risen	—	1	—	1
Not known or not male occupier		120	84	131	335
	Total	731	668	677	2,076
Superior houses not visited		153	13	150	316
Whole sample of 1 in 20 (*circa*)		884	681	827	2,392

Summary:
Working-class households (male occupier):

No children placed	1,076	
Unchanged	472 ⎫	
Down	65 ⎬	
Up	128 ⎭	665
	1,741	

The manual working class is fairly well delimitated from others in this country. The fringe of men working on their own account is small, and most of them could be readily placed in one class or the other. Shop-assistants, however, are numerous and difficult to classify. Small holders, cultivating with their families, make a difficulty in classification when they are numerous.

The manual working class is, however, very minutely graded, as has often been remarked. The fear of stepping down a rung in

the ladder of respectability is very strong, and quite free intercourse is very restricted in its scope. The division is not necessarily
by income nor by occupation, but appears to be determined by
habits and manners, which are, of course, partly dependent on income and work. The grading is very often easily observed from
the kind of house inhabited, not only from its rent and accommodation, but perhaps principally from the respectability of the
street in which it is situated. The actual locality of residence is, of
course, one of the tests for all classes. No doubt the grading is different in kind in different towns. It would probably be feasible in
any one town to mark off divisions of the working class by types:
taking the foreman, or the highly skilled artisan, perhaps owning
or acquiring house property, as one; the ordinarily skilled
journeyman as a second; the machine-tending, partly skilled
factory operative as a third; the untrained man in steady employ
as a fourth; and the man irregularly employed in muscular labour,
living from hand to mouth, as a fifth. The streets in which these
typical persons live and the people they associate with might be
found to give fairly distinct classes in many towns. The classification in the country would, of course, be different.

It is doubtful whether it is possible to divide a society into such
well-defined social classes that a useful measurement could be
made of the numbers in any class. Social structure is in a state of
flux, former divisions are breaking down, and new lines of
cleavage continually appear only to be modified within a generation. Mr. Stephen Reynolds and other writers specially well ac-
quainted with manual workers have emphasized the gulf between
"Them" and "Us," "Us" being manual workers in contact with
natural forces or working for a wage with no security of tenure,
and "Them" being persons with an adequate income and security
against future privation. This, no doubt, represents a common
attitude when the definitely rich and the less well-paid manual
workers are in contact; but in fact there are "Others" as well as
Them and Us, and classes are not separated by steep vertical
barriers, but rather there is a gentle inclined plane from the lowest
to the highest. One can perhaps extend the metaphor by suggesting that progress from class to class is like the ascent of a much-

fissured glacier, slippery and uncertain, with crevasses impossible to pass by some routes and easy by others, while from time to time the crevasses widen or close. In such a case we should make a map or plan by altitudes, and that corresponds to the method to which I now proceed.

5

L. T. Hobhouse, G. C. Wheeler, and M. Ginsberg

COMPARATIVE SOCIAL DEVELOPMENT

THEORIES of social evolution are readily formed with the aid of some preconceived ideas and a few judiciously selected corroborative facts. The data offered to the theorist by the voluminous results of anthropological inquiry on the one hand, and by the immense record of the history of civilisation on the other, are so vast and so various that it must be an unskilled selector who is unable, by giving prominence to the instances which agree and by ignoring those which conflict with his views, to make out a plausible case in support of some general notion of human progress. On the other hand, if theories are easily made, they are also easily confuted by a less friendly use of the same data. That same variety of which we speak is so great that there is hardly any sociological generalisation which does not stumble upon some awkward fact if one takes the trouble to find it. Anyone with a sense for facts soon recognises that the course of social evolution is not unitary but that different races and different communities of the same race have, in fact, whether they started from the same point or no, diverged early, rapidly, and in many different directions at once. If theorising is easy when facts are treated arbitrarily, a theory which would really grow out of the facts themselves and express their true significance presents the greatest possible difficulties to the inquirer. The data themselves are vast but chaotic,

Reprinted from *The Material Culture and Social Institutions of the Simpler Peoples: An Essay in Correlation*. London, 1915.

and at every point incomplete. They fall into two main divisions. On the one hand, there is the historical record of the civilisations; upon the other there is the immense field of contemporary anthropology. In both alike the data are equally difficult to ascertain with precision, and when ascertained to reduce to any intelligible order. In the history of civilisation we have full studies of many institutions, and we can learn something, not only of what they were at any one moment, but of their development in time, their genesis, their rise, their maturity, their decay. But even here the information often breaks off short at the most interesting point. Beginnings are frequently matter of conjecture. The nature of institutions, as they appear on paper, may be known to us, while we are left to reconstruct their actual working from casual examples, hints, and references that leave much to the imagination. We find them decaying without intelligible cause, and often enough we are faced with the fact that more thorough-going inquiry has completely revolutionised our view of an institution which had been taken as thoroughly explored and fully interpreted by earlier schools of historians. So is it also with the anthropological record. Here indeed we have a handful of monographs made by trained and skilled observers in modern times, which leave nothing to be desired excepting that the work had been carried out three or four generations ago before contact with the white man or with other more civilised races had begun to corrupt the purity of aboriginal institutions. Outside these monographs we have a vast mass of travellers' reports, good, bad, and indifferent, data which it is impossible to ignore and yet which can seldom be taken at their face value. Moreover all anthropological data of this kind, however simple the life of the people with which they deal, are modern; with the exception of the few available references that we have to the peoples that surrounded the Greeks and Romans in Herodotus, Tacitus, and other writers of antiquity, the great bulk of anthropological inquiry dates from the last three or four centuries, and it is sometimes forgotten that the peoples of whom they treat must have lived as long, must in a sense have had as extensive a tradition behind them, and to that extent are as far removed from the true primitive as civilised man himself.

Therefore when we are inquiring into development and origins we have to be careful how we take the findings of inquirers among the people of our own day, however simple, as evidence of what must have been in the beginnings of human kind. What ethnographical research yields us is not a history but a number of pictures of given peoples each taken as it were by an instantaneous photograph at a given time. It is a piece of good fortune if in any case we get successive pictures of the same people so full and true that by comparing them we can arrive directly at the actual course of the development of its institutions in a given period. Before the period of civilised influence sets in we have at best only fragments of such history, and in the main our data are descriptive rather than historical. No comparison or classification of these data can tell us offhand how institutions grew, any more than the classification of existing rocks tells the geologist how strata were formed. Yet it is in the main from the actual composition and arrangement of existing strata, assisted by what he knows of permanent physical laws and of recorded or clearly proved physical changes, that the geologist infers the history of the earth's crust, and it is on analogous methods that any scientific theory of social evolution must rely. Such a theory must rest at the outset upon the discovery of some order in the ethnological data. To this end two preliminary steps seem to be necessary. The first consists in taking the main institutions, customs, practices, and beliefs that constitute the structure of social life at any given time, and distinguishing the varieties of form which each institution actually presents in the various peoples among whom we find it. Many institutions can thus be treated from more than one point of view. Taking marriage, for example, we can obviously distinguish monogamy, various forms of polygamy and of polyandry, intermixtures or combinations of these forms, and, some may add, in addition to all some form of group marriage. Again we can treat any of these forms of marriage from the point of view of its rigidity or otherwise. We can inquire how far it is binding, distinguish cases in which it is entered into or dissolved so easily and so entirely at the will of either party that it is doubtful whether the term marriage is strictly applicable; and from this onwards we can trace every sort of gradation in the rigidity of the institution up to indissoluble monogamous marriage. Or again we can exhibit methods by which a partner is obtained, whether it be by free courtship, by child-betrothal, by the exchange of women or of gifts, or by presents to the parents or relations, by sheer purchase, by capture, and so forth. And so carrying this method through the whole field of inquiry relating to marriage, we can set up a system of forms all of which shall be illustrated somewhere in the light of human society; and in general, we can so arrange them as to show transitions from any one form to another of such a kind that we can very easily conceive an institution beginning at one end and passing through these transitional forms until it reaches the most extreme point in the opposite direction. What may be called a social morphology of this kind, that is to say, the ascertaining and classification of the actual forms of any institution known to exist may be regarded as the first step towards the introduction of order into the field of comparative sociology.[1]

But beyond this lies a second and far more difficult step. We have spoken of the form of an institution passing by gradations from one stage to another, very remote from it perhaps. It is one thing to exhibit and even to illustrate possible gradations of such a kind, and another thing to show that actual institutions do pass along such a scale of development. In some cases no doubt we can historically trace a line of change, but it would be exceedingly difficult to maintain that the line of change had always been the same in all cases, and quite impossible, we think, at the present stage of our knowledge to lay down that any given institution must take its rise in one form and must pass through a series of graded changes in a uniform direction. If indeed we could make any assumption of this kind, the process of sociological inquiry would

---

[1] The chief danger in forming any social classification is that of over-rigidity in definition. Customs and institutions vary continuously, and the lines of demarcation which any classification must draw are apt to be artificial and unreal. Moreover what is on the surface the same institution may have a different content at different stages of social development. A certain elasticity of interpretation must therefore be allowed in order to adapt any scheme of classification to the facts without forming them into unreal categories.

be enormously simplified. We should have as it were a scale of development, the direction of which would be definitely known. We should be able to assign to any form of institution credibly reported in any given society, its particular place in that scale. We should know that it had never been further on in the scale, nor yet that it had reached its particular place by any roundabout road. We should be able to infer that it had passed through the earlier phases and no other, and we could in fact treat all differences to be found in social institutions as due to a single comprehensive cause —the difference in the rate of development. In point of fact inquiry lends no countenance to any such simplicity of view. A single instance from the institution that has already been mentioned may suffice to explain this point. We commonly think of strict monogamy as the product of a high civilisation, though not necessarily the highest civilisation, and it is true that we find polygamy associated upon the whole with the lower civilisations and with the peoples whom we do not regard as civilised at all. But apart from the fact that, for fairly obvious reasons, the majority of men in all races live with one wife at a time, we find quite a number of instances in which a rigid monogamy is the established rule among some of quite the rudest races of mankind. By whatever road the Veddas, or the Semang, or the Karok, or the Dyaks have arrived at monogamy, we may be pretty sure that it was by a road quite different from that which established this system in mediæval Europe. Nor can we even infer from the fact that nations of European culture agree with the Veddas, the Semang, and the Karok, any far-reaching identity in ethical views as to the relations of the sexes, or in fact in any other social and moral customs or ideas which in many races stand closely associated with the monogamic rule. We have to recognise from the outset that two societies, as widely divergent as possible in almost every respect, may exhibit close agreement on some one or more points, and we have to learn accordingly that to infer from any single institution a general state of development is to fly in the face of the anthropological facts.

If then we cannot assume any single line of development, what use are we to make of our morphology? Let us consider where we stand. We suppose ourselves to have ascertained the forms which any given institution assumes. We have now recognised that in different societies an institution may arrive at the same form by completely different paths, and that agreement in respect of any one institution is no evidence for agreement in other respects. We cannot lay down any absolute order of development, nor can we maintain as a strict generalisation that any given form of any given institution is to be found only in some determinate stage of the development of society. Sociology in fact is not a science of rigid generalisations. Where rigid generalisation fails science resorts to statistical methods, and the question arises whether this is possible in sociology. On the practical difficulties of applying statistics to the study of social institutions, we shall speak in the next section. But if we suppose for a moment that these are not insuperable, let us see what might be gained. We might begin with any two institutional forms, A and B and find on inquiry that in 90 per cent. of the cases where we have A we also find B, and that in 80 per cent. of the cases where we have B we also find A. If that is so we can infer some connection, though probably an indirect one, between A and B, and perhaps research may show that the residual instances where we have B but not A are associated with the presence or absence of a third institution C. This would throw considerable light on the connection of these forms, and by multiplying such conditions we might obtain considerable insight into the interconnexion of certain groups of institutions. This was in fact the method applied by Dr. Tylor to the study of certain marriage customs some twenty years ago, and it is to be regretted that little has been done in the interval to extend the method of other problems.

What we propose to ask is whether it is possible to apply this line of inquiry to elucidating the changes of institution which accompany the growth of civilisation, the most important feature of social evolution. The first difficulty that occurs here is the vagueness as to the term civilisation, which, as generally used, implies elements of material, religious, artistic, and intellectual culture. If all these elements are insisted on and civilisations are judged in accordance with the level attained, not in one respect but in all, we shall of course find, if we find anything, that the most civilised race is that which has developed furthest in all these directions. We shall, in fact, achieve a purely identical proposition. The real question is how far these different developments imply one another. To attack this problem with any hope of a fruitful issue it is necessary to find some one characteristic which would be generally regarded as essential to civilisation, as possessing real significance in the life of a people, and as advancing in some determinate direction, which can be recognised and measured with some facility, and of which tangible evidence can be obtained. It will then be possible to follow other lines of development and observe the correlation of various forms of institution with successive stages in this advance. It may always be objected that we have not chosen the most essential point as the basis of our inquiry, but of that the results of the inquiry themselves will afford some test. At any rate, on these lines, if the work can be carried through, we may expect to learn something of the correlation of different elements in social growth.

The development which seems best to serve this purpose is that of material culture, the control of man over nature as reflected in the arts of life. It may be objected that this implies too materialistic a view of human society, and is too superficial a criterion of general progress. It may be replied to the latter point, in the first place that we do not use it as a criterion of general progress, but propose to inquire how far progress or (if the word be disliked) change in any definite direction is in fact associated with advance in the control over the forces of nature. On the former point it may be remarked that material culture is a fair index of the general level of knowledge and, if we may use a more general term, of mentality. The desire for comfort in his material surroundings is, with few exceptions, common to man. How much energy he will put into the business of securing it, how much organising capacity he can apply, what ideas, what knowledge, and what imagination he can bring to bear on it, what fears or scruples deter him from using all his available powers are questions which have different answers for different people, and on the answer depends in general the level of his material culture. Hence this culture does, roughly, though no more than roughly, reflect the general level of intellectual attainment. Moreover, in this case it is fairly easy to agree on the meaning of what in other instances is a very disputable term—the meaning of progress. The control of man over nature is a definite conception, and it is generally easy to recognise any advance on this particular line, while it is also the fact that it is on this particular line that the people that we call civilised show the most palpable advance over those to whom we deny the term. In the history of mankind as a whole the advance in this direction, though neither universal nor continuous, is probably more widespread and more continuous than in any other, and in modern civilisation it becomes more continuous and far more rapid. Finally the question whether there is any correlation between advance on this line and any particular movement on other sides of human life is perhaps the most important question for the general theory of social evolution. Does the advance of human knowledge which in relation to the understanding and control of natural forces seems unlimited, carry with it any distinct movement in morals, law, religion, the general organisation of society? Does it make for progress in these directions, or the reverse, or is it indifferent to them?

We do not here attempt to deal with these problems in general. To grapple with them at all would involve to begin with a definition of progress which lies outside our immediate sphere. We offer only a preliminary contribution. We do not, in fact, deal with "civilised" peoples at all, but confine ourselves to the classification of those less fortunate races which range from the lowest known *Naturmenschen* to the confines of the historic civilisation. We seek within these limits first to distinguish the advancing grades of material culture, and, secondly—without any systematic inquiry as to what constitutes "progress" or the reverse—to determine how far various forms of political and social institutions can be correlated with each grade.

The Possibility of Sociological Correlation

We have next to inquire how far it is actually possible to establish any correlations between social and political institutions on the one hand and stages of economic culture on the other, and to what extent ordinary statistical methods can be made available to forward this result. It must be replied at once that in view of the peculiar nature of the subject, and in particular of the data on which we have to rely, statistical methods can only be employed with certain reserves. All results must be rough. All are open to certain special causes of error, and any inference based on a comparison of numbers alone is dangerous. On the other hand, numerical results in combination with close analysis of accompanying conditions, are of high utility, both in checking generalisations and in measuring the value of data. This will be better understood if we study the actual difficulties which confront the inquirer who endeavours to apply the test of numbers to sociological facts.

1. The Character of the Data

If we confined ourselves to monographs compiled by skilled observers, there would be comparatively little difficulty with the data themselves, but unfortunately, as already remarked, such monographs are few and they would not in the aggregate prove sufficient to warrant any statistical calculations. Moreover, so to limit our vision would be to leave out of sight a vast amount of material which contains valuable evidence, even if the ore is sometimes difficult to sift from the dross. We are therefore forced to take account of the ordinary materials of anthropology—reports of travellers, missionaries, explorers, and casual observers, and it need hardly be said that in all such reports the problem of inferring from the statements of the observer the precise nature of the facts which he means to report, is not one which admits of an easy and straightforward solution. In particular when one endeavours to classify forms of institutions under heads, which is the necessary presupposition of any attempt at correlation, we must bear in mind that no observer has the scheme of classification in his mind, and there is considerable opportunity for error in reducing the contents of his report to the heads of any classification, however wide we may cast our net. Over and above these well-known difficulties in anthropology, there are all the sources of error, obscurity and confusion which arise from the intermixture of cultures, the rise or decay of institutions under the influence of foreigners, and in particular of the white immigrants themselves, to whom the reporter may belong, and there is always the probability that the peoples whom the reporter comes in contact with are precisely those specimens of the tribe who lie nearest to the white man or to other civilised people, and are most influenced thereby. All this, however, is common matter to anthropologists and not much of it presents any difficulty to our inquiry as compared with others.

II. The Unit

It is otherwise when we pass to the question of the unit which we must take as the basis of our calculations. Every rigid statistical inquiry supposes that the phenomena with which it deals can be stated in terms of some unit which is constant throughout its field. What is the unit social group? Let us consider a people occupying a certain area, the natives of Australia, let us say, or the Algonquin Indians. There are certain features common to the culture of these peoples, but within them there are a great many tribes and even groups of tribes. Not all that is true of one tribe will be true of others even within the same group, and certainly not all things true of a group would be true of all the Algonquins or all the Australians. And lastly, within what is called the tribe itself, there are often clans, local groups, and even sub-tribes, and even these are not always alike in all their institutions.

Now the reports of ethnographers sometimes deal with tribes, sometimes with divisions or branches of a tribe, and sometimes with groups of two or three, a dozen, or even a score of tribes taken together. We might be inclined to take the tribe as the unit. But the term tribe is used with the utmost variety of meaning by our reporters. Some apply the name to the smallest group of people living together, others to the loose unity which extends over a great area and covers all groups using a common dialect and recognising a certain affinity which distinguishes them from the rest of the world. In this wider sense tribes differ greatly in extent— one may contain a dozen or a score of subordinate groups; another may contain one or two only. And moreover, the limitations of the tribe sometimes seem to be assigned rather by the purview of the traveller or by the chance extent to which a dialect has spread than by clearly marked divisions separating it off socially or politically from its neighbours. Indeed a population which is treated as a "tribe" by one writer might be regarded as a collection of many tribes by another. Thus the statements which form our data refer to populations of different magnitude, and there is no discoverable means of reducing these to units of equal magnitude. But in fact no such reduction is necessary for our purpose. What we are examining is the correlation of social institutions with grades of economic culture. For this purpose we wish to know the number of separate social groups at any given grade possessing a given institution, and for this purpose the population or the number of subordinate bodies contained by any given social group is of secondary importance. The real question is, what constitutes a separate social group? In the higher grades of social development political independence supplies a fairly definite criterion. Yet even here it must be remembered that independence may be partial, as well as absolute, and that it might be legitimate and even necessary to count a population as forming one society for certain purposes and two or more for certain other purposes. Be this as it may, on the lower levels political unity is a much vaguer conception, and when the observer finds fundamental similarity of type and custom, uninterrupted intercourse and, in particular, free intermarriage extending over a certain area he will generally treat that area as one, whether the population corresponds to what he calls one tribe or not. In this he will not be far wrong, for the customs and institutions of such a collection of people in all probability have a common origin. They arise and flourish and decay in the main from the same causes and in close interconnection. In general we have no alternative but to follow the reporter, and take each institution that he reports as one case of the existence of that institution. Of course in so doing we are trusting to the judgment of our witness. It may be that he ought to have drawn distinctions and demarcations, and these may in fact appear when we compare his account with that of another observer, while sometimes it becomes apparent through internal evidence. In such a case we should in fact divide the group in our tables and count each of its parts as one. But in so far as groupings and divisions have been made by original observers with judgment and knowledge, it is reasonable to treat as a single instance a homogeneous population living in a continuous area enjoying regular intercourse throughout and not divided by clear lines of racial, social, or political difference.[2] The mere difference in size of these units need not greatly disturb our calculations.

On the other hand, we must recognise that the judgment of observers is not equally to be depended on in all cases, and that sometimes mere chance or the bare impossibility of obtaining detailed information as to separate communities has led our reporters to treat as one peoples who might very possibly be distributed into many distinct sections as the result of further enquiry. We note in their place certain possibilities of error in calculation that arise from this course, and throughout, as will be explained presently, we so limit our inferences as to guard against this danger in cases where its presence may have passed unnoticed.

At the same time it may be pointed out that on this side the very defects in our reports tend to cancel one another. Close inspection shows that statements made about a group of tribes are in reality based often enough on the one or two members of the group with whom the reporter has had close personal contact. Hence different reports about the same group often prove to be inconsistent and the explanation of the inconsistency not infrequently is that both are true, one of some members of the group and the other of others. Sometimes we are able to fix the exceptions, sometimes we can only table the statements as true, one of "some" members of the group and the other of "some other" members. But the repeated experience of discrepancies of this kind reduces the value of large generalisations and tends to equate the statistical value of the units with regard to which we may conceive ourselves to possess trustworthy information.

Further, it must be remembered that when we are comparing peoples at much the same level of general culture, whatever ir-

[2]   In a few cases our units are in strictness too large for this definition. Our reasons for attempting to divide them are indicated below.

regularity there is in our units will be pretty evenly distributed. Suppose we are dealing with two opposite customs, both found pretty frequently among hunting tribes. Let us say that we have 100 cases of the one and 50 of the other. The 100 will no doubt contain large groups and small, but so also will the 50. If we know of one group of special magnitude and importance, we note the fact and give it due weight in our summing up. But in general there is no reason to think that there will be any aggregation of the larger instances on one side rather than on the other. There is nothing to weight the scale, and if our numbers were sufficiently great, we might find in this consideration alone a solution of the problem so far as it depends on the inadequacy of our reports.

But in many cases our numbers are not great enough to justify us in trusting to the impartiality of chance. The probable error would be high, and we should often be unable to draw any inference at all. We therefore base no inference on small differences. The fact that a given custom is to be found, say in 55 per cent. of the instances obtained at a given level of culture, and an opposite custom in 45 per cent. must be taken as in itself insignificant. It can only mean that, roughly, there is no clear tendency to the one or the other at that stage. Such a proportion as that of 55 : 45 can be of value only if it is a link in a chain, e.g., if, at a lower level the figures were 70 : 30, and at a higher one 30 : 70. It is otherwise when we have a 2 : 1 preponderance. This is not likely to be a mere chance. But even here it is well not to be content with the gross numerical result, but also to examine the constitution of our majority and minority. Such a check is desirable, not only in view of doubts as to the equal value of our units, but to obviate a second difficulty, which has now to be examined.

This difficulty is in a manner the exact converse of the last. It may be asked whether in any cultural area—in any territory, that is, where the conditions of life are very similar, and where, though it is too large for direct intercourse between its parts, there is opportunity for institutions to propagate themselves in the course of generations by social contact—we ought to reckon distinct cases at all. Institutions and customs tend to propagate themselves indefinitely, and if we find, say, a certain form of marriage all over a sub-continent, it may be that it has had a single origin, and ought on our principles to be accounted one case rather than many. Thus we find a certain amount of polygamy—very variable it is true—common apparently, with one doubtful exception, to all Australian tribes. Shall we count this as upwards of thirty instances, or is it in reality only one instance? The reply is that whatever the degree of cultural unity among the Australian aborigines, it did not prevent their marriage customs from differing in many essential respects from one another. If that is so it seems fair to take as a unit each area which observers have, in fact, recognized as homogeneous and interconnected, and if in the matter of descent, or of capture, we get a great variation of custom as between one area and another, while in regard to the permission of polygamy we get uniformity, to let this result have its due weight by entering each instance of polygamy separately in our tables. The result at least shows that a certain degree of polygamy is suited to the conditions of Australian culture generally, while other incidents of marriage vary greatly within the limits of their culture. If an institution has, in fact, propagated and maintained itself over a great area, even though its origin be in some unitary cause, we cannot regard its extensive prevalence as unimportant or insignificant. The fact that it prevails so widely is evidence of its suitability to the conditions of life among the peoples in question, and this correlation is as suitably expressed as any other in the number of separate instances which will be counted.

If such an institution is found in all or most of the various regions of the world occupied by people of a certain industrial grade, we may fairly sum up the instances and treat the result as a measure of the correlation between that institution and the level of economic culture in question. But if all, or the great majority of instances in which it appears, are drawn from one region, it is different. To show how dangerous a simple enumeration might be in such a case we may pursue this particular instance taken a little further. When we compare the Australians with others of the same economic grade we find, for example, that the Wild Semang are monogamous. Now the Wild Semang are only entered in our table as one group. But they are very numerous and scattered, and they count as one only, because they are not sufficiently known for any one to make divisions among them. In order to compare the prevalence of monogamy and polygamy among the Lower Hunters, we cannot crudely set down the Australians as thirty cases on the one side and the Semang as one on the other. In such a case we must consider our figures from more than one point of view. We must cross-classify, and group them not only by the economic but by the geographical order. If all, or the majority of cases of any given institution come from one part of the world, we must note this fact and take it into account before drawing any inferences as to the correlation of that institution with any particular grade of culture as such. The necessity has been kept in mind, and while our geographical grouping has necessarily been rough in this experimental inquiry, we have throughout kept the different continents separate in our tables, and within these certain regions of culture contact are sufficiently apparent. Racial unity is a more problematical matter, which no doubt would explain many identities and differences if we could know all the facts, but to rely on this explanation would constantly have taken us into controversial questions, and we have been compelled for the time being to leave it aside. Meanwhile our plan is, whenever we find an accumulation of instances in a particular area to note the fact as a deduction from any generalisation that might be founded on those instances, and, if necessary, to seek some alternative method of presenting the results. For example, in the particular case referred to above, we present the totals as to polygamy and monogamy arrived at, first by taking the Australians as so many separate instances, and then by treating them as a single cultural group equated with a corresponding cultural type in Asia and Africa. This method—the details of which must vary in accordance with the nature of the concrete case—yields upper and lower limits of error, which often express the nearest approximation that we can make to the truth.

We have then two difficulties to keep in mind. The first is the imperfect precision of our units; the second is the deduction from the value of separate units to be made on account of the influence of culture contacts. Fortunately these two difficulties tend to cancel one another, for the influence of culture-contact diminishes the value of the large area relatively to the smaller. But we cannot disregard them, and to guard against them we must refrain from basing any inference on small preponderances, while if we have large differences, we must first examine the constitution of our majority and minority. When these in combination have been observed we shall in fact find that various positive results emerge.

Bibliography

1. Works illustrating the development of British sociology

Abercrombie, Patrick. *Sheffield: A Civic Survey and Suggestions towards a Development Plan*. Liverpool: The University Press, 1924.

Bateson, W. *Biological Fact and the Structure of Society*. Herbert Spencer Lecture. Oxford: Clarendon Press, 1912.

Bell, Lady Florence. *At the Works: A Study of a Manufacturing Town*. London: E. Arnold, 1907.

*Booth, Charles. "Conditions and Occupations of the People of East London and Hackney." *Journal of the Royal Statistical Society*, 1887.

———. *Conditions and Occupations of the People of Tower Hamlets*. London, 1887.

———. *Labour and Life of the People . . .* , vols. 1–2. London: Williams and Norgate, 1889–91.

———. *Labour and Life of the People . . .* , vols. 1–4. London: Macmillan, 1889–93.

———. *Life and Labour of the People in London*, vols. 1–9. London: Macmillan, 1892–97.

*———. *Life and Labour of the People in London*, vols. 1–17. London: Macmillan, 1902–3.

———. "Paupers and Old Age Pensions." *Journal of the Royal Statistical Society*, 1891.

Booth, William. *In Darkest England*. London: W. Reeves, 1890.

Bowley, A. L. *The Nature and Purpose of the Measurement of Social Phenomena*. London: P. S. King, 1915.

———. "The Improvement of Official Statistics." *Journal of the Royal Statistical Society*, 1908.

Bowley, A. L., and Burnett-Hurst, A. R. *Livelihood and Poverty*. London: G. Bell, 1915.

Bowley, A. L., and Hogg, M. H. *Has Poverty Diminished?* London: P. S. Ling, 1925.

Bowley, A. L., and Wood, J. H. "Wages in the XIXth Century." *Journal of the Royal Statistical Society*, 1906.

Brabrook, Sir Edward. "Eugenics and Pauperism." *Eugenics Review*, 1909.

———. "Social Insurances." *Journal of the Royal Statistical Society*, 1908.

Branford, S., and Farquharson, A. *An Introduction to Regional Surveys.* London: Westminster, 1924.

Branford, V. V. *Whitherward? Hell or Eutopia.* London, 1919.

———, ed. *The Coal Crisis and the Future.* London: LePlay House Press, 1926.

Branford, V. V., and Geddes, Patrick. *Our Social Inheritance.* London: Williams and Norgate, 1923.

———. *The Coming Polity.* London: Williams and Norgate, 1921.

Brock, A. J. *Health and Conduct.* London: Williams and Norgate, 1919.

Butler, C. V. *Social Conditions in Oxford.* London, 1919.

Cadbury, Edward. *Experiments in Industrial Organization.* London: Longmans, Green, 1912.

Cadbury, Edward, and Matheson, M. C. *Women's Work and Wages: A Phase of Life in an Industrial City.* London: T. F. Unwin, 1906.

Chadwick, Edwin. "On the Best Modes of Representing the Duration of Life, and the Pressure and Progress of the Causes of Mortality amongst Different Classes and Different Districts and Countries." *Journal of the Statistical Society*, 1845.

———. "The Results of Different Principles of Legislation and Administration in Europe." *Journal of the Statistical Society*, 1860.

Chapman, S. J., and Marquis, F. J. "The Recruiting of Employers from Wage Earners in the Cotton Industry." *Journal of the Royal Statistical Society*, 1912.

*Clay, Rev. John. "The Relation between Crime, Popular Instruction, Attendance on Religious Worship and Beer Houses." *Journal of the Statistical Society*, 1859.

———. "The Social and Moral Statistics of Criminal Offenders." *Journal of the Statistical Society*, 1839.

*D'aeth, J. W. "Present Tendencies of Class Differentiation." *Sociological Review*, 1910.

Danson, J. T. "Investigation of the Changes in the Condition of the People of the United Kingdom during the Eight Years 1839–47, and of the Connection between Those Changes and the Variations Occurring during the Same Years in the Prices of Food." *Journal of the Statistical Society*, 1849.

Darwin, Leonard. "Eugenics in Relation to Economics and Statistics." *Journal of the Royal Statistical Society*, 1909.

Davies, M. F. *Life in an English Village*. London: T. F. Unwin, 1909.

*Dickinson, R. E. "The Commercial Functions of the Nuclei of the English Conurbations." *Sociological Review*, 1929.

———. *The LePlay Method in Regional Survey*. London: LePlay House, n.d.

Drummond, Henry. *The Ascent of Man*. London: Hodder and Stoughton, 1894.

Dundee Social Union. *Social Conditions in Dundee*. Dundee, 1905.

Edgeworth, F. Y. "The Generalized Law of Error." *Journal of the Royal Statistical Society*, 1906.

———. "On Methods of Statistics." *Journal of the Statistical Society*, 1885.

———. Presidential Address. *Journal of the Royal Statistical Society*, 1913.

Edinburgh Charity Organization Society. *Report on the Condition of 14,001 School Children—Their Homes and Surroundings*. London, 1906.

Elderton, W. P. "Modern Methods of Treating Observations." *British Association Report*, 1907.

Elliott, J. H. "Increase of Material Prosperity and Moral Agents Compared with the State of Crime and Pauperism." *Journal of the Statistical Society*, 1869.

Everest, R. "The Influence of Social Degradation in Producing Pauperism and Crime." *Journal of the Statistical Society*, 1855.

*"The Eugenics Education Society, Its Origin and Work." *Eugenics Review*, 1909.

Farr, William. "The Influence of Scarcities and of High Prices of Wheat on Mortality in England." *Journal of the Statistical Society*, 1847.

———. Presidential Address. *Journal of the Statistical Society*, 1872.

Fletcher, Joseph. "Moral and Educational Statistics of England and Wales." *Journal of the Statistical Society*, 1850.

Flux, A. W. "Urban Vital Statistics in England and Germany." *Journal of the Royal Statistical Society*, 1910.

Frazer, J. G. *The Golden Bough*. London: Macmillan, 1900.

———. *Lectures on the Early History of Kingship*. London: Macmillan, 1905.

*Galton, Francis. *English Men of Science*. London: Macmillan, 1874.

*———. *Essays in Eugenics*. London: The Eugenics Education Society, 1909.

*———. *Hereditary Genius*. London, 1875.

———. *Natural Inheritance*. London: Macmillan, 1881.

———. "The Relative Supply from Town and Country Families to the Population of Future Generations." *Journal of the Statistical Society*, 1874.

Galton, Francis, and Schuster, E. J. *Noteworthy Families*. London: J. Murray, 1906.

Gatliff, Charles. "Improved Dwellings and Their Beneficial Effects on Health and Morals." *Journal of the Statistical Society*, 1876.

*Geddes, Patrick. *Cities in Evolution*. London: Williams and Norgate, 1915.

———. "The Classification of Statistics." *Nature*, 1884.

———. "Social Evolution: How to Advance It." *Sociological Review*, 1929.

———. "The Survey of Cities." *Sociological Review*, 1905.

Geddes, Patrick, and Mears, F. C. *The Civic Survey of Edinburgh*.

Giffen, Robert. "The Progress of the Working Classes in the Last Half Century." *Journal of the Statistical Society*, 1883.

———. "The Utility of Common Statistics." *Journal of the Statistical Society*, 1882.

Glass, D. V., and Gray, J. L. "Opportunity and the Older Universities." In *Political Arithmetic*, ed. L. Hogben. London: G. Allen & Unwin, 1938.

*Gray, J. L., and Moshinsky, P. "Ability and Opportunity in English Education." In *Political Arithmetic*, ed. L. Hogben. London: G. Allen & Unwin, 1938.

Guy, W. "The Duration of Life as Affected by the Pursuits of Literature, Science and Art and the Duration of Life among the Upper and Middle Classes." *Journal of the Statistical Society*, 1847–60.

———. "The Influence of Employments upon Health." *Journal of the Statistical Society*, 1844.

*———. "The Proper Function of a Statistical Society." *Journal of the Statistical Society*, 1844.

———. "Tabular Analysis." *Journal of the Statistical Society*, 1865.

Hamilton, Lord George. Presidential Address. *Journal of the Royal Statistical Society*, 1910.

Harrison, F. *The Meaning of History*. New York: Macmillan, 1894.

———. *On Society*. London: Macmillan, 1918.

———. "Sociology, Its Definition and Limits." *Sociological Review*, 1915.

Hawkins, C. B. *Norwich: A Social Study*. London: P. L. Warner, 1910.

Heywood, J. "Report of a House to House Inquiry . . . of 176 Families in Miles Platting, Manchester." *Journal of the Statistical Society*, 1838.

Hobhouse, L. T. *Development and Purpose*. London: Macmillan, 1913.

———. Editorial. *Sociological Review*, 1908.

———. *The Metaphysical Theory of the State*. London: G. Allen & Unwin, 1918.

———. *Mind in Evolution*. London: Macmillan, 1901.

———. *Morals in Evolution*. New York: H. Holt, 1906.

———. *The Rational Good*. New York: H. Holt, 1921.

———. "The Roots of Modern Sociology." Inaugural lecture, reprinted in *Sociology and Philosophy*, 1966.

*———. *Social Development*. London: G. Allen & Unwin, 1924.

———. *Social Evolution and Political Theory*. New York, 1911.

———. "Sociology." Article for the *Encyclopaedia of Religion and Ethics*, reprinted in *Sociology and Philosophy*, 1966.

Hobhouse, L. T.; Wheeler, G. C.; and Ginsberg, M. *The Material Culture and Social Institutions of the Simpler Peoples*. London: Chapman & Hall Ltd., 1915.

*Hogben, L. T., ed., *Political Arithmetic*. London: G. Allen & Unwin, 1938.

Hooper, W. "The Method of Statistical Analysis." *Journal of the Statistical Society*, 1838.

*Howarth, E. G., and Wilson, M. *West Ham: A Study in Social and Industrial Problems*. London: J. M. Dent, 1907.

Hutchins, B. L. "Women's Life and Employment." *Journal of the Royal Statistical Society*, 1909.

Huxley, T. H. *Evolution and Ethics*. 1893.

*———. *Lay Sermons*. New York: D. Appleton, 1871.

Inge, W. R. "Some Moral Aspects of Eugenics." *Eugenics Review*, 1909.

Ingram, J. K. Presidential Address. *Report of the Proceedings of the British Association*, 1878.

Iwan-Müller, E. B. *The Cult of the Unfit*. 1909.

Jebb, E. *Cambridge: A Brief Study in Social Questions*. Cambridge: Macmillan & Bowes, 1906.

Jones, D. C. "The Census of Occupations for England and Wales." *Journal of the Royal Statistical Society*, 1915.

Kidd, B. *Social Evolution*. New York: Macmillan, 1894.

Lefevre, G. J. Presidential Address. *Journal of the Statistical Society*, 1878.

Liverpool Statistical Society. *How the Casual Labourer Lives*. 1909.

Lubbock, Sir J. *The Origin of Civilisation*. London, 1870.

McLennan, J. F. *Primitive Marriage.* Edinburgh, 1865.

*Maine, Sir Henry. *Ancient Law.* 1864.

———. *Village Communities in the East and West.* London: J. Murray, 1871.

Mallock, W. H. *Aristocracy and Evolution.* New York: Macmillan Co., 1898.

Mann, H. H. "Life in an Agricultural Village." *Sociological Papers,* 1904.

Marr, T. R. *Housing Conditions in Manchester and Salford.* Manchester, 1904.

Martineau, H. *Autobiography.* Boston: J. R. Osgood, 1877.

*Mill, J. S. *August Comte and Positivism.* 1865.

———. *A System of Logic.* 1843.

*Mouat, F. J. "History of the Statistical Society of London." *Journal of the Statistical Society, Jubilee Volume,* 1885.

Neilsen, F. G. P. "A Method for Conducting Inquiries into the Comparative Sanitary Condition of Various Districts." *Journal of the Statistical Society,* 1845.

———. "Vital Statistics." *Journal of the Statistical Society,* 1846.

*Newmarch, W. "The Progress and Present Condition of Statistical Inquiry." *Journal of the Statistical Society,* 1869.

Newsholme, A. *The Declining Birth Rate.* New York: Moffat, Yard, 1911.

———. *The Prevention of Tuberculosis.* 1909.

Pearson, Karl. *The Groundwork of Eugenics.* London: Dulau, 1909.

Penstone, M. M. *Town Study.* London: National Society's Depository, 1910.

Peverett, G. T., and Pike, A. T. *Social Survey: A Guide to Good Citizenship.* 1923.

Pitt-Rivers, A. H. *The Evolution of Culture.* Oxford, 1906.

*Porter, G. R. *The Progress of the Nation.* London: C. Knight, 1838.

Purdy, F. "The Preparation and Printing of Parliamentary Statistics." *Journal of the Statistical Society,* 1872.

Rawson, R. W. "The Condition of Criminal Offenders." *Journal of the Statistical Society,* 1841.

Reeves, M. S. *Round about a Pound a Week.* London: G. Bell, 1913.

Ritchie, D. G. *Darwinism and Politics.* New York: Scribner & Welford, 1889.

Rosenbaum, S. "The General Election of 1910." *Journal of the Royal Statistical Society,* 1910.

*Rowntree, B. S. *How the Labourer Lives.* 1911.

*———. *Land and Labour: A Study of Belgium.* 1913.

*———. *Poverty.* London: Macmillan, 1901.

Rowntree, B. S., and Lasker, B. *Unemployment: A Social Study*. London: Macmillan, 1911.

Saleeby, C. W. *Parenthood and Race Culture*. New York: Moffat, Yard, 1909.

Seward, A. C., ed. *Darwin and Modern Science*. Cambridge: The University Press, 1909.

Sherwell, A. *Life in West London*. London: Methuen, 1897.

Spencer, Herbert. *Autobiography*. New York: D. Appleton, 1904.

———. *Descriptive Sociology*. 1931–34.

———. *Essays, Scientific, Political and Speculative*. 1858–74.

———. *The Principles of Sociology*. London, 1876.

*———. *The Study of Sociology*. 1873.

Spiller, G. "Darwinism and Sociology." *Sociological Review*, 1914.

Statistical Society of London. "Report of . . . an Investigation into the State of the Poorer Classes in St. Georges-in-the-East." *Journal of the Statistical Society*, 1849.

———. "Report . . . upon the State of the Working Classes in . . . Westminster." *Journal of the Statistical Society*, 1840.

———. "Third Report . . . upon the State of Education in Westminster." *Journal of the Statistical Society*, 1838.

Stevenson, T. H. C. "English Vital Statistics—Suggested Lines of Advance." *Journal of the Royal Statistical Society*, 1910.

Tawney, R. H. "The Theory of Pauperism." *Sociological Review*, 1909.

*Tylor, E. B. "A Method for Investigating the Development of Social Institutions." *Journal of the Anthropological Institute*, 1881.

*———. *Primitive Culture*. 1871.

———. "Quetelet and the Science of Man." *Nature*, 1876.

———. *Researches into the Early History of Mankind and the Development of Civilization*. 1865.

Urwick, E. J. "Sociology and Social Progress." *Sociological Review*, 1910.

Wallas, G. *Human Nature in Politics*. 1908.

*Webb, B., and Webb, S. *Methods of Social Study*. London: Longmans, Green, 1932.

Whetham, W. C. D., and Whetham, C. *The Family and the Nation*. London: Longmans, Green, 1909.

2. Secondary Sources

Abrams, M. A. *Social Surveys and Social Action*. London: Heinemann, 1951.

Annan, N. G. *The Curious Strength of Positivism in English Political Thought.* 1959.

Barnes, H. E. "The Fate of Sociology in England." *Sociological Review,* 1928.

———. *Historical Sociology.* New York: Philosophical Library, 1947.

Beveridge, Lady Janet. *An Epic of Clare Market.* London: G. Bell, 1960.

Beveridge, Lord William. *The London School of Economics and its Problems.* London: G. Allen & Unwin, 1960.

———. *Power and Influence, an Autobiography.* London: Hodder and Stoughton, 1960.

Boardman, Philip. *Patrick Geddes.* Chapel Hill: University of North Carolina Press, 1946.

Branford, V. V. "The Sociological Work of L. T. Hobhouse." *Sociological Review,* 1929.

Briggs, Asa. *A Study of the Work of Seebohm Rowntree.* London: Longmans, 1961.

Burrow, J. W. *Evolution and Society.* London: Cambridge University Press, 1966.

Caine, S. *The History of the Founding of the London School of Economics.* London: London School of Economics and Political Science, 1963.

Ginsberg, M. *Reason and Unreason in Society.* London: Longmans, Green, 1948.

Glass, Ruth. "Urban Sociology in Great Britain." *Current Sociology,* 1955.

Hobson, J. A., and Ginsberg, M. *L. T. Hobhouse: A Memoir.* London: G. Allen & Unwin, 1931.

Marret, P. *Patrick Geddes, Pioneer of Sociology.* 1948.

Parsons, T. *The Structure of Social Action.* New York: McGraw-Hill, 1937.

Rumney, J. *Herbert Spencer's Sociology.* London: Williams and Norgate, 1934.

Simey, T. S., and Simey, M. B. *Charles Booth, Social Scientist.* Oxford, 1960.

Webb, Beatrice. *My Apprenticeship.* 1936.

Wells, A. F. *The Local Social Survey in Great Britain.* London: G. Allen & Unwin, 1935.